The Art of Credit Derivatives:
Demystifying the Black Swan

João Garcia and Serge Goossens

A John Wiley and Sons, Ltd., Publication

Registered office
John Wiley & Sons Ltd, The Atrium, Southern Gate, Chichester, West Sussex, PO19 8SQ, United Kingdom

For details of our global editorial offices, for customer services and for information about how to apply for permission to reuse the copyright material in this book please see our website at www.wiley.com.

Library of Congress Cataloging-in-Publication Data

Garcia, João.
The art of credit derivatives : demystifying the black swan / João Garcia, Serge Goossens.
    p.   cm.
Includes bibliographical references and index.
ISBN 978-0-470-74735-3
1. Credit derivatives.   2. Securities.   3. Portfolio management.   I. Goossens, Serge.   II. Title.
HG6024.A3G367 2010
332.63′2–dc22   2009039208

A catalogue record for this book is available from the British Library.

ISBN 978-0-470-74735-3 (H/B)

Typeset in 10/12pt Times by Aptara Inc., New Delhi, India
Printed in Great Britain by CPI Antony Rowe, Chippenham, Wiltshire

Contents

About the Authors

João Garcia is the Head of the Credit Modeling team at the Treasury and Financial Markets of Dexia Group in Brussels. His current interests include credit derivatives, structured products, correlation mapping of credit portfolios in indices, developing strategies and trading signals for credit derivatives indices and pricing distressed assets. Before that he worked for four years on the construction of a grid system for strategic credit portfolio management of the whole Dexia Group. He has experience in methodologies to rate and price cash flow CDOs. He also worked on the allocation of credit economic capital and the pricing of exotic interest rate derivatives. He is an Electronic Eng. from Instituto Tecnológico de Aeronáutica (ITA, Brazil), with an MSc in Physics (UFPe, Brazil) and a PhD in Physics (UA, Belgium).

Serge Goossens is a Senior Quantitative Analyst working in the Front Office of Dexia Bank Belgium. He has vast experience with credit derivative instruments, both rating and pricing for hedging and trading. He has also focused on mark to model of hard to value distressed assets and on restructuring the capital structure of large portfolios. From his previous positions he has extensive expertise in parallel large-scale numerical simulation of complex systems, ranging from computational fluid dynamics to electronics. Serge holds an MSc in Engineering and a PhD from the Faculty of Engineering of the K.U. Leuven, and a Master of Financial and Actuarial Engineering degree obtained from the Leuven School of Business and Economics. He has published a number of papers and presented at conferences worldwide.

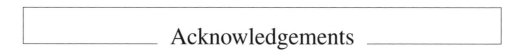

Acknowledgements

Choose a job you love, and you will never have to work a day in your life.
Confucius

This work could not have been realized without the direct and indirect support of several people. First of all we thank Mathijs Dreesen for his numerous valuable contributions. On the trading side we would like to express our gratitude to Claude Njikam. We are grateful to Igor Toder for many fruitful conversations and for bringing up the credit valuation adjustment for protection bought from a non-collateralized counterparty. His initial work on this problem really got us off to a flying start.

Special thanks go to Pete Baker and the publishing staff at John Wiley and Sons Ltd.

João would like to express his deepest gratitude to Marijke for neverending love and support and dedicate this book to her, Ilya, Hendrik and Elliot.

Finally, Serge would like to reserve his biggest thanks for Katrien and dedicate this book to her and to Elise, Wout and Klara.

João Garcia
Serge Goossens

Preface

Technology has no respect for tradition.
Peter Lee

Some people say that this book has been written during unusual market conditions. Securitization activity was designed to bring liquidity for the collateral in the portfolio. Investing in securitization instruments is a diversification and it reduces idiosyncratic risk. Combined with credit derivatives, securitization led to increased leverage in financial institutions. The high leverage levels affected liquidity, bringing the financial system to the brink of collapse.

Innovation plays a crucial role in society and leverage allows economic activity to be speeded up. However, all leveraged positions need to be carefully managed, as can be seen by the dramatic events that followed the summer of 2007. Standardized credit indices are the instruments to foster the securitization business model, playing a central role in the pricing discovery. Transparency in the pricing algorithms and the underlying parameters is key to the activity.

Our main objective in this book is to present the framework to manage this leverage. Many quantitative analysts and market practitioners have contributed to the development of the toolkit for credit derivatives described here. Despite their enormous contribution, many of them have faced hard times during the dramatic market correction that began in 2007. The quotes at the begining of each chapter have been selected to honour their work.

Nowadays, the metaphor of the black swan is sometimes used to describe the credit crunch. It is the fruit of the imagination of Taleb (2007). The underlying idea is that the credit crunch was highly improbable and constituted an extreme event. However, highly improbable under the Gaussian distribution does not mean unlikely under other distributions. Moreover, improbable does not mean undetectable. Physicists doing quantitative trading in the foreign exchange and equity markets have been using ideas inspired by the work of Mandelbrot for quite some time. We did so in September 2002 for credit portfolio management and in March 2007 for CPDOs.

Instead of assuming that a process is Brownian motion-driven, one should first get an in-depth understanding of the underlying dynamics. In this book, we show that the ones who had a sufficiently long memory have seen that the alleged *black* swan is in fact *white*. Seek and ye shall find!

For other titles in the Wiley Finance series
please see www.wiley.com/finance

List of Tables

List of Figures

1

Introduction

If you put the federal government in charge of the Sahara Desert, in five years there'd be a shortage of sand.

Milton Friedman

The credit derivatives market surged from USD 200 billion in 1997 to an astonishing USD 55 trillion in 2008. The largest growth happened in 2006 and 2007. When associated with the *securitization* process, the CDS asset class was in the driving seat of the enormous economic and consumption expansion that took place in the world economy in the post-internet bubble years.

A proper and detailed introduction to credit derivatives can be found in many books already on the market. For an overview of the credit derivatives market, the available instruments, their valuation and trading strategies we refer to the JP Morgan *Credit Derivatives Handbook* (JP Morgan, 2006) and to the Morgan Stanley *Structured Credit Insights* books (Morgan Stanley, 2007a; 2007b). For an introduction to stochastic calculus for finance we refer to Shreve (2004a; 2004b), and to Bingham and Kiesel (2004). For an introduction to credit risk modeling we refer to Bluhm et al. (2003). We refer to Schönbucher (2003) and O'Kane (2008) for credit derivatives pricing. A classic work on options, futures and other derivatives is the book by Hull (2003). For an overview of the bond market we refer to Fabozzi (2004).

This book complements the above references in many respects. First, we focus on the standardized credit indices. Second, we try not to focus only on the instrument and the models but also on the market developments, attempting to adopt a very critical view when using a model. Third, we show models to price instruments, both standardized credit indices and bespoke tranches. Fourth, we show models for portfolio management purposes of bespoke credit portfolios. Fifth, we position the securitization business model as key to the world economy and we describe the processes underlying the activity that need to be well understood. Sixth, we propose a framework to be put in place in financial institutions in order to manage the activity.

When pricing a single name credit derivative instrument, known as a *credit default swap* (CDS), one needs to have a default model. There are two widespread approaches in the industry for doing this. The first is based on the equity market, and in the second a default process is postulated. The two approaches are briefly described in Chapter 2. Initially, the market was predominantly a single name protection instrument. However, in the last few years there has been a drive for multiname instruments for portfolio risk management purposes, rating of whole portfolios and for pricing of multiname CDSs, raising the necessity of models for default dependency within a portfolio. The classical solution has been to use the concept of copulas, and this is described in Chapter 3. In both cases we keep the description to the minimum required to understand the remaining chapters.

We then move forward to Part II of the book where we focus on the pricing of single name credit instruments. In Chapter 4 we show how to price a CDS, the simplest synthetic credit instrument, using the intensity model described in Chapter 2.

We develop two approaches to calibrate the model to observed market spreads. A first taste of the book can be seen when we go one step further and describe practical reasons why one model is chosen over another. Additionally, we show a table comparing the recovery rates on some defaulted bonds during the credit crunch.

In Chapter 5 we price a single name credit spread option using trinomial trees typically used for interest rate processes. Although the chapter is based on a published work (see Garcia et al., 2003), and on data from 2001, the study is still very relevant as the option market is still OTC and not yet fully developed. We show again a comparison between model and reality. In addition, we highlight the parallels in terms of modeling purposes between interest rate and the default intensities, and between discount factors and survival probabilities. The subject will become more relevant once the market comes to use the indices for active portfolio management purposes, a key proposal of this book, in which case one will certainly evolve in the direction of term structure of volatilities of the expected loss.

The collapse of Bear Stearns and the bankruptcy of Lehman Brothers served to highlight the importance of counterparty risk in CDS contracts. In a very short time, protection buyers of CDSs sold by Lehman Brothers realized that their contracts were not as safe as they thought. In order to understand the complex nature of those events, consider a retail bank that sold to its wealthy clients USD 200 million of a capital guaranteed instrument structured by Lehman Brothers (LB). Suppose, for example, that the instrument was a credit constant proportion portfolio insurance (CPPI) issued by LB. The sudden bankruptcy meant that the retail bank got all the exposure to a complex product it might not be able to manage being potentially exposed to any trading loss on the product. The issue of counterparty risk and the so-called credit valuation adjustment (CVA) is addressed in detail in Chapter 6.

Part III of the book is dedicated to corporate multiname credit derivatives. In Chapter 7 we describe what *collateralized debt obligations* (CDOs) are, giving a brief overview of the instrument. The chapter addresses very important issues that underlie the current credit crunch. That is, we show the differences between cash and synthetic deals, the cost of regulatory capital showing explicitly how the instrument is suitable for leveraged positions at the cost of systemic risk. Moreover, we point out the issues of concentration, correlation and diversification inherent to the instrument. The chapter is important in order to understand how CDOs can lead to liquidity problems and why the standardized credit indices are needed.

In Chapter 8 we give a description of the corporate standardized credit indices iTraxx and CDX, focusing on the importance of standardization. In that chapter we give a first intuitive way of pricing the index. The widely-used one factor Gaussian copula algorithm to price tranches of the standardized credit index is described in detail in Chapter 9. We also show how to adapt the model to use Lévy processes. The importance of using Lévy models cannot be emphasized enough. The need for it can be seen in the work of Mandelbrot who was among the first to have studied Lévy processes in finance. We first describe the algorithms used by practitioners. The discussion about self-organized criticality and Mandelbrot is postponed to the final part of the book. The chapter describes the problems of implied compound and base correlation, pointing out the interpolation problems, central to any pricing algorithm for tranches of CDOs.

A more in-depth study comparing Gaussian copula with Lévy base correlation is presented in Chapter 10. The concept of base correlation solves the problem of pricing bespoke tranches. The problem with the base correlation approach, however, is that it is not an intuitive concept, and neither is it straightforward to guarantee arbitrage free pricing. Those issues can only be guaranteed within the concept of base expected loss described in more detail in Chapter 11.

One of the most important applications of the standardized credit indices is the pricing and hedging of bespoke portfolios and for this one needs the concept of correlation mapping. In Chapter 12 we show different methodologies available in the market for choosing the appropriate correlation for pricing purposes of a bespoke tranche. It should be clear that pricing is currently more an *art* than a science and the user needs to understand the implications prior to choosing one particular algorithm over another.

In Chapter 13 we show how correlations among tranches are impacted by the assumptions on systemic risk for the underlying collateral. This chapter is very important for risk, regulatory capital and accounting purposes.

In Chapter 14 we describe cash flow CDOs, presenting a waterfall or indenture in detail. We describe one of the first methodologies to analyze CDOs, the Binomial Expansion Technique (BET), first developed by Moody's. Although it is current best practice to use Monte Carlo (MC) simulation, we decided to describe the old BET approach in some detail due to its central role in the risk analysis of CDOs that led to the failure of a certain large company during the credit crunch. The curious reader is advised to rush to that chapter.

Structured credit products such as Constant Proportion Portfolio Insurance (CPPI) and Constant Proportion Debt Obligation (CPDO) are described in Chapter 15. With the credit crunch and the enormous losses suffered by CPDO investors, this instrument became a symbol of a risky product in which models failed. We had foreseen this danger. It could have been detected by comparing the results of simulation driven by Brownian motion with simulations based on jump-driven Lévy processes. This is yet more evidence that pricing means first understanding the nature of the product and only then selecting an appropriate model to catch possible features and hidden risks.

In Part IV we address CDOs of Asset Backed Securities (ABS). The different protocols used in the market for ABCDSs, that is CDSs of ABSs, are described in Chapter 16. In Chapter 17 we present one credit event model to price CDOs of ABSs, showing the complex problems faced by the industry associated with the input parameters. Given the importance of the asset class, one needs standardized credit indices for pricing and hedging purposes. Some of those indices are described in Chapter 18 and we focus on ABX.HE and TABX.HE, the standardized credit indices for subprime Mortgage Backed Securities (MBSs). In Chapter 19 we show how to adapt the standard market approach for pricing tranches of corporate credit indices to price TABX.HE, the tranches of ABX.HE, both under the Gaussian copula and Lévy models. The deterioration in the subprime MBSs was visible in the TABX.HE tranches. Additionally, we show that, when using the prepayment assumptions taken from the remittance reports there was no value of correlation that would recover observed market prices. An important message of this chapter is that, in order to be able to foster the securitization business model at low cost of capital, key ingredients are the standardized credit indices and transparency in the methodologies for pricing purposes. This also implies the ability to map portions of the bespoke portfolio into the capital structure of standardized credit indices. If the pricing algorithm is one factor then one may use the techniques described in Chapter 12. This implies the assumption by the market of a risk neutral prepayment assumption for pricing purposes. One of the current difficulties in pricing CDOs of ABSs is the input spread parameter from which probabilities of default are implied. Differences in probabilities implied from an ABS bond and ABCDS are due to the cost of funding of the former, the mark to market nature of the latter, and liquidity issues. In Chapter 20 we adapt the techniques widely used for the corporate case to come up with the basis between ABCDSs and the ABS bonds.

In Part V we point out that a solution for the securitization business model for financial institutions requires understanding the relation between widespread investment in apparently safe AAA securitization instruments and its catastrophic impact on the stability of the whole financial system. To this end, we discuss long-term memory processes and self-organized criticality central to the work of Benoit Mandelbrot and others. An intuitive description of those processes is given in Chapter 21. We also mention the inappropriateness of the Gaussian framework for pricing and portfolio management purposes. We then move to Chapter 22 where we address in detail the credit crunch and its link with securitization. We show via an intuitive example that the process to be followed is the dynamic of systemic correlation that can be monitored via the standardized credit index. It turns out that the dynamics of correlation follow a long-term memory process. We know that the probability of extreme events is much higher than expected under the Gaussian framework. One solution to the stability problem is to significantly increase the cost of capital for securitization instruments.

This medicine kills the sickness – instability – but also the patient – the securitization activity – and with it a large part of the world economy as we know it. One cannot expect the world to stop thinking in Gaussian terms overnight as all the systems and the mathematical framework in the heads of the practitioners are based on Gaussian distributions. In Chapter 23 we present a solution for the whole puzzle. We show the inadequacy of a regulatory capital framework that is portfolio independent. Moreover, we show the inadequacy of the correlation values that have been used for securitization instruments for both risk management and rating purposes. Next we unveil the implicit assumptions of liquidity adopted by practitioners when rating agency models are used for structuring purposes. This leads us to the necessity of exchange traded standardized credit indices. Continuing along this path, we propose a mark to market approach for securitization instruments within a dynamic credit portfolio management framework as one possible solution for the securitization business model.

Part I
Modeling Framework

2

Default Models

Genius, that power that dazzles mortal eyes, is oft but perseverance in disguise.
Henry Austin

2.1 INTRODUCTION

A credit derivative is a derivative whose payoff depends on the credit risk of an underlying reference. In several places in this book we show that the market for credit derivatives has grown enormously in recent years since its formal inception in the mid 1990s. As a consequence of this growth there has been a demand for default models to be used for the evaluation of those instruments. The increased level of sophistication of the credit instruments, as evidenced by the credit crunch of June 2007, brought up the necessity for credit risk systems and models for default probabilities for credit risk purposes. These models do not need to be the same.

There is already a lot of literature available on this subject and we do not intend to repeat it here. We will give a very brief description of what is behind the modeling approaches in a way that the reader can follow through the remaining chapters. Two traditional references are Schönbucher (2003) and de Servigny and Renault (2004). Additional references will be given at the appropriate place. The chapter is structured as follows. In Section 2.2 we discuss what is called a default. In Section 2.3 we present the two approaches most used to model the default process.

2.2 DEFAULT

Generally speaking, an obligor is said to be in *default* when she cannot honor her legal contractual obligation in a debt instrument. Although intuitively speaking the concept is quite simple, in practice however the *default process* may be quite complex, and the catch is in the word *legal*.

In practice, one says that an obligor is said to be in default when a contractually specified *credit event* has been triggered. Possible credit events are: bankruptcy, failure to pay, moratorium, debt restructuring, rating downgrade, acceleration of debt payment, or even moves on the credit spread. In order to standardize those contracts and bring liquidity into the market the definitions of what is called a credit event have been documented by the International Swap Derivatives Association (ISDA) and we refer to this organization for legal detail on this topic.

The importance of those contractual definitions should not be underestimated. Consider, for example, that an insurance portfolio manager sells default insurance on a portfolio of five references, an instrument known as a *basket*. At the same time, the manager buys individual protection on the entities in the portfolio she feels are most likely to default. Assume, for example, that the entity for which the manager had bought individual protection has a debt restructuring event. Under the single name CDS contract, the seller has the right to call the credit event and, in case of noncash settlement, receive a bond of the buyer. However, it sometimes happens that a debt restructuring may turn out to be a good deal for a company.

For the basket contract the one who triggers the default event, however, is the protection buyer and not the seller. In that case it can happen that the manager will have to go in the market and buy underlying name to be able to deliver it to the CDS seller, while still keeping its exposure in the basket open. She will probably have lost money on the deal. The restructuring clause is present in Europe and not in the US and has been the cause of many contentious issues.

In what follows we do not enter into the legal details of what has triggered a credit default. We define it phenomenologically and assume that the meaning of a credit default is well understood.

2.3   DEFAULT MODELS

2.3.1   Overview

One of the main problems with modeling defaults is that default events are rare and as such not much data is available. Moreover, even if more data becomes available, it will typically represent an historical perspective, more appropriate for a buy and hold strategy. For pricing purposes, however, one is interested in the probabilities of default implied in the prices of instruments available in the market. This means *risk neutral* measures. From the start, one is left with two possibilities, using information embedded in the prices of either equity or debt instruments. For this reason, for pricing purposes there are basically two widespread approaches to model a default. One approach is called *firm* or *asset value models* (AVM) and is based on the original work of Merton (1974) and Black and Scholes (1973). Those are equity market-based models. In the second approach one models the default process explicitly. It is based on the original work of Duffie and Singleton (1999). Those models use debt instruments directly for calibration purposes. In what follows we give a very brief description of the ideas and principles behind those approaches.

2.3.2   Firm value models

Firm value models have been around for a long time and the literature is very extensive. They have been very influential in many products available in the market. Both Moody's KMV and CreditGrade from CreditMetrics are firm value-based models.

In firm value models, a company is in default when a latent variable, the asset value, breaches some barrier, typically the debt book value. In this approach one needs an assumption for the asset value process and an assumption for the capital structure of a company. Denote by V_t the value of a company, S_t its equity price and B_t the value of its outstanding debt at time t. Additionally D is the par or notional value of the debt at maturity. The value V_t of the company is given by

$$V_t = S_t + B_t. \tag{2.1}$$

Under Merton's assumptions V follows the usual geometric Brownian motion and is given by

$$dV = \mu V \, dt + \sigma V \, dW \tag{2.2}$$

where μ is the drift, σ is the volatility and W is the driving Brownian motion.

In the original Merton model the value of the company should not fall below the outstanding debt at *maturity*. From (2.1) we have that the value of the equity of a company at maturity

T is given by

$$S_T = \max(V_T - D, 0) \tag{2.3}$$

which is the payoff of a call option with strike set at D. Analogously for the debt of the company at time T we have:

$$D_T = \min(D, V_T). \tag{2.4}$$

From BS formula one has for S_t and D_t:

$$S_t = V_t N\left(x + \sigma_V \sqrt{(T - t)}\right) - D \exp\left[-r(T - t)\right] N(x) \tag{2.5}$$

and

$$D_t = D \exp\left[-r(T - t)\right] N(x) + V_t N\left(-x - \sigma_V \sqrt{T - t}\right) \tag{2.6}$$

where

$$x = \frac{\ln \dfrac{V_t}{D} + \left(r - \dfrac{1}{2}\sigma_V^2\right)(T - t)}{\sigma_V \sqrt{(T - t)}} \tag{2.7}$$

and r is the risk free interest rate, and N is standard normal cumulative distribution function. Observe that in the Merton model default is associated to the value of the company at the maturity of the debt (T). Over the years several extensions have been proposed. In one such an extension, proposed by Black and Cox (1976), the default process would be triggered in case the barrier is crossed at any time between t and T.

Despite its use by some market participants there are very practical problems with this approach. First, the asset value of a company is not an observable, its equity value is. This means that it is common market practice to use the equity process as a proxy for the asset value. Second, the barrier that determines default is not a clear cut value and one needs to have access to the whole capital structure of a company. That is, a real company has several outstanding bonds at different maturities and with different subordination levels, making the model assumptions on the capital structure too simplistic. Third, the model is not easily adaptable for illiquid nonlisted companies for which both equity and debt information is not easily known. Fourth, one cannot use it directly for other asset classes such asset backed securities. Fifth, as we have seen during the credit crunch, many companies have their stock below the supposed book value, and default has not been triggered. That is, the relation between an equity process, the barrier level and default may be a very strong assumption. Sixth, the way to use those models for companies that are typically leveraged, such as financials, is still a matter of discussion.

An example of a very practical problem using the link between equity and credit for trading purposes is the following. Assume a bank sells an insurance contract on the default of a certain reference name, while deciding to hedge the exposure by buying deeply out of the money equity put options. The rationale behind the strategy is simple. In the case of a default event, share prices fall and the money lost in the insurance side is gained on the put side as the share price will have gone close to zero. As we have seen in the last section, however, the insurance contract gives protection not only to default but also to credit events such as restructuring of debt. Where the company goes through a debt restructuring there are cases in which the credit event is seen as good by the equity holders. In this case the insurance contract may be exercised while the share price will go up. The protection seller will have lost money on both sides of the deal.

The ultimate problem facing firm value models for pricing purposes is linked to issues of calibration. The link between equity and the default process is in fact a very strong assumption. There is nothing that guarantees that the equity market will move in synchronization with the credit market, such that default probabilities follow the quotes in the credit market.

A final point on asset value models is as follows. Structured credit products are typically *correlation* instruments. If one is modeling for pricing purposes the correlation should come from the prices of available liquid market instruments. In Chapter 23 we explain that for doing portfolio analysis one may need to have correlation numbers that do not necessarily need to come from pricing instruments. Given that joint default data is very rare, a framework justifying the use of equity data for the evaluation of correlation is a welcome feature. This justification is addressed via firm value models.

In this book we do not explore the use of firm value models. The literature is very large and we refer to Chapter 9 of Schönbucher's book (2003) and to Chapter 3 of O'Kane's book (2008) and the references therein for additional literature. In the next section we address the ideas behind intensity-based models.

2.3.3 Intensity models

In *intensity* or *reduced form* models one explicitly proposes a model that is capable of recovering the characteristics of the default process. A first characteristic is that defaults are rare events and the probability of more than one default at the same point in time is assumed to be zero. A second point is that with time going to infinity the probability of default should go to one. A desirable property of the model is a straightforward calibration. Poisson processes are a class of well-known stochastic processes that fit this description. A *counting process* $N(t)$ for $t \geq 0$ is said to be a *Poisson process* with a rate $\lambda \geq 0$, if it has the following properties:

1. $N(0) = 0$;
2. Stationary and independent increments $P(t + \Delta t, t) = P(\Delta t)$;
3. $P\left[N(t + \Delta t) - N(t) = n\right] = \frac{1}{n!}(\lambda \Delta t)^n \exp(-\lambda \Delta t)$

where, $P(t + \Delta t, t)$ and $P(\Delta t)$ are the probabilities of an event occurring between t and $t + \Delta t$, and in an interval Δt at any point in time. $P\left[N(t + \Delta t) - N(t) = n\right]$ represents the probability of n events taking place in the interval $[t, t + \Delta t]$. These properties have several important consequences (see e.g. Ross, 1996). First, Poisson processes are memoryless as stated by item 2. This means that what happens between t and $t + \Delta t$ does *not* depend on what happened prior to time t. Second, the inter-arrival times of a Poisson process are exponentially distributed. Third, item 3 implies that the probability of two or more events happening at the same time is zero. Poisson processes are widely used in modeling queuing processes (Wolff, 1989), or point processes (Bremaud, 1981). They have many applications in engineering and physics. Typical examples are the number of clients arriving at a gas station, the flux of cars in a highway, and radioactive decay.

One may extend the definition above by making the intensity time dependent. For pricing CDS instruments it is standard market practice to assume the default process follows an inhomogeneous Poisson process and as such for any $0 \leq t \leq T$ the default time τ and default intensity $\lambda(t)$ satisfy

$$\mathbb{P}(\tau > t) = \exp\left(-\int_0^t \lambda(u)\, du\right) \tag{2.8}$$

where $\mathbb{P}$ is the risk-neutral probability measure and T is the final maturity. As outlined in Chapter 4 the single name survival probabilities $\mathbb{P}(\tau > t)$ are typically implied from the credit default swap (CDS) market. We note that the intensities above are deterministic. A generalization of the model is to make the intensities stochastic and the process is called a *Cox process*. An example can be found in Chapter 5.

There are several important references for reduced form models and among them we mention Duffie and Singleton (1999) and Jarrow et al. (1997) and the references therein. In the remaining chapters of this book we show that reduced form models are a standard component used by practitioners for pricing purposes of credit derivatives instruments. For an extensive description of the models we refer to O'Kane (2008).

3
Modeling Dependence with Copulas

Great spirits have always encountered violent opposition from mediocre minds.
Albert Einstein

3.1 INTRODUCTION

In order to generate the joint loss distribution of a credit portfolio one needs a framework to express the *dependency* or *correlation* between the underlying references which may be either single name instruments or asset backed securities. In order to be usable in practice, the adopted approach should have a few desirable features. First, it needs to be as simple and easy to understand as possible. That is, error checking is not overly complex. Second, calibration to available market data should be tractable. There is no point in generating a loss distribution that one cannot relate to observable market data. Additionally, the adopted approach should be scalable, that is, applicable to a small portfolio involving a couple of references as well as to very large portfolios. Finally, the generated loss distribution for the whole portfolio has to be compatible with the marginal loss distributions of the underlying references. This needs to be so as in a liquid market the dynamics of one reference does not change because it is in the portfolio of a certain institution. If the last two conditions are not fulfilled coherence problems between the two loss distributions may be encountered when trying to hedge a single name or a subportfolio exposure within a larger portfolio.

In practice, the dependence relation within a portfolio is generated using a *copula* function. In this chapter we briefly address the concept of copulas focusing on what is most used in practice. The remainder of this chapter is organized as follows. In Section 3.2 we describe copulas and their use in practice. In Section 3.3 we describe a copula algorithm and show how it is used in practice. For a general reference on the subject we refer to Nelsen (1999), and for more specialized literature about the use of copulas in insurance and finance we refer respectively to Frees and Valdez (1998) and Cherubini et al. (2004).

3.2 COPULA

Consider a basket of M entities and denote by $P_1(x_1)$, $P_2(x_2)$, $\ldots$, $P_M(x_M)$ the *marginal* distributions of default times, implied from quotes on the CDS market for each entity. We refer to Chapter 4 for details. A copula function C is defined as

$$C : [0, 1]^M \to [0, 1] : C(P_1(x_1), P_2(x_2), \ldots, P_M(x_M)) = P(x_1, x_2, \ldots, x_M), \qquad (3.1)$$

where P is the *joint* distribution of default times. A well-known result by Sklar (1973), states that, under some technical conditions such as continuity of the marginal distributions, the following theorem holds:

> Given the marginal distributions any multivariate distribution function can be written in the form of a copula function.

That is, given the joint distribution $P(x_1, x_2, \ldots, x_M)$ and the marginal distributions $P_1(x_1)$, $P_2(x_2), \ldots, P_M(x_M)$, a *unique* copula function C as defined by (3.1) exists.

The use of copulas can be a complex issue due to the following problem. In practice, as is the case in financial applications, the marginals are known or can be estimated, and we are interested in a possible candidate for the joint probability distribution. However, *given the marginals one cannot guarantee that the copula is unique*. That is, for a set of marginals there are several copula candidates that one can use to generate a possible joint probability distribution.

The Gaussian copula is the copula most used by market practitioners. It has been adopted by Li (1999) for pricing a basket of credit derivatives and in a risk management context by Gupton et al. (1997) and in Moody's KMV (2002).

In this case the copula is defined as:

$$C(N(x_1), N(x_2), \ldots, N(x_M)) = N_M(x_1, x_2, \ldots, x_M, \Sigma) \tag{3.2}$$

where N is the standard normal cumulative distribution function and N_M is the multidimensional Gaussian distribution function with average 0, standard deviation 1 and correlation matrix Σ.

Several elements have led to the wide dissemination of the Gaussian copula amongst practitioners. First, the normal and multinormal distributions are very well known and are usually readily available in numerical packages. A second and important practical reason is that one can use assumptions on the firm value model to justify the use of equity data to determine the correlation matrix Σ. Where one uses an alternative copula one still has to calibrate the parameters for that copula. In what follows we briefly discuss alternative copulas and the issues related to it.

The following well-known result (see e.g. Lucas, 1995), is widely used for calibration purposes. Denote by $P_2(x_1, x_2, \Sigma)$, $P(x_1)$ and $P(x_2)$ the joint and the marginal default probabilities of the references S_1 and S_2, and by Σ their correlation parameter. The default correlation ρ_{12} between S_1 and S_2 is given by

$$\rho_{12} = \frac{P_2(x_1, x_2, \Sigma) - P(x_1)P(x_2)}{\sqrt{P(x_1)(1 - P(x_1))P(x_2)(1 - P(x_2))}}, \tag{3.3}$$

which results from a straightforward application of the definition of correlation

$$\rho_{xy} = \frac{\text{cov}(X, Y)}{\sigma_X \sigma_Y} = \frac{\mathbb{E}[XY] - \mathbb{E}[X]\mathbb{E}[Y]}{\sqrt{\mathbb{E}X^2 - (\mathbb{E}X)^2}\sqrt{\mathbb{E}Y^2 - (\mathbb{E}Y)^2}} \tag{3.4}$$

to the default indicators, which are binary variables taking the value one with a probability equal to the default probability.

Where a copula other than the Gaussian is chosen, one still needs to calibrate the parameters of the new copula. A simple approach for that calibration is to calculate the default correlation under the Gaussian copula using (3.3) and to use that result to evaluate the parameters, represented here as Σ, for the alternative copula.

An important point related to the use of this approach for calibration purposes is that the relation is only valid for *elliptical distributions* and that it is in fact not appropriate for distributions that do not fall into this class. As a matter of fact, the concept of *linear correlation* as a measure of dependence makes sense only for elliptical distributions. For other families of distributions other measures such as *rank correlation* and *tail dependence* coefficients need to be used (see Embrechts et al., 2002 and the references therein). Alternative calibration approaches would be to imply the parameters from observed market instruments. Ideally the observed dynamics of expected losses are recovered and the resulting copula parameters are more in touch with reality.

In practice, however, we need to have a credit option market on the standardized indices that are traded in exchange to be able to have the dynamic of the expected loss and, as such, calibrating the parameters of alternative copulas. Those instruments are certainly not yet available in the market. It means that when choosing alternative copulas one may be driven by mathematical tractability, making the choice rather arbitrary. In this case we should be very careful when using a model that is not the same as the one used by the market in general. This sort of event happened in May 2005 when the downgrade of auto companies took the market by surprise, causing the unwinding of trading positions in the correlation market. The rush to the exit generated unexpected movements in the correlation market.

In the next section we explain the necessity of factor analysis-based models for portfolio management purposes. We also show the steps on the use of the Gaussian copula for simulating default times for a certain portfolio.

3.3   USING COPULAS IN PRACTICE AND FACTOR ANALYSIS

In this section we describe factor analysis and show how to use it in the context of copula functions to generate correlated default times for a credit portfolio. We also present a step-by-step algorithm.

3.3.1   Factor analysis

At least three good reasons can be given for adopting dimensionality reduction techniques when generating the loss distribution of a portfolio: the *size* of the portfolio, the need for *simplifying assumptions* and, last but not least, *performance*. We note that credit portfolios can vary in size from a couple of references, as is common in a first to default basket, to hundreds of thousands of credit instruments for the portfolios of financial institutions. Simplifying assumptions are also necessary for feasibility reasons and for improving the understanding of the behavior of a portfolio. Performance issues become important when one needs to stress parameters or test different scenarios.

Factor Analysis (FA) or *Principal Component Analysis* (PCA) is a statistical technique whose objective is to reduce the dimension of a problem by identifying the *drivers* or the *factors* that have the largest impact on the observed process. The main objective of using factor analysis is to make the correlated dynamics of the names in a portfolio depend on a limited set of common factors. Ideally, the factors should be intuitive enough to provide easy explanations for their impact on the dynamics of the underlying references. It has become standard market practice to make the return of a reference entity dependent on what are called *systemic* and *idiosyncratic* factors. The systemic factors affect all the companies in general and represent the market forces. The idiosyncratic factors represent particularities of the observed company itself. Using factor analysis the return Y of a reference entity C is given by

$$Y_C = \rho X_C^M + \beta \xi_C \tag{3.5}$$

where X_C^M is the systemic factor and ξ_C is the idiosyncratic factor. In practice, the number of factors driving the market depends on the application. For pricing standardized credit indices and for Basel II purposes, it is common to have only one factor driving the systemic factor. That is, all the references in the market are supposed to be affected by market movements in the same way and the correlation between any two references C_1 and C_2 is given by ρ^2. For risk management and rating purposes the market parameter is represented by two factors in which one represents the industry sector and the other one represents the region. In that case the correlation between two references is more complex and will depend on the sectors and industries that drive the reference returns.

3.3.2 Simulating default times using the Gaussian copula

Assume a portfolio with several references is given for which one also knows the correlation matrix Σ. Further, we also assume CDS quotes for different maturities, e.g. the 1, 3, 5, 7 and 10 year tenors to be known. The algorithm to generate the default times is as follows:

1. For each reference i in the portfolio estimate the default probability distribution

$$F_i(t) = \mathbb{P}\left[\tau_i < t\right], \tag{3.6}$$

   where τ_i is the default time. We refer to Chapter 4 for more details on how to extract the default probabilities from CDS quotes.

2. Generate correlated random numbers from a multivariate Gaussian distribution with correlation matrix Σ. If the correlation Σ has been evaluated specifically for the reference entities then a factor model is not needed. In general, however, the portfolio is very large and a factor model is used. In this case one still needs to generate individual normally distributed random numbers for the idiosyncratic factors in order to evaluate the return. Denote by $Y = [y_1, y_2, \ldots, y_M]$ the vector of generated returns.

3. For each random number generated in step 2, evaluate the default probabilities p_i using a standard normal distribution function such that

$$p_i = N(y_i) = \int_{-\infty}^{y_i} n(x)\, \mathrm{d}x \tag{3.7}$$

   where $n(x)$ is the standard normal density function and $N(x)$ is the cumulative standard normal distribution function.

4. For each evaluated probability p_i in (3.7) and the marginal distributions F_i evaluated in step 1 evaluate the time t_i such that

$$p_i = F_i(t_i). \tag{3.8}$$

   The vector of points $T = [t_1, t_2, \ldots, t_M]$ are the simulated default times.

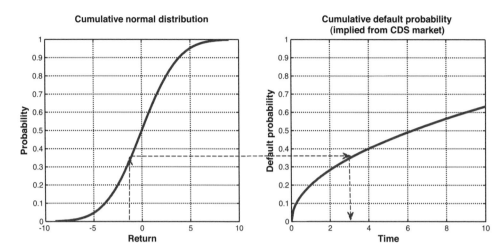

Figure 3.1　Generating default times using a Gaussian copula.

The algorithm described above is depicted in Figure 3.1. The return generated for one of the references y_i is shown on the x-axis in the left graph. That return corresponds to a certain probability of default p_i evaluated in (3.7), and it corresponds to a certain default time t_i taken from the probability distribution implied from the CDS market in this case. In the case of rating algorithms the probability of default may have been estimated from historical data on rating statistics, reflecting a buy and hold perspective.

Part II
Single Name Corporate Credit Derivatives

4

Credit Default Swaps

The four most expensive words in the English language are "This time it's different."
John Templeton

4.1 INTRODUCTION

The most fundamental credit derivative instrument is the *credit default swap*. In its plain form the instrument provides single name insurance in case of a default event of an underlying reference. The importance of this instrument to the recent financial activity can be seen by the sheer speed of its growth. As Table 22.1 shows, the market for individual name CDSs has grown from about USD 200 billion in 1997 to around USD 25 trillion in 2008, according to ISDA.

To understand how a CDS functions, consider an investor who has bought a 10-year bond from a company X. In order to protect herself against a default event on the reference entity of the bond the investor buys a 10-year CDS from a counterparty on the specific bond she has bought. Under the CDS contract the investor pays a fee, usually every quarter, until the end of the contract or until a credit event on the bond happens. Where there is a credit event the protection seller pays par to the protection buyer while receiving the defaulted bonds. In the case of cash settlement the protection seller pays par minus the *recovery* value of the bond, that is, she pays the *loss given default* (LGD).

Observe that a CDS is a synthetic instrument or, more precisely, it is an insurance contract, and no cash may need to be put up front, that is, there is *no cost of funding*. Depending on specific details of the CDS contract, one may not need to specify exactly which bond needs to be delivered in case of default, and in that case the protection buyer would deliver the *cheapest to deliver*. Additionally, the payoff of the contract is exactly the same as for a bond. In a bond the investor loses the LGD where there is a default. Just like in a bond the CDS seller loses the LGD where there is a default. With the same payoff and no cost of funding investors would rather sell a CDS than buy a bond. There is a difference, however, in the accounting process. CDSs need to be marked to market while a bond may be put on buy and hold. This is an important issue for many banks, especially in volatile markets.

Assume, for example, that a bank has a portfolio of USD 100 billion on bonds and it has bought CDS protection on at least USD 20 billion on the underlying portfolio. The bond portfolio may be put on buy and hold and, due to problems of liquidity, bankers may essentially keep the prices significantly higher than market prices would suggest. On the portfolio of CDSs, however, the bank needs to be pricing it on mark to market. This may essentially generate volatility on the profit and loss (P&L) numbers of the activity, and as such it becomes an issue of intense debate on possible conflict of interests. For the shareholders that sort of volatility may provide important information on the the the nature of the activity of the financial institution. For the management, however, this may be an embarrassing point. The issues and implications behind mark to market are more general than addressed here and will be dealt with in Part V when we deal with dynamic portfolio management as the solution for the securitization business model of financial institutions.

The remainder of this chapter is organized as follows. In Section 4.2 we describe the contract in more detail. The standard process used for pricing purposes is outlined in Section 4.3. In Section 4.4 we discuss very practical issues behind calibration. In Section 4.5 we show the results of the auction processes and the resulting recovery rates.

4.2   CREDIT DEFAULT SWAP: A DESCRIPTION

A *credit default swap* (CDS) is an insurance contract in which a credit protection buyer buys credit protection from a protection seller on a credit event of a reference entity on a contract specified notional amount. That is, the protection buyer pays a fee, usually quarterly, to the protection seller for the life of the CDS contract or until a credit event happens. Usually the CDS contract specifies a *reference obligation* to which the contract is an insurance. The reference obligation is usually senior unsecured although one also sees CDSs on subordinated obligations. It is important to note, however, that the focus is on the underlying obligor name. That is, once a CDS is bought on a senior unsecured note of an underlying obligor, any senior unsecured note of that obligor can be a candidate for settlement in the case of a credit event. Where a credit event is triggered the protection seller needs to make a payment to the protection buyer, and this settlement can be done in two ways, usually contract specified.

1. *Cash settlement*. In this case a pool of dealers determines the market value of the underlying reference obligation. The protection seller pays to the protection buyer the cash difference between the contract notional and the market value of the reference obligation.
2. *Physical delivery*. The protection buyer selects a reference obligation, usually the so-called *cheapest to deliver*, and delivers it to the protection seller who pays the contract notional to the protection buyer.

An important legal issue on a CDS contract is the precise definition of what is considered a *credit event*. Although ISDA gives six possibilities for the corporate credit events, the following three are the most important:

1. *Failure to pay*. The reference entity fails to pay interest or principal on at least one of its obligations.
2. *Bankruptcy*. The reference entity officially files for bankruptcy protection, voluntarily or not.
3. *Debt restructuring*. This refers to changes in the terms of outstanding debt contracts, usually in the form of reducing the amount of principal or interest to be paid by the obligor.

We refer to the ISDA website (www.isda.org) for additional details on those issues.

The seller of protection is said to be the seller of the CDS, meaning that she is *long* the CDS as she is long the credit risk in the underlying reference. That is, the risk taken by the protection seller is analogous to the *buyer* of a bond. In ISDA documentation the protection seller is said to be the *float* payer. The important difference between the bond buyer and the protection seller is that the first one needs to fund the buying of the bond. The protection seller needs to offer the commitment to cover the losses in the case of a future credit event.

In the same way, the protection buyer is said to be the buyer of the CDS, meaning that she is *short* the CDS as she is short the credit risk of the underlying reference. That is, the risk taken by the protection buyer is analogous to the *seller* of a bond. In an ISDA documentation the protection buyer is said to be the *fixed* payer. By selling protection the investor is taking a short position on a bond without having to jump all the hurdles of taking a real position in the cash instrument.

The fact that the instrument permits one to take credit risk on a reference without having to fund it has been responsible for the enormous growth of the credit derivatives market as shown in Table 22.1. Typical trades involving CDSs are the following. Consider an investor that funds at (L + 10) bp and invests in a bond receiving (L + 200) bp. The investor may buy protection on the default of the underlying bond obligor paying a margin of 170 bps. The investor will have funded at (L + 10) bps while receiving a margin of (L + 30) bps. The problem with this trade, however, is the cost of counterparty risk (CVA), that is, the risk that the CDS seller defaults resulting in the CDS becoming worthless. The problem of CVA is treated in more detail in Chapter 6. A second investment strategy using individual name CDS would be the following. Assume a well rated holding company funds at (L + 30) bps, with a subsidiary that funds at (L + 200) bps. As the holding company has full information on the subsidiary it can profit from the high spread by selling funded protection on the default of the subsidiary. The funded CDS protection is a new instrument called a *Credit Linked Note* (CLN). Assume, for example, that the risk-free investment would give (L − 15) bp. The net margin made by the holding company would be 155 bps. One should be aware that before the credit crunch that began in June 2007 the risk-free investment was AAA commercial paper, an instrument that has certainly had its bad days during the credit crunch.

4.3 MODELING CDSs

As discussed in Chapter 2 there are two widely used techniques for modeling credit events, the *latent variable* or *structural model* based on the original work of Merton (1974) on the one hand and the *reduced form models* based on the original work of Duffie and Singleton (1999) on the other hand.

It is standard market practice to use reduced form models to price a CDS. As mentioned in Chapter 2, we assume the default process to follow an inhomogeneous Poisson process and as such for any $0 \leq t \leq T$ the default time τ and default intensity $\lambda(t)$ satisfy

$$P_S(t) = \mathbb{P}(\tau > t) = \exp\left(-\int_0^t \lambda(u)du\right) \tag{4.1}$$

where $\mathbb{P}$ is the risk-neutral probability measure and T is the final maturity. The single name survival probabilities $\mathbb{P}(\tau > t)$ are typically implied from the credit default swap (CDS) market.

The fair spread of a CDS balances the present value of the contingent leg C, given by

$$C = N(1 - R)\sum_{i=1}^{n} d(t_i)(P_S(t_{i-1}) - P_S(t_i)) \tag{4.2}$$

and the present values of the fee leg F, given by

$$F = NS\left(\sum_{i=1}^{n} P_S(t_i)d(t_i)\Delta t_i + A_D\right), \tag{4.3}$$

where N is the CDS notional and A_D is the accrual on default

$$A_D = \frac{1}{2} \sum_{i=1}^{n} N d(t_i) (P_S(t_{i-1}) - P_S(t_i)) \Delta t_i. \tag{4.4}$$

In these equations the summations run over the payment dates, S is the spread premium on a yearly basis, paid quarterly, $P_S(t_i)$ is the survival probability at time t_i, R is the recovery rate, $d(t)$ is the risk-free discount factor and $\Delta t_i = t_i - t_{i-1}$ is the year fraction, corresponding to an Actual/360 day counter. The standard maturity dates on a corporate CDS contract are the 20th of March, June, September and December. The fee leg can be written as

$$F = NSB, \tag{4.5}$$

where $B = \text{BPV}(0, T)$ is the present value of 1 basis point (bp) paid from time zero until maturity T. It is given by

$$\text{BPV}(0, T) = \sum_{i=1}^{n} P_S(t_i) d(t_i) \Delta t_i + \frac{1}{2} \sum_{i=1}^{n} N^{CDS} d(t_i) (P_S(t_{i-1}) - P_S(t_i)) \Delta t_i. \tag{4.6}$$

4.4   CALIBRATING THE SURVIVAL PROBABILITY

4.4.1   Bootstrap method

We now turn to the problem of determining the survival probability in (4.1) from the observed CDS market quotes. This is done by specifying the intensity $\lambda(u) \geq 0$ for $0 \leq u \leq T$. We assume the function $\lambda(u)$ to be piecewise constant between the maturities of the CDS contracts. As an example, assume 5-year and 10-year CDS quotes are available. In that case the function $\lambda(u)$ is as follows:

$$\lambda(u) = \begin{cases} \lambda_{0-5} & 0 \leq u \leq 5, \\ \lambda_{5-10} & 5 < u \leq 10. \end{cases} \tag{4.7}$$

The process of implying default probabilities from CDS market quotes is called *calibration* and in general there are two main approaches. First, the parameters in (4.7) from the market quotes are determined via a *bootstrapping technique* as follows. From the 5-year CDS quote we find the value of λ_{0-5} which determines the survival probability in (4.1) up to 5 years. Next, we find the λ_{5-10} parameter, determining the survival probability in (4.1) between 5 and 10 years, from the 10-year CDS quote.

Finding the parameters λ_{0-5} and λ_{5-10} can be done using a straightforward root finding algorithm that for a given market observed spread, equates the contingent and fee legs. We note that in the bootstrap approach the intensities are determined in a sequential way, that is, in the example above we used the 5-year CDS quote to determine the λ_{0-5}, and then used it together with the 10-year CDS quote to determine the λ_{5-10}.

4.4.2   Optimization method

The second approach uses an optimization algorithm to determine all the probabilities of default simultaneously. The algorithm we present below is due to Martin et al. (2001). Absence of arbitrage at the start of a CDS means that both sides, the fee and the contingent legs, must be equal and from (4.2) and (4.3) we have that the spread at time zero is given by

$$S = \frac{(1 - R) \sum_{i=1}^{n} d(t_i) (P_S(t_{i-1}) - P_S(t_i))}{\left(\sum_{i=1}^{n} P_S(t_i) d(t_i) \Delta t_i + A_D \right)} \tag{4.8}$$

Consider there are CDS quotes associated with several maturities, say 3, 5, 7 and 10-year maturities. All the CDSs at inception follow (4.8). In an optimization algorithm the set of survival probabilities at each point in time is determined such that the error in recovering the observed CDS quotes is minimized. Obviously, probabilities are constrained between zero and one. Assume $Y[P_S(t_1), P_S(t_2), \ldots, P_S(t_n)]$ is a possible set of survival probabilities, S_is are the market CDS rates at time zero with maturity T_i, Z_i is the value of the spread using Y. The objective function $T[P_S(t_1), P_S(t_2), \ldots, P_S(t_n)]$ to be minimized is given by

$$T [P_S(t_1), P_S(t_2), \ldots, P_S(t_n)] = \frac{1}{2} \sum_{i=1}^{m} \left(\frac{S_i - Z_i}{\sigma_i} \right)^2 + \mu \sum_{i=0}^{n-1} d^2(p_{i+1}, p_i), \tag{4.9}$$

where $d(p_i, p_{i+1})$ is a probability distance measure given by

$$d(p_i, p_{i+1}) = \sqrt{(p_{i+1} - p_i) \ln \left(\frac{p_{i+1}}{p_i} \right) + (p_i - p_{i+1}) \ln \left(\frac{1 - p_{i+1}}{1 - p_i} \right)}. \tag{4.10}$$

The weights σ_j serve to adjust the importance given to the different quotes when implying the probabilities. The 5- and 10-year contracts may be expected to be more liquid than the 3 and 7-year contracts. Additionally, depending on market conditions we may expect that the 5-year contract is more liquid than the 10-year contract. The $d(p_i, p_{i+1})$ is an *entropic distance measure* (see e.g. Cover and Joy, 2006, for details), and serves to guarantee smoothness between two adjacent points in time of the probability distribution. Additionally, when a probability moves close to zero or close to one the parameter d will increase enormously guaranteeing that the probabilities stay constrained. The importance of the continuity part of the error function is controlled via the parameter μ.

4.4.3 Comparison

Both approaches have their advantages and disadvantages. The bootstrap method has the advantage of simplicity. There are, however, some important disadvantages. First, if the 3-year quote is unreliable, due to illiquidity, any mistakes on the determination of the short-term probabilities are propagated to the subsequent ones. Second, depending on the form of the CDS curve, one may come up with negative probabilities, and this issue needs to be properly addressed. In the optimization algorithm one searches for the distribution of probabilities that minimize CDS errors and obey some constraints, for example that probabilities remain positive and smooth. One can also control which quotes are reliable and which are not. The problem with the algorithm, however, is the following.

Assume a position has been taken on a long dated CDS, say 10 years, and it is being hedged using a short-term instrument, say a 1-year future contract on a bond. Under the constrained optimization algorithm variations on the 10-year CDS quotes will have an impact on the whole default probability curve, including the 1-year quote. In reality, however, a move on the 10-year CDS quote may not have any impact on the 1-year quote used as a hedge. By using the optimization algorithm, however, one will certainly make mistakes on the hedge parameters.

We conclude this section with a subtle and quite important point related to choosing between the bootstrap and the optimization method. Negative probabilities indicate that the market probably does not want to trade a short-term CDS on the underlying reference entity. This may signal an arbitrage opportunity. But it may also be a warning or red flag signal. In any case, the traders and the decision makers should be aware of it. This is detected by the bootstrap method and all people involved are aware of the solution. If the optimization algorithm is used the solution is implicitly taken by selecting model parameters and this event may pass unnoticed. Chances are that even the quantitative analyst may not remember the decision she has taken to address this issue. In this book the bootstrap algorithm is used.

4.5 2008 AUCTION RESULTS

In order to price a CDS an assumption for the recovery rate needs to be made. Around 2002 it was market practice to consider recovery rates of approximately 20%; recently this has become 40%. In this section we show some of the results of the recovery rates for defaults that occurred in 2008.

Table 4.1 shows the 2008 CDS auction results. Observe that Fannie Mae and Freddie Mac had high recovery rates of more than 90%. Several other names had recoveries well below 10%. The net open interest on Fannie Mae and Freddie Mac was on the buy side, pushing the final prices very high in a delivery squeeze. Note that the subordinated paper ended up higher than the senior paper. This is counterintuitive as the senior paper is deliverable in a subordinated contract, but not vice versa. Hence the senior recovery should not be lower than the subordinated. The obvious explanation for this result is that there was clearly no interest in selling subordinated paper. It should not come as a surprise that the Icelandic banks had an open interest to sell, flooding the auction with paper, pushing the final price very low. It is worthwhile comparing these numbers with the study of defaulted corporate bonds over the period 1971–1995 published by Altman and Kishore (1996). Based on 66 observations they estimate the recovery rate for financial institutions at $R = 35.7\%$.

We conclude this chapter with the following observation. The ABX.HE.AAA 7–2 index was trading at 34% on 30 January 2009, that is, a loss of 66%. This 7–2 vintage has been the worst performing AAA-rated index related to subprime mortgage loans. The paper may still

Table 4.1 2008 CDS auction results

Date	Underlying	Price (%)	Open interest
6 Oct 2008	Fannie Mae Senior	91.51	Buy
	Fannie Mae Subordinated	99.9	Buy
	Freddie Mac Senior	94	Buy
	Freddie Mac Subordinated	98	Buy
10 Oct 2008	Lehman Brothers	8.625	Sell
23 Oct 2008	Washington Mutual	57	Sell
4 Nov 2008	Landsbanki Senior	1.25	Sell
	Landsbanki Subordinated	0.125	Sell
5 Nov 2008	Glitnir Senior	3	Sell
	Glitnir Subordinated	0.125	Sell
6 Nov 2008	Kaupthing Bank Senior	6.625	Sell
	Kaupthing Bank Subordinated	2.375	Sell

recover depending on the actions of the US government. This still compares favorably with the 91% loss on a Lehman bond investment, putting the ABS investor in a far better position.

4.6 THE BIG BANG PROTOCOL

The Auction Hardwiring Supplement Protocol, a.k.a. The Big Bang protocol, was launched by ISDA on 12 March 2009. It is a supplement to the 2003 credit derivatives definitions and covers three major changes. First of all, it adds the auction settlement method as a new settlement method. This should not have any real impact on the market. Although existing CDS contracts specify physical settlement, market participants have generally agreed on cash settlement. Second, it adds an ISDA credit derivatives determination committee to the definitions. This committee will determine if credit events and succession events have occurred and if an auction should take place in the case of credit events. Their decisions are binding. Finally, some of the definitions relating to when a credit event or succession event has occurred will be amended. This addresses a problem related to backstop dates. Consider an investor who first sells protection, and later buys it back. She may still be at risk of a credit event over a certain period of time, because credit events are usually recognized and notified a short time after they actually occur.

5

Pricing Credit Spread Options:
A 2-factor HW-BK Algorithm

When you are one step ahead of the crowd, you're a genius. When you are two steps ahead, you are a crackpot.
Rabbi Shlomo Riskin

5.1 INTRODUCTION

In this chapter we describe what a *credit spread option* (CSO) is and show a tree algorithm to price it. The tree algorithm we have opted for is a two factor model composed by a Hull and White (HW) (Hull and White, 1994a) one factor for the interest rate process and a Black-Karazinsky (BK) (Black and Karazinsky, 1991) one factor for the default intensity. As opposed to the tree model of Schönbucher (1999a), the intensity process cannot become negative. Having as input the risk-free yield curve and market implied default probability curve, the model by construction will price correctly the associated defaultable bond. We then use market data to calibrate the model to price an at the money (ATM) CSO call and then test it to price an out of the money (OTM) Bermudan CSO call on a CDS. Furthermore, the discussions in this chapter show in practice the difficulties and challenges faced by financial institutions in marking to market those instruments. This chapter is based on Garcia et al. (2003). Although the paper is from 2003 the price exercise shown was made in 2001. We have kept the same numerical example to show that many of the same issues persisted until the end of 2008 – that is, the fact that the credit derivatives markets is still OTC and there is no liquid option market available.

In this chapter we show a Cox-based model for the dynamic of the intensity of default to the pricing of a *credit spread option* (CSO) on a CDS. The model has been based on the work of Schönbucher (1999a). The additional features of the model presented are as follows:

1. We use the HW model for the interest rate and the BK model for the hazard rate process, while Schönbucher uses the HW model for both processes.
2. We show in practice the difficulties involved in the calibration of the algorithm.
3. After the calibration is done (using market data) we use the model to price a Bermudan CSO on a CDS and compare the price given by the model with the price given by a market maker.
4. We give a practical view of the problems financial institutions still face when keeping track of marking to market of CSOs.

Although the model may certainly accommodate a correlation function between the dynamics of interest rates and hazard rates we will consider that both processes are not correlated. The main reason for this is that the CSO market is not yet mature and there is not enough data available to make the calibration to correlation reliable enough. Moreover, as mentioned in Schönbucher (1999a), the impact of uncertainties in recovery rates is much higher than the impact of correlation. Back in the early 2000s it was normal market practice to consider recovery rates of 20%. More recently, the standardized corporate credit indices are priced with recoveries of 40%. We refer to Table 4.1 for the 2008 CDS auction results.

The remainder of this chapter is organized as follows. In Section 5.2 the model used for the credit process is presented. In Section 5.3 we describe a credit spread option and show how this instrument is related to the stochastic processes for the risk-free rate and the default intensity. The integration of interest and hazard rates in a two factor Hull-White and Black-Karazinsky is briefly outlined in Section 5.4. Section 5.5 presents the numerical results for a Bermudan CSO on a CDS and Section 5.6 provides some concluding remarks.

5.2   THE CREDIT EVENT PROCESS

The default process here used is the intensity model described in Chapter 2. We will assume, however, that the default event follows a Poisson process with stochastic hazard rates. In the literature this is called a Cox process, and we refer to Bremaud (1981) or Lando (1998) for details.

Consider that $Q(t, T)$ is the cumulative default probability viewed at time t for the period [t, T]. In a Cox process $Q(t, T)$ is given by

$$Q(t, T) = 1 - \exp\left(-\int_t^T \lambda_t(u)\, du\right) \tag{5.1}$$

where $\lambda_t(u)$ is the instantaneous forward rate of default at time u viewed at time t. If one has $Q(t, T)$ then $\lambda(t, T)$ will be given by

$$\lambda(t, T) = -\frac{\partial}{\partial T} \ln\left(1 - Q(t, T)\right). \tag{5.2}$$

In the next section we show how the hazard rate and the cumulative default probability are used to price a credit spread option.

5.3   CREDIT SPREAD OPTIONS

Credit spread options (CSO) are designed to give cheap protection in case of spread changes. As the bond market is less liquid than the CDS market, instead of buying a put option on a bond one might want to buy a call option on a CDS. Alternatively an investor might decide to sell a CDS instead of investing in a bond, thus eliminating the funding costs. One of the possible hedges for the open CDS position is a call option on a CDS.

5.3.1   Credit spread put option on a bond

Consider $B_D(t, T)$ the price at time t of a defaultable bond with maturity T. Assume that at time t the bond is being traded at a yield spread of y_t above the yield on a risk-free identical bond ($B_{RF}(t, T)$). A credit spread put option with expiry date T_{exp} ($T_{exp} < T$) gives the holder the right to sell the bond for a prespecified yield spread K (the strike of the option) in case the yield spread y_t goes higher than K.

Consider that at the time of default the bond will be worth a recovery factor (1-L) multiplied by the notional, where L is the loss factor. Any expected accrued interest is supposed to have been accounted for in the recovery factor. We refer to Duffie and Singleton (1999) for a time deterministically dependent loss factor. For a description of alternative models of recovery rate we refer to Schönbucher (1999b).

Consider that $r(s)$ is the continuous short-term interest rate at time s, and as before $\lambda(s)$ is the hazard rate for the given entity at time s seen at the time of pricing (for simplicity the second index has been omitted). In what follows we have assumed the usual technical assumptions and the expectations are taken with respect to the equivalent martingale measure. The price of the defaultable bond is given by

$$B_D(t, T) = \mathbb{E}_t \left[\exp \left(- \int_t^T r(u) + L\lambda(u) \, du \right) \right]. \tag{5.3}$$

We refer to Duffie and Singleton (1999) or Schönbucher (1999b) for the derivation of the equation above. If one assumes independence between the intensity and the risk-free rate processes we have:

$$B_D(t, T) = B_{\mathrm{RF}}(t, T)\mathbb{E}_t \left[\exp \left(- \int_t^T L\lambda(u) \, du \right) \right]. \tag{5.4}$$

For the payoff of a CSO suppose K is the strike spread and T_{exp} the expiry date. The payoff of the credit spread (put) option at the expiry date is given by

$$\mathrm{CSO}_{\mathrm{payoff}}(T_{\mathrm{exp}}) = \left[\exp(-K(T - T_{\mathrm{exp}}))B_{\mathrm{RF}}(T_{\mathrm{exp}}, T) - B_D(T_{\mathrm{exp}}, T) \right]^+ \tag{5.5}$$

where $[x]^+$ denotes the maximum of x and zero. The price of the option at time t is given by

$$\mathrm{CSO}(t) = \mathbb{E}_t \left[\mathrm{CSO}_{\mathrm{payoff}}(T_{\mathrm{exp}}) \right] \tag{5.6}$$

where as before $\mathbb{E}_t$ is the expectation at time t under the equivalent martingale measure.

5.3.2 Credit spread option on a CDS

A call option on a CDS gives the holder the right to buy a CDS with a certain strike rate K at (or until, depending on the nature of the option) a certain date T_{exp}. With this instrument the buyer acquires the right of buying protection on the default of a general bond (which is detailed in the CDS contract).

In this study we will assume that one can replicate a CDS by taking positions in a defaultable and a risk-free *floating rate note* (FRN). An option on a CDS is approximated by using the algorithm described in the last section using FRNs instead of bonds. The results of the approximation are discussed in Section 5.5.

A short position in a CDS can be synthetically built by a short position in a defaultable FRN and a long position in a risk-free FRN. In order to see it, consider the cash flows of each side of the position: where there is no default the short side will pay the risk-free forward rate plus the (CDS) spread, while from the long side one will receive risk-free forward, generating a net position of the CDS spread. Where there is default the short side will deliver the recovered value of the defaulted FRN while receiving (in full) the notional, the net value for the short side is the loss in case of default. We refer to Schönbucher (1999b) for additional details.

In this way a call on a CDS rate is identical to a put on a defaultable FRN note, and we use (5.5) above except that in place of a bond we have an FRN. In this case the call on the CDS is then given by

$$\mathrm{CSO}_{\mathrm{payoff}}(T_{\mathrm{exp}}) = \left[\exp \left(-K(T - T_{\mathrm{exp}}) \right) \mathrm{FRN}_{\mathrm{RF}}(T_{\mathrm{exp}}, T) - \mathrm{FRN}_D(T_{\mathrm{exp}}, T) \right]^+. \tag{5.7}$$

5.4   HULL–WHITE AND BLACK–KARAZINSKY MODELS

In order to price a credit derivative security one generally needs at least a two-factor model: one for the interest rate and the other for the intensity process. In what follows we first show how to build the risk-free and the intensity process separately, then we show how the two are integrated in a three dimensional tree.

The assumption of independence between interest rates and intensities makes it possible to de-couple the payoff of a derivative so that one does not need to build a tree for the interest rate process. However, this is not the most general case, so, in what follows, we show how to develop a model which involves both a tree for the interest rate and a tree for the intensity process.

The whole algorithm follows very closely the 2-factor process algorithm described in Hull and White (1994b). In the next section we give a brief description of the HW and BK models and how they are integrated in a 2-factor model for credit derivatives (see Schönbucher, 1999a, for more details).

5.4.1   The risk-free interest rate tree

The interest rate process is modeled using the HW model which is basically an Ornstein-Uhlenbeck process. We refer to Øksendal (1998) and Karatzas and Shreve (1991) for a general treatment of the Ornstein-Uhlenbeck process. We assume

$$\mathrm{d}r = (\theta_r(t) - a_r r)\ \mathrm{d}t + \sigma_r\ \mathrm{d}B \tag{5.8}$$

where r, a_r and σ_r are the unobserved instantaneous short rate, mean reversion and volatility respectively.

The algorithm builds the dynamic of the interest rate process in a recombining trinomial tree structure. For each time step of length Δt the short rate will assume values of the form $r(t + \Delta t) = r(t) + k\Delta r$, where k might be negative or positive integer and Δr is given by

$$\Delta r = \sigma_r \sqrt{3\Delta t}. \tag{5.9}$$

The branching probabilities at the nodes are evaluated by the use of three constraints: the first two moments of the process and the fact that probabilities add up to 1. One more constraint on the whole tree might be added: it may not grow indefinitely otherwise probabilities might become negative.

The steps in building the tree are as follows:

- Suppose in (5.8) that $\theta_r(t)$ is zero and build a symmetric tree for the r process.
- Evaluate the value of $\theta_r(t)$ to be added at each node such that one may price correctly zero coupon bonds.
- Evaluate the values of a_r and σ_r which would correctly price swaptions, caps or floors or any derivative which may be linked with the securities one needs to price.

The third step above is called *calibration*. Observe that by construction any values of mean reversion and volatility will lead to the correct prices of zero coupon bonds. The determination of the mean reversion and volatility to be used in each case is done by searching the values of the two parameters which give acceptable prices of market available interest rate options.

In principle one could also use the HW model above to model the evolution of the hazard rate (the default intensity). Indeed, this was the approach proposed by Schönbucher (1999a).

The HW model, however, does not preclude the values in the tree nodes from becoming negative. As default intensities are related to default probabilities we see from (5.1) that negative intensities would lead to negative default probabilities.

In the next section we briefly describe the BK tree model.

5.4.2 The default intensity tree

The default intensity process follows the stochastic differential equation:

$$d \ln \lambda = (\theta_\lambda(t) - a_\lambda \ln \lambda) \, dt + \sigma_\lambda \, dB \tag{5.10}$$

where, as before, a_λ and σ_λ are the mean reversion and volatility for the intensity process, λ is the intensity and ln is the natural logarithm.

The steps in building the tree are basically the same as described above and we refer to Hull and White (1994b) for details. There are, however, two important points worth mentioning.

The first is that (see Section 5.4.1 above) in order to evaluate $\theta_\lambda(t)$ *one needs the cumulative probability of non-default curve*. In our case we implied this cumulative probability from the CDS spreads observed at the CDS market using one of the algorithms described in Chapter 4.

The second, and no less important aspect, is how to calibrate the model. One should remember that by construction any value of a_λ and σ_λ will reproduce the cumulative probability given. That is, by construction one prices exactly the defaultable bond associated with the cumulative default probability given as input. But in order to price options one still needs the option market to determine the values of the mean reversion and volatility (calibration). In here, however, there is no liquid option market for credit products. The approach we have used for the calibration is the following: we got from the market a price for an at the money (ATM) and an out of the money (OTM) CSO. The model was calibrated for the ATM and the parameters so determined have been used to price an OTM option. Later on we comment on this approach and discuss an alternative methodology for the calibration.

5.4.3 The credit tree HW and BK

The new integrated tree, referred to as the *3D tree* in what follows, has the same number of time steps as the other two trees, referred to as *2D trees*. One should make sure that both 2D trees have the same time step interval. At each node in the new tree one may go to 9 possible nodes if there is no default, or to one node in case of default – i.e. 10 possible nodes in total.

A node in the 3D tree will be represented by $n_{3D}(x, y, z)$, where the first index represents time step and the other two indexes are the interest rate coming from the node $n_{RF}(x, y)$ in the interest rate tree, and the default intensity $n_D(x, z)$ in the intensity tree.

The branching probabilities in the 3D tree are given in Table 5.1 and the default probability in node $n_D(x, y, z)$ is given by

$$P_{\text{default}}(x, y, z) = 1 - \exp(-n_D(x, z)\Delta t). \tag{5.11}$$

From Table 5.1 it is clear we are assuming independence between the two processes. We comment on this in Section 5.5.

Table 5.1   Branch probabilities in the 3D tree

	UP	Middle	Down
Up	$p_{R,u} \times p_{D,u}$	$p_{R,u} \times p_{D,m}$	$p_{R,u} \times p_{D,d}$
Middle	$p_{R,m} \times p_{D,u}$	$p_{R,m} \times p_{D,m}$	$p_{R,m} \times p_{D,d}$
Down	$p_{R,d} \times p_{D,u}$	$p_{R,d} \times p_{D,m}$	$p_{R,d} \times p_{D,d}$

5.4.4   Using the tree to price a CSO

In this section we explain in more detail how to price a CSO on a CDS. Consider that one wants to evaluate a 1-year call CSO with strike K on a 6-year CDS. As we have already mentioned we will approximate it by pricing a put option on a defaultable FRN. For simplicity, consider that the notional of the contract is N, the recovery rate supposed fixed is α. In what follows, we will call the interest rate and the default intensity trees as 2D trees. The steps are as follows:

- Build a tree for the 6-year risk-free FRN. Consider that $n_{RF}(x, y, z)$ and $n_{RF}(x, y)$ represent the node of the 3D and the 2D risk-free FRN trees. Then we have:

$$\text{FRN}_{RF}(x, y, z) = \text{FRN}_{RF}(x, y). \tag{5.12}$$

In this way the value of the risk-free FRN depends only on the values it has in the 2D tree nodes.
- Build a tree for the defaultable FRN (represented as FRN_D). Let T be the maturity of the FRN_D, in case $T = 6$. At time T we have:

$$\text{FRN}_D(x_T, y, z) = N + C, \ \forall y, z \tag{5.13}$$

where x_T is the time step corresponding to time T. C is the coupon of the floater. The remaining nodes in the tree are calculated by backward induction as follows:

$$\text{FRN}_D(x_n, y, z) = \exp(-\lambda(x_n, z)\Delta t)$$
$$\left(\sum_{i,j} \left(p(x_n, y_i, z_j)\text{FRN}_D(x_{n+1}, y_i, z_i)\exp(-r(x_n, y)\Delta t) \right) + I(x_n)C \right)$$
$$+ (1 - \exp(-\lambda(x_n, z)t))\alpha N \tag{5.14}$$

where $\lambda(x_n, z)$ and $r(x_n, y)$ are the values of the default intensity and risk-free rate at nodes (x_n, z) and (x_n, y) in their respective trees. The notation $p(x_n, y_i, z_j)$ is shorthand for the following more cumbersome notation $p((x_n, y, z)|(x_{n+1}, y_i, z_j))$ which means the probability in node (y, z) at time x_n of going to node (y_i, z_j) at time x_{n+1}. $I(x_n)$ is the indicator function which is 1 if there is a coupon payment at time x_n and 0 otherwise. The first factor in (5.14) is the value of the bond in case there is no default while the second factor gives the value in the case of default.
- Build a tree for the CSO. Consider that T_{CSO} ($T_{CSO} < T$) is the expiry time of the option and that this corresponds to node x_{CSO} in the 3D tree. Assuming that the strike in the option is K at the expiry of the (put) option we have that:

$$\text{CSO}(x_{T_{\exp}}, y, z) = \left[\exp(-K(T - T_{\exp}))\text{FRN}_{RF}(x_{T_{\exp}}, y, z) - \text{FRN}_D(x_{T_{\exp}}, y, z) \right]^+. \tag{5.15}$$

Assuming that in case of default of the FRN_D the option holder gets the recovery rate on the FRN, then the remaining nodes in the tree are calculated as:

$$\text{CSO}^{\text{eur}}(x_n, y, z)$$
$$= \exp(-\lambda(x_n, z)\Delta t) \sum_{i,j} [p(x_n, y_i, z_j)\text{CSO}(x_{n+1}, y_i, z_j)\exp(-r(x_n, y)\Delta t)]$$
$$+ (1 - \exp(-\lambda(x_n, z)t)\alpha) \tag{5.16}$$

for the case of an European option. If the option is American (or Bermudan) we have

$$\text{CSO}^{\text{am}}(x_n, y, z) = \exp(-\lambda(x_n, z)t)$$
$$\times \max\left(\sum[p(x_n, y_i, z_j)\text{CSO}(x_{n+1}, y_i, z_j)\exp(-r, x_n, y)t],\right.$$
$$\times \exp(-K(T - T_{\text{exp}}))\text{FRN}_{\text{RF}}(x_{\text{CSO}}, y, z) - \text{FRN}_D(x_{\text{CSO}}, y, z))$$
$$+(1 - \exp(-\lambda(x_n, z)\Delta t)\alpha N) \tag{5.17}$$

In the above formulation we have made the simplifying assumption that the option premium is paid up front. We also decided to count the defaultable coupon as being the risk-free forward rate plus the spread.

A simplifying assumption is that the risk-free forward rate will be evaluated using the current yield curve, avoiding the option to become path dependent. In this way the coupon of the FRN_D is given by

$$C(t_n) = (f(0, t_{n-1}, t_n) + K)(t_n - t_{n-1}) \tag{5.18}$$

where t_{n-1} and t_n are the dates when the coupon rate is determined and paid respectively; $f(0, t_{n-1}, t_n)$ is the forward rate observed at time zero for the period between t_{n-1} and t_n, and K is the CDS strike rate in the option.

Moreover, we will be pricing a Bermudan CSO and allowing the exercise dates to be taken on payment dates only. The reason for this is that the value of the floater immediately after the coupon payment is face value. Otherwise, to be absolutely precise, one would need to determine the value of the coupon of the floater making the option to be path dependent.

In the next section we give results of the pricing of a Bermudan call CSO on a CDS with the model being calibrated to market prices. Observe that, as mentioned before, a call on a CDS rate is a put on the defaultable FRN.

5.5   RESULTS

In this section we show the results of pricing a Bermudan call CSO on a CDS. As already mentioned, we have calibrated the HW interest rate tree for swaptions and then calibrated the intensity in the BK tree to an ATM American CSO and both prices have been taken from a market participant.

The mean reversion and volatility for the interest rate tree are respectively 0.012 and 0.009. The risk-free discount curve of the day is shown in Table 5.2

In order to build the BK intensity tree one will need to imply default probabilities. In Table 5.3 we show the CDS credit spreads. The implied default probabilities are shown in Table 5.4.

The prices for the ATM and the OTM CSO obtained from the market and from the tree are shown in Table 5.5. Both market prices are the bid prices by a large financial institution.

Table 5.2   Risk-free discount factors

Date	Discount factor
16/8/2001	1.0000000
17/8/2001	0.9998747
20/8/2001	0.9994978
27/8/2001	0.9986182
3/9/2001	0.9977382
20/9/2001	0.9956654
22/10/2001	0.9919294
22/11/2001	0.9886339
20/2/2002	0.9785173
20/5/2002	0.9695015
20/8/2002	0.9600748
20/8/2003	0.9205583
20/8/2004	0.8793688
22/8/2005	0.8371468
21/8/2006	0.7947228
20/8/2007	0.7521805
20/8/2008	0.7102778
20/8/2009	0.6695355

Table 5.3   CDS quotes used to determine the default probability

Time (yr)	1	2	3	4	5	6	7	8	9	10
Spread (bp)	175	241	264	276	285	293	300	302	304	306

Table 5.4   Cumulative default probability curve

Date	Default probability
16/08/2001	0
16/08/2002	0.0342510
16/08/2003	0.0920711
16/08/2004	0.1474603
16/08/2005	0.1996514
16/08/2006	0.2505164
16/08/2007	0.3004684
16/08/2008	0.3487388

Table 5.5   ATM and OTM CSO prices

Strike (bp)	Market price (bp)	HWBK price (bp)
285 (ATM)	160	–
340 (OTM)	105	135

As can be seen from Table 5.5 the bid price from the model for the OTM CSO is higher than the one given by the market. Should one then conclude that the model is inadequate? Is there any utility in the model? How should the results be interpreted?

There are several reasons for the discrepancies in the prices between the model and the market. One is that the credit derivatives market for single name options is still quite illiquid and an OTC market. A second reason for the discrepancy in prices is that the model might systematically overprice OTM CSO calls. Indeed, if the market was using a BS-like approximation we would have calibrated the model for a higher volatility, the ATM option, than the one used in pricing the OTM option, assuming smiles effects. As the BK process presents fatter tail distributions than the one expected by the BS process, one again would expect higher prices for the OTM call.

A third reason would be the effect of an error on the assumed recovery rate when implying default probabilities from the CDS quotes. A fourth is the independence assumption between interest and intensity rates. We had only one option available for calibraton purposes as we had only one ATM CSO available. This is linked to the difficulty in getting market quotes. Alternatively, instead of getting market quotes (to be used for calibration) one could use the Black-Scholes formula (see Schönbucher, 2003) for European CSOs and calibrate the model to it. It happens that the BS model depends on default intensity volatilities and those volatilities are not yet available in the market.

One last remark: most of the questions above might only be answered when the credit derivatives market becomes more mature and data becomes available. In the present situation, practitioners will have to continue coping with models that are only half understood in order to mark to market CSO exposures.

5.6   CONCLUSION

In this chapter we have developed a 2-factor tree model to price Bermudan call CSOs on a CDS. Some approximations are done in considering the CSO as options on the spread between a defaultable and a risk-free FRN. Although we have assumed independence between interest and default intensity rates, for completeness we have shown how to model the two processes and put them together. The model uses a HW tree for the interest rate dynamics and a BK tree for the intensity process.

The HW tree has been calibrated to swaption prices.

In the construction of the BK tree we have used a default probability curve that was implied from observed market CDS rates at the time of pricing. Once the BK tree is constructed it is then calibrated to an (ATM Bermudan) call CSO market quote. The parameters so determined are then used to price an (OTM Bermudan) call CSO.

Although we have observed that the model overprices the bid price of the OTM option we cannot say that the price is out of the bid offer spread. The CSO market is still very illiquid and prices might vary considerably from bank to bank. Several problems need to be addressed when trying to model a CSO, of which we mention four:

- lack of reliable intensity volatilities or even CDS rates;
- uncertainties about recovery rates;
- lack of CSO quotes for which to calibrate the model;
- uncertainties about correlation parameters between interest and intensity rate processes.

The way these uncertainties affect the price of a CSO will continue to be an area for future research.

As a final remark, this chapter showed the difficulties faced by practitioners who have to mark to market portfolios of CSOs. Most of them might be pricing via the hedge instruments and running the problems of imperfect hedges.

6

Counterparty Risk and Credit Valuation Adjustment

Hell is other people.
Jean-Paul Sartre

6.1 INTRODUCTION

Derivatives are marvelous as they enable hedging different specific risks. The result is a portfolio that *may seem safer*. However, this comes at the cost of replacing fairly common, well-understood risks with the exceptional risk that the counterparty may fail.

Counterparty credit risk is defined as the risk that a counterparty in an over the counter (OTC) derivative transaction will default prior to the expiration of the contract and hence will be unable to make all contractual payments. Credit value adjustment is the price of counterparty credit risk. It can be calculated as the risk-neutral expectation of the discounted loss over the life of the transaction. The exposure to a counterparty at any future time is the loss experienced where the counterparty defaults at that time, assuming zero recovery rate. In this chapter, we address the problem of credit valuation adjustment (CVA) for a credit default swap (CDS). As an example, we consider a CDS intermediation business case.

A typical transaction in the CDS intermediation business is built as follows. On the one hand, the intermediator (I) sells (collateralized) protection on a reference entity to a collateralized counterparty (CC). On the other hand, the intermediator buys protection on the same reference entity for a noncollateralized counterparty (NCC) to hedge this position. Such a transaction has an asymmetric risk profile. The favorable outcome is a tightening of the CDS on the reference entity, resulting in a positive mark to market (MtM). In this case, a default of the NCC is harmless to the intermediator. There are two nonfavorable outcomes for the intermediator. First, if the CDS spread on the reference entity widens, the intermediator will have to post collateral to the CC whereas the NCC does not have to post collateral. In this case, a default of the NCC will affect the intermediator as it is obliged to unwind the CDS with the CC, paying the due mark to market. Second, if there is a default of the reference entity and a default of the NCC during the settlement period of the CDS on the reference entity, the intermediator is in a dangerous position as the intermediator owes the CC the CDS notional. The CVA can be computed as the risk-neutral expectation of the discounted loss of the CDS contract.

Recently, the bilateral nature of counterparty risk has been considered (see e.g. Gregory, 2009). Taking this bilateral nature into account would result in an institution reducing its counterparty risk in line with its own default probability. Note that it means that economic value is attached to the fact that a gain is made when the institution itself defaults, just as a loss is made when the counterparty defaults. Taken to the extreme limit, this would imply that a derivatives portfolio with counterparty risk would be more valuable than the equivalent risk-free portfolio. In this chapter, we assume that the institution itself does not default during the lifetime of the contract. This assumption dates back from the times that iTraxx Financials was trading at around 8 bp and should be revised given the market developments since June 2007. However, this is outside the scope of this book.

General references for credit derivatives modeling include Arvanitis and Gregory (2001), Bluhm et al. (2003) and Schönbucher (2003), amongst others. A more detailed coverage of counterparty credit risk is covered in Pykhtin (2005). Brigo and Chourdakis (2008) have also considered counterparty risk for CDS in the presence of correlation between default of the counterparty and the reference entity. The correlation models presented here are semi-static alternatives to simulation of default intensities, such as e.g. using trinomial trees. We also refer to our earlier publication (Garcia et al., 2008).

The remainder of this chapter is organized as follows. The CVA methodology is outlined in Section 6.2. In Section 6.3 we develop a Monte Carlo simulation for the CVA on a CDS. A semi-analytic correlation model is presented in Section 6.4. Results are given in Section 6.5. In Section 6.6 we decompose the spread paid to the counterparty into the real protection payment – that is, the *true CDS* – and the *CVA* – that is, the price of the counterparty risk. We argue in Section 6.7 that counterparty risk needs to be observable and measurable. Finally, our conclusions are presented in Section 6.8.

6.2 VALUATION OF THE CVA

As mentioned in the introduction, there are two nonfavorable outcomes. First, we address the calculation of the expected loss ($\mathbb{E}L_1$) due to the deterioration of the CDS with the NCC. Second, we focus on the determination of the expected loss ($\mathbb{E}L_2$) for the joint default of the reference entity and the NCC.

For the determination of the CVA, three ingredients are required: the probability of default between the payment dates at time t_i and t_{i-1}; the loss given default; and the future expected (positive) exposure at time t_i. The future expected positive exposure (EPE) can be written as an European swaption with a strike equal to the issue spread of the reference entity. Hence we can write the expected loss due to the absence of collateral during the life of the transaction as follows:

$$\mathbb{E}L_1 = (1 - R_{\text{NCC}}) \sum_{t_i \in [0,T]} \mathbb{P}^{\text{NCC}} [t_i \leq \tau_{\text{NCC}} < t_{i+1}] \max(\text{MtM}_{\text{CDS}}(t_i), 0). \tag{6.1}$$

The future expected positive exposure in (6.1) is calculated using the general methodology for swaption valuation, i.e. Black's formula. For more details we refer to Schönbucher (2003). Moreover, this is similar to a CDS European call option of maturity t_i and strike K whereas the value of the contract at time t_i equals the amount of collateral posted. The future expected positive exposure is determined as follows:

$$\text{CDS}_{\text{Option}}(K, t, T) = \text{EPE}_t = \text{BPV}(t, T) \, \text{Black}(F_{t,T}(0), K, \sigma_{t,T}, \sqrt{T - t}) \tag{6.2}$$

where $F_{t,T}(0)$ is the CDS forward rate at time t, with maturity $(T - t)$, K the strike of the option (issue spread) and $\sigma_{t,T}$ is the volatility of the forward rate. The present value of 1 basis point (bp) paid from time t until maturity T is denoted by $\text{BPV}(t, T)$ and is computed as in (4.6) summing over the relevant payment dates.

In the case of a joint default, the expected loss is the following:

$$\mathbb{E}L_2 = (1 - R_{\text{NCC}})(1 - R_{\text{RE}}) \sum_{t_i \in [0,T]} \mathbb{P}^{\text{NCC,RE}} [t_i \leq \tau_{\text{NCC}}, \tau_{\text{RE}} < t_{i+1}] \tag{6.3}$$

where R_{RE} and R_{NCC} are respectively the recovery rate of the reference entity and the NCC.

In the case where the default times of the reference entity and the NCC are assumed to be independent, the joint default probability can be obtained as the product of the individual probabilities:

$$\mathbb{P}^{NCC,RE}[t_i \leq \tau_{NCC}, \tau_{RE} < t_{i+1}]$$

$$= \mathbb{P}^{NCC}[t_i \leq \tau_{NCC} < t_{i+1}]\,\mathbb{P}^{RE}[t_i \leq \tau_{RE} < t_{i+1}]. \tag{6.4}$$

Under the assumption of independence the value of $\mathbb{E}L_2$ is significantly smaller than $\mathbb{E}L_1$ and the contribution of the joint default scenario to the CVA could be neglected.

The CVA is the upfront fee U, which is the sum of $\mathbb{E}L_1$ and $\mathbb{E}L_2$:

$$U = \mathbb{E}L_1 + \mathbb{E}L_2. \tag{6.5}$$

A running fee R equivalent can be defined by dividing the upfront fee by the present value of 1 basis point (bp) paid over the life of the contract subject to the survival probability of the NCC

$$R = \frac{U}{\mathrm{BPV}^{NCC}}. \tag{6.6}$$

6.3   MONTE CARLO SIMULATION FOR CVA ON CDS

We simulate correlated default times for the reference entity and the NCC. To this end we generate the following random variates:

$$X_1 = N^{[-1]}(U_1) = Z_1, \tag{6.7}$$

$$X_2 = N^{[-1]}(U_2) = \rho Z_1 + \sqrt{1 - \rho^2} Z_2, \tag{6.8}$$

in which $X_1, X_2, Z_1, Z_2 \sim \mathcal{N}(0, 1)$ are standard normal distributed variates and $U_1, U_2 \sim$ Uniform$(0, 1)$ are uniformly distributed variates. We denote by $N(x)$ and $N^{[-1]}(p)$ the standard normal cumulative distribution function and its inverse respectively. Moreover Z_1 and Z_2 are independent. Hence X_1 and X_2 are correlated with a correlation factor ρ:

$$\mathrm{corr}(X_1, X_2) = \rho. \tag{6.9}$$

Setting the survival probabilities for the reference entity and the NCC equal to U_1 and U_2, the corresponding default times can be found by solving equation (4.1) for τ_{RE} and τ_{NCC} respectively. In the special case of a single constant default intensity λ, an explicit solution is readily available:

$$\tau = \frac{-1}{\lambda} \log u. \tag{6.10}$$

Starting from the generated default times τ_{NCC} and τ_{RE}, we first check if

$$\tau_{RE} \leq \tau_{NCC} \leq \tau_{RE} + S, \tag{6.11}$$

in which S is the settlement period for the CDS on the RE, typically three months. If this is the case we have a joint default, since the NCC defaults during the settlement for the CDS on the RE, which has defaulted. In this scenario a loss of $(1 - R_{NCC})(1 - R_{RE})$ is incurred, as in (6.3). Otherwise, a loss equal to $(1 - R_{NCC})\text{EPE}_{\tau_{NCC}}$, in which $\text{EPE}_{\tau_{NCC}}$ is computed using (6.2), is incurred at τ_{NCC}, as in (6.1).

It is straightforward to apply importance sampling. Given that the contract has a fixed finite maturity T, we only have to generate uniform random variates larger than the survival probability at maturity $P_S(T)$ as given by (4.1). In this application our interest is clearly in the default time of the NCC.

6.4   SEMI-ANALYTIC CORRELATION MODEL

The survival probability $P_S(t)$ is modeled as described by (4.1) and the default probability $P_D(t)$ can be obtained from $P_D(t) = 1 - P_S(t)$. A default threshold is defined by

$$X_t = N^{[-1]}(P_D(t)). \tag{6.12}$$

The joint probability of default $\mathbb{P}^{NCC, RE}$ $[t_i \leq \tau_{NCC}, \tau_{RE} < t_{i+1}]$ is computed using a Gaussian copula:

$$P_J = N_2\left(N^{[-1]}(P_{D,1}), N^{[-1]}(P_{D,2}); \rho_C\right) \tag{6.13}$$

where $N_2(x, y; \rho_C)$ denotes the bivariate normal distribution with correlation parameter ρ_C.

The correlation parameter ρ_C addresses the joint probability of default. We could also consider a correlation between the default probability of the NCC and the evolution of the forward spreads. To this end we introduce the correlation parameter ρ_C in the methodology outlined below. Correlation is modeled using a one factor model, in which Z is the common market factor. We decompose the default barrier for the NCC as

$$X_M = \sqrt{\rho_F}Z + \sqrt{1 - \rho_F}\varepsilon_{X_M}. \tag{6.14}$$

All variates X_M, Z and ε_{X_M} are standard normal distributed and Z and ε_{X_M} are independent. The parameter $0 \leq \rho_F \leq 1$ controls the correlation.

We now revisit the computation of $\mathbb{E}L_1$ in light of this added correlation model. An individual term in (6.1) reads

$$\begin{aligned}
E &= \mathbb{E}\left[1_{\{t_{i-1} < \tau_{NCC} < t_i\}} A (F - K)_+\right] \\
&= \mathbb{E}\left[\mathbb{E}\left[1_{\{t_{i-1} < \tau_{NCC} < t_i\}} A (F - K)_+\right] | Z\right] \\
&= \mathbb{E}\left[\mathbb{E}\left[1_{\{t_{i-1} < \tau_{NCC} < t_i\}} | Z\right] \mathbb{E}\left[A (F - K)_+ | Z\right]\right].
\end{aligned} \tag{6.15}$$

We denote by τ_{NCC} the default time of the NCC and by t_i payment dates, or option dates. The risky annuity is denoted by A, while F denotes the forward spread and K is the strike, i.e., the contractual spread.

The evolution of the forward spreads follows a driftless geometric Brownian motion:

$$F_t = F_0 \exp\left(-\frac{\sigma^2}{2}t - \sigma\sqrt{t}W\right) \tag{6.16}$$

in which $W \sim \mathcal{N}(0, 1)$ is a standard normal distributed random variable and σ is the volatility. The driving Brownian motion is correlated to the common market factor Z as well.

$$W = \sqrt{\rho_F}Z + \sqrt{1 - \rho_F}\varepsilon_W \tag{6.17}$$

All variates W, Z and ε_W all standard normal distributed and Z and ε_W are independent. As a result of this construction the correlation between X_M and W is ρ.

Table 6.1   CVA upfront fee for a notional of 10^4 as a function of the strike K and the spread s of the NCC for a 10-year contract, assuming the default times of the NCC and the RE are independent

s	350 bp	585 bp	2000 bp
$K = 18$ bp	7.65	11.08	18.97
$K = 20$ bp	6.82	9.83	16.18

Table 6.2   Probability of joint default and CVA upfront fee for a notional of 10^4 as a function of the correlation factor ρ using the Monte Carlo method

ρ	p_{JD}	U
0	0	15.73
5%	0.1%	16.40
10%	1.8%	26.18
15%	4.8%	42.94
20%	8.0%	60.44
25%	11%	76.03
30%	13%	89.23

6.5   NUMERICAL RESULTS

Table 6.1 shows the CVA upfront fee for a notional of 10^4 as a function of the strike K and the flat spread s_{NCC} of the NCC for a 10-year contract, intermediating between the CC at 20 bp and the NCC at 18 bp, assuming the default times of the NCC and the RE are independent. The present value of this contract is 16.40. The forward rate F is flat at 20 bp and the volatility σ is 50%. The recovery rates are $R_{RE} = 90\%$ and $R_{NCC} = 40\%$ respectively. All quotes are supposed to be valid for a CC, unless stated explicitly.

The CVA upfront fee U is the price of the (exotic) option to replace a CDS contract with another one. Our interest is in the option to replace the CDS with the NCC struck at $K = 18$ bp. Replacement contracts can come from both the CC and NCC markets. Note that replacing the contract with another NCC does not solve the collateral posting mismatch; only replacing the contract with a CC addresses this issue. In order to estimate the cost of this collateral posting mismatch we can try to compute the CVA using forward spreads on the NCC side. In the absence of sufficiently liquid quotes at the NCC side, we can also use the CC forward spreads to compute a CVA upfront fee for a contract struck at $K = 20$ bp, although this is not the contract we are seeking to replace. Note that this is a very crude approximation.

Table 6.2 shows the probability of joint default and CVA upfront fee for a notional of 10^4 as a function of the correlation factor ρ. These results have been computed using the Monte Carlo simulation approach. The forward rate F is flat at 50 bp and the volatility σ is 50%. The strike is $K = 45$ bp. The recovery rates are $R_{RE} = 90\%$ and $R_{NCC} = 40\%$ respectively.

6.6   CDS WITH COUNTERPARTY RISK

In this section we address the problem of buying protection on a reference entity from a counterparty that may be correlated to the underlying reference entity. The spread paid to the counterparty is decomposed into the real protection payment – that is, the *true CDS* – and the risky counterparty fee (RCF). Note that this RCF is not the price of counterparty risk as in the classical sense of CVA. We assume that the single name survival probabilities as in (4.1) are available, both for the reference entity and the counterparty. The *true CDS value* is calculated using the classical formulas (4.2) for the contingent leg and (4.3) for the fee leg. The difference, however, is that in the contingent leg (4.2) the probability of default of the reference entity is calculated using a Gaussian copula as in (6.13). In this case we are interested in the probability that the reference entity defaults between t_{i-1} and t_i and the counterparty does not default before t_i. It is given by

$$P_S(t_{i-1}) - P_S(t_i) = N_2\left(N^{[-1]}(P_{S,m}(t_i)), N^{[-1]}(P_{S,r}(t_{i-1})); \rho\right)$$
$$- N_2\left(N^{[-1]}(P_{S,m}(t_i)), N^{[-1]}(P_{S,r}(t_i)); \rho\right) \qquad (6.18)$$

which in the case of independence becomes

$$P_S(t_{i-1}) - P_S(t_i) = P_{S,m}(t_i)\left(P_{S,r}(t_{i-1}) - P_{S,r}(t_i)\right). \qquad (6.19)$$

The fee leg (4.3) is not modified. The probability appearing there is the single name survival probability of the reference entity. It is clear that this approach carries over to other copula functions as well.

As an example, we consider buying noncollateralized protection on a super senior tranche from a monoline insurer. When spreads were tight, this could be done at a spread of $s_r = 5$ bp and the CDS on the AAA monoline insurer would be around $s_m = 10$ bp. The maturity of the contract is $T = 5$ years. The assumed recovery rate is $R = 40\%$ both for the tranche and insurer. A flat interest rate curve $r = 0\%$ has been used.

The impact of correlation on this counterparty risky CDS is shown in Table 6.3. Observe that above a certain value for the correlation one is paying more for the counterparty risk than for the true value of the CDS on the underlying reference entity. Consequently, it becomes more interesting to *hedge the default risk of the insurer* than to buy protection from the insurer.

Table 6.4 shows the sensitivity of the counterparty risky CDS to the spread s_m of the monoline insurer for different values of the correlation. Obviously the counterparty risk as measured by the RCF increases as the CDS spread of the counterparty goes up. It is interesting to see that the boundary, above which one is paying more for the counterparty risk than for the

Table 6.3 Impact of correlation on counterparty risky CDS

ρ (%)	RCF	CDS
0	0.0214	4.9786
50	0.4089	4.5911
75	1.1759	3.8241
90	2.3276	2.6724
91.3	2.5010	2.4990
95	3.1731	1.8269
96	3.4329	1.5671
97	3.7537	1.2463
98	4.1665	0.8335
99	4.7000	0.3000
100	5.0000	0.0000

Table 6.4 Sensitivity analysis of CDS with counterparty risk

s_m (bp)	RCF	CDS	RCF	CDS	RCF	CDS
10	0.0214	4.9786	0.4089	4.5911	1.1759	3.8241
40	0.0860	4.9140	1.0411	3.9589	2.5662	2.4338
100	0.2121	4.7879	1.7767	3.2233	3.6351	1.3649
200	0.4130	4.5870	2.5065	2.4935	4.3003	0.6997
500	0.9524	4.0476	3.5642	1.4358	4.8076	0.1924
1 000	1.6766	3.3234	4.2459	0.7541	4.9486	0.0514
2 000	2.6652	2.3348	4.6855	0.3145	4.9897	0.0103
3 000	3.2751	1.7249	4.8296	0.1704	4.9965	0.0035
6 000	4.1246	0.8754	4.9493	0.0507	4.9996	0.0004
10 000	4.5157	0.4843	4.9826	0.0174	5.0000	0.0000
	$\rho = 0$		$\rho = 50\%$		$\rho = 75\%$	

true value of the CDS on the underlying reference entity, comes down very quickly if the correlation goes up. This happens at 1794 bp under independence and at 199 bp where the correlation is 50%. Even more striking is that this breakeven occurs at 38 bp for 75% correlation and at 11 bp for 90% correlation.

It is clear that the correlation between the portfolio of the insurer and the underlying reference entity is the key parameter. We address this problem in Chapter 13 and find that the correlation between *two* super senior tranches is 84% for 5-year contracts where the underlying asset correlation is 20%. Consequently, the correlation between a portfolio that already has a lot of super senior tranches and one additional super senior tranche is extremely high!

We conclude this section with a trivia question. Choosing between buying *noncollateralized* protection on a super senior tranche from an AAA-rated insurer or buying a CDS on it from a BBB counterparty that *posts collateral* should not be too difficult, should it?

6.7 COUNTERPARTY RISK MITIGATION

A counterparty default index can be constructed using a very simple methodology. The index value is defined as the arithmetic average of the 5-year CDS spreads of the constituents. Obvious candidates for the constituents are the top dealers operating in the market. At the time of writing the constituents were Bank of America, Barclays, BNP Paribas, Citigroup, Credit Suisse, Deutsche Bank, Goldman Sachs, HSBC Bank, JPMorgan Chase, Morgan Stanley, Royal Bank of Scotland, Société Générale and UBS.

Clearly this methodology requires updating the index when a credit event occurs. Bear Stearns was removed on 17 March 2008, as it was acquired by JPMorgan. On 25 April 2008, ABN Amro was replaced by RBS, following the acquisition of ABN by RBS. Lehman Brothers was removed on 15 September 2008. Merrill Lynch was removed on 2 January 2009, as it was acquired by Bank of America.

The historical evolution of such an index is shown in Figure 6.1. Given a counterparty default index, counterparty risk can be measured. The next step is to build products based on the index to hedge against it.

The classical approach to counterparty risk mitigation is collateral posting. The obvious benefits of collateral management are that it reduces the credit risk and that it frees up lines with counterparties. On the other hand, the process exhibits some weaknesses. First of all,

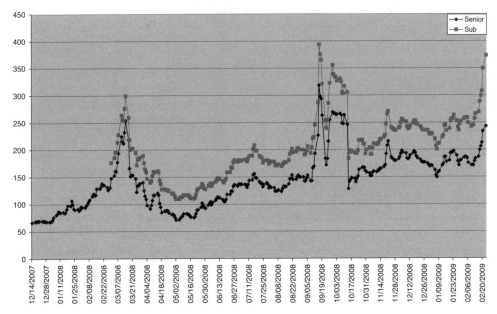

Figure 6.1   Counterparty default index

the dispute resolution processes can be enhanced. Second, the collateral may not be worth what it is claimed to be worth and its value may decline over time. Third, as it is peer to peer, the relation between the counterparties may play. As an example, consider a weak player buying protection from a stronger counterparty. Suppose that at some time the trade has a positive mark to market for the weak player. Clearly the weak player is entitled to collateral. However, the stronger counterparty threatens to cut its (short term) funding to the weak player. As funding is very important to the weak player and he is forced to choose between collateral and funding, he decides to drop his collateral claims and is left with a risk that in theory could have been mitigated.

It is advantageous to have a central counterparty. In the wake of the financial crisis, pressure is mounting on users in the over-the-counter (OTC) markets to increase transparency. Trading on an exchange with a central counterparty clearly increases transparency. Moreover, having a central counterparty should help alleviate long-standing concerns over the way collateral has been handled in the OTC environment.

6.8   CONCLUSIONS

In this chapter we have described a methodology for credit valuation adjustment on credit default swaps. Given the absence of market data for the volatilities of forward CDS spreads, one should be careful when applying these models.

Part III
Multiname Corporate Credit Derivatives

7
Collateralized Debt Obligations

It wasn't raining when Noah built the ark.
Warren Buffet

7.1 INTRODUCTION

In this chapter we start with the analysis of multiname credit derivatives. In those contracts the payoff is contingent on the credit events in a portfolio of reference entities. Typical examples are collateralized debt obligations (CDO), first loss on a basket, and first or nth to default swaps.

In a *first to default swap* the protection buyer pays a fee in return for a lump payment by the protection seller for the first entity to default in the portfolio. The instrument offers cheaper protection than buying individual protection. Consider, for instance, an investor who wants to hedge the credit exposure on a portfolio of five bonds. She feels that for her investment horizon the risk on more than one default is rather small, and instead of buying protection on each single name in the portfolio she chooses to buy protection against one default. In a *first loss basket* the protection buyer pays a fee to receive protection up to a certain amount on a certain portfolio. Instead of buying protection on the number of entities to default this derivative allows the investor to focus directly on the possible amount lost. As a consequence, the losses in the portfolio may be reduced, improving its rating and ultimately the cost of *regulatory* capital. Here we see again how the cost of regulatory capital became an important point for decision-making purposes and the development of the credit derivatives market.

In general, basket instruments involve small portfolios from five up to 10 or 20 references. The powerful role of *innovation* and its impact in the market can be seen in the evolution from a basket to a CDO. One can extend the ideas above in two ways.

First, instead of buying or selling protection on the first loss piece of a small portfolio, a (hedge) fund manager could buy or sell protection on any piece of the *capital structure* of a reference portfolio that could eventually end up having hundreds to some thousands of references. This instrument is known as a *synthetic CDO* and the piece of the capital structure is called a *tranche*. Those portfolios, however, are still *bespoke* and the rather illiquid transactions are still over the counter (OTC). Moving one step further, we have *standardized* portfolios, known as *standardized credit indices*, with standardized tranches.

Second, financial institutions can build a full business model based on the idea of optimizing the use of regulatory capital centralized on securitization. In such a business model standardized credit indices play a key role as will be seen later in this book.

In this chapter we briefly introduce the subject of CDOs and we call attention to neglected aspects that ultimately led to the credit crunch which began in June 2007. The remainder of the chapter is structured as follows. In Section 7.2 we give a brief overview of CDOs. In Section 7.3 we highlight differences between cash and synthetic CDOs. We move one step further and, through an example, we show how regulatory capital and the ideas above have evolved to become the so-called *securitization business model of financial institutions*. The treatment of the standardized credit indices is deferred to later chapters.

7.2   A BRIEF OVERVIEW OF CDOs

Instruments whose cash flows are backed by portfolios of bonds first appeared during the 1980s. The underlying portfolio (collateral) was composed by mortgages and called *Collateralized Mortgage Obligations* (CMOs). In what follows we give a brief overview of the CDO basics. We refer to Lucas (2001) for more detail on the structure of the contracts, to Hill and Vacca (1999) for arbitrage CDOs, to Goodman (2002) for synthetic CDOs, to Goodman and Fabozzi (2002) for a wider description of the instruments and to Kothari (2006) for a more general and recent reference.

The collateral on a CDO can be of very different types of securities: high yield bonds and emerging market debts (CBOs), bank and syndicated loans (CLOs), ABS/MBSs (Structured Finance CDOs), CDSs (synthetic CDOs), equity funds or, more recently, notes of other CDOs (CDO^2, called CDO *squared*). The instrument is set up as a *special purpose vehicle* (SPV), also called *special purpose entity* (SPE). The idea behind the SPV, an entity especially created for the purpose of the transaction, is that it is bankruptcy remote, meaning that it is immune to insolvency of the originator. The SPV will issue CDO notes that are bought by investors who will receive the proceedings coupons and principal of the pool. The interest and principal payments from the collateral pool are allocated to the notes following a certain prioritization schedule. The prioritization schedule is known a priori and is detailed in the prospectus of the CDO (see Part V for more detail).

A typical CDO structure can be seen in Figure 7.1. The notes to be issued by the SPV are tranched into different rating classes. The rating of each class is determined by the seniority of the note in the schedule of receiving principal and interest payments. The senior notes are rated from AAA to A, the mezzanine notes from BBB to B being subordinated to the senior notes. Finally, the equity holders generally named on the subordinated notes receive the residual on the CDO cash flow scheme. The equity holders are supposed to absorb the first losses in the whole structure.

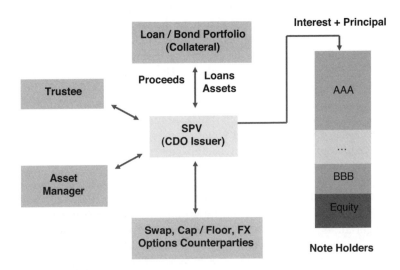

Figure 7.1   Typical CDO structure

The function of the *trustee* is to perform oversight on the CDO manager and to make sure that the rules specified in the contract are not breached. The asset manager is responsible for the management of the collateral portfolio. Swaps, caps and floors are there to hedge the interest rate risks in the product. The note holders are the investors.

Depending on the purpose of the CDO issuer there are basically two main classes of CDOs: *balance sheet* and *arbitrage*. In a balance sheet CDO a financial institution securitizes loans in its balance sheet with four immediate purposes: capital relief, increase in liquidity of the loans, improve performance measurement ratios, and transfer risk off balance sheet. In an arbitrage CDO one intends to get the difference between the cost of funding and the return on high yield investing. This means that in an arbitrage CDO the yield on the assets has to be higher than the total fees and the cost of funding the instrument. Banks and financial intermediaries will be the typical issuers of balance sheet CDOs, while the sponsors of the arbitrage deals will be insurance companies and asset managers (e.g. mutual and hedge funds).

Depending on the way the collateral pool is managed, a CDO may be one of two types: *cash flow* and *market value*. In a cash flow CDO the manager is not supposed to engage in actively trading the assets in the collateral and there are very strict rules on buying and selling collateral. Uncertainties in the payments of cash flow CDO's are related to the number and the timing of defaults. In a market value CDO, on the other hand, the payments are determined by gains on the mark to market value of the collateral pool. The return on a market value CDO is determined by the trading performance of the CDO manager. From the modeling point of view, an algorithm to price a market value CDO would ideally have to take into account the trading behavior of the collateral manager. In this book we will not be dealing with market value CDOs.

Depending on the nature of the assets, a CDO can be of three types: *cash*, *synthetic* or *hybrid*. In a cash transaction the assets – that is, the bonds – are acquired via the funding required to buy the instruments. The bonds are then removed from the portfolio of the originator in the case of balance sheet CDOs or bought directly from the market for arbitrage CDOs. For a synthetic CDO, on the other hand, the assets are built by selling protection – that is, using CDSs on the underlying reference entities. One very important difference between the two is the level of funding necessary to build the instrument. A cash deal requires raising cash in order to buy the instruments for the collateral. The protection seller in a synthetic deal will need to raise cash only when a credit event on a reference entity has been triggered. In practice, however, a synthetic transaction needs to have an amount of cash equal to the necessary credit enhancement to absorb losses to guarantee an AAA rating for the senior notes, as this is a desirable feature to get the deal moving forward. The cash used to fund the instrument is then invested on a highly rated collateral; prior to the credit crunch this would typically be AAA commercial paper.

Given the importance of the difference between cash and synthetic deals we elaborate on it in the next section.

7.3   CASH VERSUS SYNTHETIC CDOs

In a cash CDO there is a *legal transfer* of an asset from the originator to the SPV. Additionally, one needs to fund an amount of cash equal to the value of the assets transferred to the portfolio. Hence when issuing a cash deal one needs to solve two problems at the same time: the funding of the deal and the legal transfer of the assets. There are many legal and quite complex issues when transferring a cash instrument.

Some countries require that the obligor is advised and needs to give the approval for the legal transfer of its bonds to another company, in this case the SPV. It means that before issuing the cash CDO the originator needs to get the approval of every bond issuer in the collateral portfolio. This can potentially damage the relationship between the bank and the obligors, not to mention that it is a time-consuming process. In many countries the law requires that once a loan has been transferred the collateral that backs the deal should also be transferred. Consequently, not only the loans but also the collateral supporting the loans should be transferred.

The legal characterization of the transfer as *true sale* is a major source of difficulties. In the legal concept of true sale the originator is supposed to eliminate any risk once the assets have been transferred. Any support of the assets in the SPV with the own credit of the originator can be interpreted as the SPV being used as a source of funding for the originator instead of true sale. The legal issue called *consolidation* is another source of difficulty. This happens when the SPV and the originator are legally considered as one entity, even in the case that one has made a true sale. Issuing more than one SPV using intermediate SPVs has been a common solution for this problem, although it increases considerably the levels of complexity and legal costs. Another set of complicated issues comes up when the assets are originated in different jurisdictions, which may imply different sets of legal principles.

Where there is any profit on the true sale of the collateral, the originator needs to realize it and pay the upfront tax on the profits. A more recent example related to capital restructuring solutions during the credit crunch has to do with the *booking* of realized losses. Assume a portfolio of subprime ABS bonds, e.g. credit card loans, auto loans, mortgages, whose nominal is USD 20 billion. Assume that prices have fallen and, due to liquidity issues, the price counterparties would be willing to pay is USD 12 billion. Consider a capital restructuring situation in which investors agree to take the risk in the portfolio. The SPV of a cash CDO that would remove the assets from the balance sheet of the institution would pay USD 12 billion for something whose notional is USD 20 billion causing the financial institution to *realize a loss of USD 8 billion* potentially impacting its level of capital and eventually its survival. Additional issues related to a cash flow CDO are double taxation of residual profits, time and flexibility in structuring the deal, and amount of notionals involved.

All the above issues point to the advantages of synthetic CDOs and have been the reason for their enormous growth. There is one very important point, however, that makes synthetic CDOs a far more complex instrument than what had been recognized before the credit crunch: its leverage nature. As already mentioned, the amount of cash to be put in a synthetic CDO is just enough to guarantee the AAA rating of the super senior tranches. If the whole market acts in the same way, investing in synthetic CDOs at some point in time, the leverage issue may cause the problems of liquidity observed since June 2007. In the next section we deal with the issue of leverage underlying synthetic CDOs.

7.4 SYNTHETIC CDOS AND LEVERAGE

In the last section we mentioned that one advantage of using a synthetic CDO is that it is not necessary to have the whole funding for the structure to move forward. In a synthetic CDO one needs to fund enough to have a cushion to guarantee the AAA level of the super senior tranches.

When investing on a single instrument a financial institution needs to keep track of the risk underlying the reference. When investing in an ABS/CDO instrument, the financial institution

Table 7.1 Regulatory cost of capital

Rating	Bond/CDO %	Bond %	CDO %	SS CDO %
AAA	100	20	20	7
AA	100	20	20	8
A	100	50	50	12
BBB	100	100	100	60
	Basel I		Basel II	

is exposed to a diversified portfolio of references. Additionally, given that the CDO instrument has a synthetic format, one may increase the levels of return for a certain level of funding, potentially increasing its return on regulatory capital. Additionally, if the tranche invested is very high in the capital structure – that is, if the tranche expected loss is very remote – the institution may take a leveraged position.

Table 7.1 shows the costs of regulatory capital for a single name bond, for a CDO note and for a leverage super senior CDO note. We observe that *the super senior (SS) tranches are supposed to be characterized by attachment points that significantly exceed the level of losses consistent with the AAA rating* (see Kalra et al., 2006). A leveraged SS is a leverage position in a super senior note. Assume an investment of USD 100 million on an AAA bond, an AAA CDO tranche or AAA leveraged super senior. The spreads one would make are respectively (1 bp = 0.01%) 10 bps, 20 bps and 10 bps on an exposure of USD 100 million. In the case of a bond one needs to fund and invest USD 100 million. For the AAA CDO tranche and for the LSS the investor may need to put USD 10 million up front (USD 10 million needs to be funded). The results of the return on regulatory capital are shown in Table 7.2. We did not subtract the cost of funding. If the cost of funding of the investor is higher than 10 bps (its rating is lower than AAA) then it would not be possible to make the AAA bond investment unless via AAA CDOs.

Given the results above we see that financial institutions may have had an enormous incentive to invest in synthetic CDO instruments. From an investment point of view the institution does not need to have specialized credit personnel to follow up the idiosyncratic risks involved in single name transactions. By investing on an AAA CDO note it has the benefit of a diversified portfolio of credit, and a higher return for the same level of risk with a lower cost of capital (compare the return on an AAA CDO note and on an AAA bond). Additionally, if it decides for a LSS position the return on regulatory capital is even higher for an even lower risk.

The process described above can easily become a full business model in which the whole system aims at substituting idiosyncratic risk for systemic risk. Underlying this business model there are three important points. First, the idiosyncratic for systemic substitution is done at the cost of increased leverage. Second, up to now we have not mentioned any mechanism or

Table 7.2 Return on regulatory capital

Investment	Funding	Cost of capital	Return (bps)	ROC (bps/USD)
AAA Bond	100%	1.60 m	10	6.25 m
AAA CDO	10%	0.16 m	20	125 m
LSS CDO	10%	0.056 m	10	178.6 m

instrument available in the market by which one could measure any market-wide variation of systemic risk. Third, it raises important questions regarding correlation between the underlying instruments in the CDO portfolio.

In the next section we show an example of the issues underlying diversification, concentration and correlation.

7.5   CONCENTRATION, CORRELATION AND DIVERSIFICATION

We finish this chapter with an example. Consider a portfolio manager with USD 1 billion to invest. His first option is to invest in only two companies of two uncorrelated sectors: say USD 500 million in an insurance company and USD 500 million in a semiconductor company. His second option is to invest in the same two sectors but this time in 10 companies of each sector, resulting in 20 investments of USD 50 million each. The question, then, is which of the two portfolios would be more correlated?

We observe that the latter portfolio is much more diversified than the former. The issue, however, is that as each company is correlated with the market as a whole, the level of correlation between the two subportfolios is much higher in the latter portfolio than in the former!

We note that going from the former to the latter portfolio the manager may have *increased the level of diversification* but he also *increased the level of correlation in the portfolio*! In the ABS market the same process takes place on a very large scale. By downloading idiosyncratic risk into the market and uploading systemic risk the diversification may have increased at the cost of a higher exposure to systemic correlation.

For the equity market the VIX index has been the instrument used by market participants to quantify the level of systemic risk. Before the credit crunch levels of VIX above 40 would indicate high systemic risk and an oversold market. Levels below 10 would indicate complacency and an overbought market.

In the credit market the instruments to monitor the level of systemic risk is not yet well known and widespread. However, these instruments exist. They are the standardized credit indices. In the next chapters we show the importance of those indices for financial activity and for the securitization business model.

8
Standardized Credit Indices

Mediocrity does not see higher than itself. But talent instantly recognizes the genius.

Sir Arthur Conan Doyle

8.1 INTRODUCTION

In order to help us understand the rationale behind the standardized credit indices, we will begin by discussing the well-known equity stock market indices. There are several reasons why the equity indices are there. They help investors track the performance of sectors, ultimately serving as a *mechanism for pricing discovery* of the sectors they represent. The performance of a portfolio of equity instruments is usually compared with a passive index representing the sector in which the manager is supposed to invest.

Technically speaking, the idea of an index is backed by Markowitz; instead of taking idiosyncratic risk on one company, an investor is better off taking a sector diversified risk by buying the sector index to which the company belongs. Back in the 1970s, *innovation* brought the options market as a tool for portfolio managers and investors alike to hedge their risks. The simple existence of an equity index with an *exchange traded liquid option market* increases liquidity as investors have access to more information on the underlying market. *Exchange traded funds* (ETF) are further examples of the impact of *innovation* underlying the financial activity. They are the ultimate commoditization of the idea of indices as they make indices easily accessible to individual investors.

Standardized credit indices are for the credit market what the equity indices are for the stock market. From 1997 to 2003 the synthetic CDO market had grown quite fast both in quantity and complexity but it was still fragmented and diverse. The indices and their tranches brought liquidity into the market by putting in place standardization in terms of capital structures, underlying portfolios and pricing algorithms. Simply stated, they are tradable products that permit an investor to take long and short credit positions on a well-defined credit portfolio.

The credit indices are not perpetual, but rather they have fixed maturities and compositions. Hence new series are launched periodically while the older ones continue to exist until their final maturity. In this chapter, we describe the basics of some of the corporate credit indices and their tranches. The remainder of the chapter is structured as follows. In Section 8.2 we briefly describe the CDS indices. In Section 8.3 we describe the concept of standardization and explain the necessity for it. In Section 8.4 we extend the concepts to the tranches on the capital structure of the indices, demonstrating the leap in innovation behind these instruments. In Section 8.5 we show simple relations between the CDS quotes of the collateral and the index spread.

8.2 CREDIT DEFAULT SWAP INDICES

A standardized CDS index is made up of a portfolio of single name CDS contracts. They have been designed to bring liquidity and serve as an information mechanism of the market activity for the underlying asset class. Asset managers, corporate treasuries and bank proprietary trading desks may use the indices to take diversified outright credit positions or as a hedge tool to their portfolios. Hedge funds and proprietary trading desks have used the index to take credit positions on obligors versus sectors, or sectors versus sectors. Additionally, the indices are useful for executing trades without exposing the underlying strategies. Insurance companies use it for hedging parts of their capital structure.

There are two broad families of indices. The iTraxx family covers Europe and Asia. The CDX family covers North America and Emerging Markets. The top 125 European references in terms of CDS volume traded in the six months prior to the roll of the index constitute the Markit iTraxx Europe Main index. The iTraxx Financial covers senior and subordinated debt. Both indices have 25 underlying references. The Nonfinancials covers autos, consumers, energy, industrial and TMT and has 100 references. Additionally, the iTraxx HiVol index contains the 30 largest spread references from the iTraxx Main. Fifty European subinvestment grade reference entities constitute the Crossover index. After the roll on 20 March 2009, the Crossover index constituted only 45 reference entities. Trading on tranches of the capital structure also exists, primarily on the main indices (see Section 8.4 for details). The iTraxx futures are currently offered on Main, HiVol and Crossover.

On the Asian market the following indices are available: iTraxx Asia ex-Japan with 70 references; iTraxx Australia with 25 references; iTraxx Japan with 50 references; iTraxx Japan 80 with 80 references; and iTraxx Japan HiVol with 25 references.

The CDX family also consists of investment grade, crossover and HY indices. Similar to iTraxx Main, the CDX North America Main contains 125 references. They are supposed to be investment grade rated by Moody's and S&P. For each new series, credits with low liquidity in the old series are replaced by better underlying credits. The CDX HiVol series contains the subset of the 30 credits with largest spreads from CDX Main. The CDX Crossover contains 35 references. The CDX HY index contains 100 references. The indices are all traded on a spread basis, except for the High Yield (HY) which is traded on price basis.

By buying protection on an index, an investor is insuring against defaults on the underlying portfolio of the index. The protection buyer pays the premium on a quarterly basis to the protection seller. In the case of default and physical settlement, the protection seller pays par and receives from the protection buyer the underlying reference obligation or any bond deliverable into the contract.

8.3   STANDARDIZATION

The standardization of the indices manifests itself in several elements:

1. *Static reference portfolio*. The composition of the underlying portfolio is *fixed* both in *number* and in *weight*. Once a reference defaults it is removed from the index and no new obligor replaces it (see more details in the next section).
2. *Fixed maturity and payment dates*. Cash flow dates occur every quarter, on the 20th day of March, June, September and December, the date convention is modified following. For the iTraxx family of Main, HiVol and Crossover, the maturities are 3, 5, 7 and 10 years, while the sector indices have maturities of 5 and 10 years. In practice, however, the liquidity of the contracts depends on market conditions.
3. *Rollover mechanism*. As *maturity* is a part of the standardization process, and given that the maturity of the old index is decreasing with time, a new index is launched every six months. The purpose is to bring a liquid credit index whose duration is approximately constant to the market. The old index continues to exist until its maturity, although with a

lower liquidity. The old (new) index is said to be *off the run* (*on the run*). Investors who decide to stay with a liquid index need to take a position on a new index in a process called *rollover*.

4. *Fixed coupon/spread*. The corporate indices are traded on spreads. At inception, it starts with a predetermined fixed coupon. With time, trading will evolve and the market spread move above or below the index coupon. As an example, if the market spread moves tighter than the coupon the protection seller (buyer) will be required to pay (receive) an upfront amount as they will be receiving a higher (lower) amount than the current cost of protection. On the other hand, if market spreads move wider the protection seller (buyer) will be receiving (paying) an upfront amount to compensate for the higher risk being taken. Where an index contract is issued between payment dates, an accrual interest should still be paid upfront.

The theoretical spread of an index is the duration weighted average spread of the CDS spreads of the constituents of the index. In practice, however, the spread is given by the forces of supply and demand. It means that one needs to adjust the collateral CDS spreads before pricing tranches in the index. The factor used for adjustment is given by the ratio between the *index reference* (available in the market) and the arithmetic averaged CDS spreads.

5. *Legal debt conventions*. Generally speaking, a default credit event is settled either in cash or physically. The International Swaps and Derivatives Association (ISDA) has published five cases of US company defaults in which the auctions were administered by Markit and Creditex. The protocols and the auction procedures are available at www.isda.org and www.markit.com respectively. The main objective of the whole process is to determine one recovery rate (the result of an industry-accepted auction mechanism) to be used to cash settle the credit event for all index transactions and also determine the losses for equity and nonequity tranches.

There are additional and quite important legal aspects underlying the indices, as for example the convention used for debt restructuring. The conventions adopted for the index are not the same as for the underlying CDSs. Moreover, there are differences between the indices themselves. For example, credit event convention for North American, single-name, high grade credits usually includes *Modified Restructuring* (MR) while high yields do not (no restructuring (NR)). European single name credits, on the other hand, generally use the *Modified Modified Restructuring* (MMR), allowing a larger range of deliverable obligations in the case of a debt restructuring credit event than MR. We refer to www.isda.org for more on the legal details.

Note that with an index trade a position is taken on a whole portfolio. It means that in a volatile market indices react faster than the underlying CDSs and are therefore more liquid than the underlying CDSs. Table 8.1 shows that, indeed, from 2004 to 2006 trading on indices increased sharply compared to single names.

Table 8.1 Credit derivatives by products

Type	2004	2006
Single name CDS	*51.0%*	32.9%
Full Index	9.0%	*30.1%*
Synthetic CDO	16.0%	16.3%
Tranched Index	2.0%	*7.6%*
CLN	6.0%	3.1%
Others	*16.0%*	10.0%

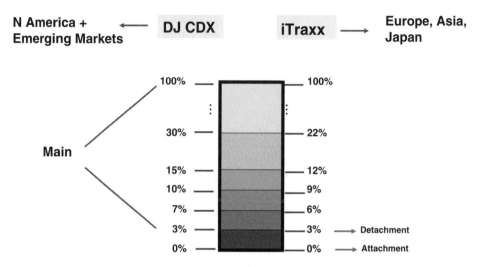

Both indices have 125 references in the collateral portfolio

Figure 8.1   Standardized credit indices corporates: iTraxx and CDX and the tranches

8.4   ITRAXX, CDX AND THEIR TRANCHES

The enormous amount of innovation brought by the indices can be seen if we enlarge the definition given in Section 8.2 to encompass tranches. Broadly speaking, credit indices are tradable products that permit an investor to take a long or short synthetic credit view on different portions of the capital structure of a standardized credit portfolio.

The iTraxx and CDX indices and their tranches are shown in Figure 8.1. They are the most liquid standardized indices currently in the market. Both are traded in spreads. An important difference between the two concerns the debt restructuring convention. The CDX.NA Main is such that the protection leg is triggered only in the case of default or failure to pay, not debt restructuring. The CDX.NA Main spread is said to trade using a No-Re spread curve. For the iTraxx Main, however, debt restructuring is taken into account.

There are several uses for the indices and their tranches. Investors may need instruments to hedge different portions of their own capital structure. Consider an investor who is ready to accept losses up to 10% of her own portfolio, but wants to hedge losses between 10% and 30%. Therefore she may contact a bank and buy protection on the [10%–30%] tranche. A cheaper solution may be to take appropriate positions on the tranches of the standardized indices. An asset manager may be willing to take positions on the underlying references but may only be allowed from some point up in the capital structure. Hedge funds may want to take a position on a low level of the capital structure against a high level of it betting that systematic risk will decrease, or the other way around betting that the market expectation of defaults will increase.

8.5   THEORETICAL FAIR SPREAD OF INDICES

The index spread is driven by the *supply and demand of the market*, and as such it is not calculated directly from the spreads of the underlying credit default swaps. Consequently, the index spread can be different from both the average spreads of the underlying credit default swaps and its theoretical fair value. The *theoretical fair value* is the duration weighted average of the underlying credit default swaps.

The first point that comes to mind when comparing the index spread to the spreads of the underlying credit default swaps is average spread s_a of the basket

$$s_a = \sum_{i=1}^{N} \alpha_i s_i, \tag{8.1}$$

where s_i is the spread of the ith underlying credit default swap and the weighting coefficients $\alpha_i = 1$ sum to 1:

$$\sum_{i=1}^{N} \alpha_i = 1. \tag{8.2}$$

For an equally weighted index, such as the iTraxx index, we have

$$\alpha_i = \frac{1}{125}. \tag{8.3}$$

The clear disadvantage of the average spread is that it does not account for the fact that spread payments end when a name defaults. Consider a name that is near default. Its high spread is paid only for a very short time, which is not reflected in (8.1).

A far better criterion is to state that the *expected loss* of the index should be equal to the expected losses on the underlying credit default swaps. As the expected loss is the product of the spread times the corresponding risky duration DV01, we have that the index spread s should satisfy

$$\sum_{i=1}^{N} \alpha_i s_i \text{DV01}_i = s\text{DV01}_{\text{Index}}. \tag{8.4}$$

This justifies the definition of *theoretical fair value* as the duration weighted average of the underlying credit default swaps. The duration weighted average spread of the basket: weighting each name by its risky duration clearly accounts for the fact that spread payments end when a name defaults.

Finally, we consider the prices of the index and the underlying basket and state that the *mark to market value* of the index should be equal to the mark to market value of the underlying credit default swaps.

At inception a fixed premium or *strike* s_0 is set for the index. As by the supply and demand of the market the index moves away from this strike, there is a nonzero mark to market and consequently an upfront fee. However, the market quotes the spread which reflects both the strike and the upfront fee, where by market convention the upfront fee is computed using a flat credit curve and a fixed recovery rate. Hence the index spread s should balance:

$$\sum_{i=1}^{N} \alpha_i (s_i - s_0) \text{DV01}_i = (s - s_0) \text{DV01}_{\text{Index}}. \tag{8.5}$$

Observe that if the risky duration of the index is equal to the weighted average of the risky durations of the underlying credit default swaps:

$$\sum_{i=1}^{N} \alpha_i \text{DV01}_i = \text{DV01}_{\text{Index}}, \tag{8.6}$$

the strike s_0 cancels in (8.5) and this equations reduces to (8.4). However, for single name credit default swaps, a more accurate model is often used to account for steep credit curves. Where different methodologies are used for the computation of the risky durations (8.6) does not hold and hence different theoretical fair values are implied by (8.4) and (8.5).

It should be clear that risky duration weighted averages as implied by (8.5) and (8.4) should be smaller than the average spread in (8.1) because the weights of the riskiest names are smaller.

The effect of risky duration weighted averaging is even larger with inverted credit curves. The use of a flat curve for the index results in a longer duration for the index than for the underlying credit default swaps. Hence the theoretical fair value will be lower.

No-arbitrage arguments lead one to expect the observed market quotes to satisfy (8.4) and/or (8.5). However, arbitraging the index and the underlying credit default swaps may not be easy in practice for several reasons.

At present both the index and the underlying credit default swaps are traded over the counter (OTC) and OTC products are subject to counterparty risk, which has received more attention since Lehman's failure. The potential profit needs to cover at least the transaction costs, so the bid and ask spreads should be considered in (8.4) and (8.5). A profitable trade may be carry positive, but require an upfront payment which may be undesirable. As spreads are driven by supply and demand, launching and unwinding structured products can result in increased liquidity. The market may shift from being driven by indices to being driven by single names and vice versa. As an example, consider the CPPI and CPDO structured products on the indices and the activity in single names after Lehman's failure.

Proprietary trading desks of banks are obvious candidates to be executing this arbitrage. However, their activity can be expected to have decreased since the credit crunch.

Pricing Synthetic CDO Tranches

The finest thought runs the risk of being irrevocably forgotten if it is not written down.
Arthur Schopenhauer

9.1 INTRODUCTION

Since the introduction of the 1-factor Gaussian copula model for pricing synthetic Collateralized Debt Obligation (CDO) tranches by Andersen et al. (2003), correlation is seen as an exogenous parameter used to match observed market quotes. First the market adopted the concept of *implied compound correlation*. In tandem with the concept of volatility in the Black-Scholes option pricing framework, compound correlation was the parameter to be put in the model to match observed market prices of tranches.

One of the problems of this approach resides in its unsuitability for interpolation. We have seen in the last chapter that the standard attachment points are 3%, 6%, 9%, 12% and 22% for iTraxx Europe Main and 3%, 7%, 10%, 15% and 30% for CDX.NA.IG. Given the implied compound correlations for the [3%–6%] and [6%–9%] tranches of iTraxx Europe Main it is not clear which value to use for a nonstandard tranche such as, e.g. [5%–8%]. Besides the problems of interpolation we can also mention that during some market events correlation may receive non-meaningful values (e.g. during the auto crisis of May 2005).

The current widespread market approach is to use the concept of *base correlation* (BC) introduced by McGinty et al. (2004). In the base correlation methodology only equity or base tranches are defined, where base or equity tranches are defined as tranches with attachment point 0. The price of a tranche [A–D] is calculated using the two equity tranches with A and D as detachment points. Using BC it is quite straightforward to bootstrap between standard attachment points. Additionally the BC concept is quite adapted to interpolation for nonstandard tranches. Hence the [5%–8%] tranche would be priced by interpolating the BC curve for values at 5% and 8% respectively.

Another characteristic of the standard market approach is its reliance on the Gaussian copula. In this chapter we introduce the concept of Lévy base correlation as a possible alternative to the Gaussian framework.

This chapter will be organized as follows. In Section 9.2 we review the generic 1-factor model for valuation of CDO tranches, using both Gaussian and Lévy processes. In Section 9.3 we give numerical results on the use of implied or compound and base correlation and we also show the impact of adopting different recovery rates for pricing purposes.

9.2 GENERIC 1-FACTOR MODEL

The 1-factor Gaussian copula model using the so-called *recursion algorithm* was first introduced by Andersen et al. (2003) and is in widespread use by market participants. In what follows we give a brief description of the generic 1-factor algorithm. Consider a portfolio of N firms and fix a time horizon T. We assume the default process to follow an inhomogeneous

Poisson process (see Chapter 2), and as such for any $0 \le t \le T$ the default times τ_i and default intensities $\lambda_i(t)$, $i = 1, \ldots, N$, satisfy

$$\mathbb{P}(\tau_i > t) = \exp\left(-\int_0^t \lambda_i(u)\mathrm{d}u\right) \tag{9.1}$$

where $\mathbb{P}$ is the risk-neutral probability measure. In a 1-factor model of portfolio defaults, a single systemic factor X is introduced, conditional upon which all default probabilities are independent. As shown in Chapter 4, the single name survival probabilities $\mathbb{P}(\tau_i > t)$ are typically implied from the credit default swap (CDS) market.

The key step in valuing CDO tranches is to compute the joint loss distribution. In the recursion algorithm one computes a discretized version of the conditional loss distribution by means of a simple recursion formula. The unconditional loss distribution is found by integrating over the market factor. Analogous to the CDS case the fair spread of a CDO tranche balances the present value of the fee leg F and the present value of the contingent leg C. In the base correlation framework, the expected loss on a tranche is computed as the difference of the expected loss of two equity tranches.

9.2.1   CDO tranche valuation

The key step in valuing CDO tranches is to compute the joint loss distribution. In the recursion algorithm one computes a discretized version of the conditional loss distribution by means of a simple recursion formula. A loss unit u is chosen so that, within a certain tolerance, losses can be represented by integers. For the iTraxx Europe Main portfolio with an assumed uniform recovery rate of 40%, the loss unit is 0.48%. We denote by $P^{(i)}(l, t|X)$ the probability of l losses (in terms of the loss unit u) at time t with i names conditional on the market factor X. Recalling that conditional on X all default probabilities are independent, we can write that $P^{(i)}(l, t|X)$ is the sum of two terms:

$$P^{(i)}(l, t|X) = P^{(i-1)}(l, t|X)\mathbb{P}(\tau_i > t|X) + P^{(i-1)}(l - \omega_{(i)}, t|X)(1 - \mathbb{P}(\tau_i > t|X)), \tag{9.2}$$

where $\omega_{(i)}$ is the number of loss units incurred by a default of the ith name. The unconditional loss distribution is found by integrating over the market factor

$$P(l, t) = \int_{\Omega_X} P(l, t|X)f(X)\mathrm{d}X, \tag{9.3}$$

where $f(X)$ is the density of the probability distribution of the market factor X. Analogous to the CDS case (see Section 4.3), the fair spread of a CDO tranche balances the present value of the fee leg F, given by

$$F = S \sum_{i=1}^{n} (N^{(\mathrm{Tr})} - \mathbb{E}[L_i^{(\mathrm{Tr})}])d(t_i)\Delta t_i \tag{9.4}$$

and the present value of the contingent leg C, given by

$$C = \sum_{i=1}^{n} d(t_{i+\frac{1}{2}})\left(\mathbb{E}[L_i^{(\mathrm{Tr})}] - \mathbb{E}[L_{i-1}^{(\mathrm{Tr})}]\right). \tag{9.5}$$

In these equations the summations run over the payment dates, S is the spread premium on a yearly basis, $d(t)$ is the risk-free discount factor, $\Delta t_i = t_i - t_{i-1}$ is the year fraction, $\mathbb{E}[L_i^{(\mathrm{Tr})}]$ is the expected loss on the tranche at time t_i and $N^{(\text{Tr})}$ is the tranche size.[1] In the base correlation framework, the expected loss on a tranche is computed as the difference of the expected loss of two equity tranches

$$\mathbb{EL}[A - D] = \mathbb{EL}[0 - D; \rho_D] - \mathbb{EL}[0 - A; \rho_A]. \tag{9.6}$$

For more details on base correlation we refer to McGinty et al. (2004) and to O'Kane and Livasey (2004).

9.2.2   Latent variable models

In the so-called *latent variable* model default occurs when a certain (latent) variable A_i (usually the return) falls below a certain threshold K_i that is implied from CDS prices. This idea has been discussed in Chapters 2 and 3 and has been inspired in the work of Merton (1974). Using factor analysis the *market* or *systemic* factor X and the *idiosyncratic* factor $X^{(i)}$ are random variables whose functional form depends on model assumptions.

9.2.3   Gaussian copula

In the 1-factor Gaussian copula setting the latent variable A_i is given by:

$$A_i = \sqrt{\rho}X + \sqrt{1 - \rho}X^{(i)}, \quad i = 1, \ldots, N \tag{9.7}$$

where the systemic factor X and the idiosyncratic factor $X^{(i)}$ are taken to be independent standard normal random variables. Gauss-Hermite quadrature can be used to evaluate the integral in (9.3). Note that the Gaussian copula model is a special case of the generic 1-factor Lévy model, in which the normal distribution is used.

The threshold implied from the CDS risk-neutral probability of defaults $p_i(t)$ is given by

$$K_i(t) = N^{[-1]}(p_i(t)). \tag{9.8}$$

This is the specialization of (9.11) for the normal distribution. The conditional default probability $p_i(y;t)$ given the value y for the systemic factor

$$p_i(y; t) = N\left(\frac{N^{[-1]}(p_i(t)) - \sqrt{\rho}y}{\sqrt{1 - \rho}}\right). \tag{9.9}$$

We recognize this specialization of (9.12) for the normal distribution as the classical formula for the conditional default probability in the Gaussian copula algorithm.

9.2.4   Generic 1-factor Lévy model

If for every positive integer n, the characteristic function $\phi(u) = \mathbb{E}[iuX]$ is also the nth power of a characteristic function, the distribution is said to be *infinitely divisible*. Given an infinitely divisible distribution, a stochastic process, $X = \{X_t, t \geq 0\}$, can be constructed. This so-called Lévy process starts at zero $X_0 = 0$, has independent and stationary increments and the distribution of the increments $X_{t+s} - X_s$, has $(\phi(u))^t$ as characteristic functions.

---

[1] The [0–3%] equity tranche is quoted as an upfront payment plus 500 basis points (a basis point is equal to 0.01%) running.

The cumulative distribution function of X_t and its inverse are denoted by H_t and $H_t^{[-1]}$ respectively. We normalize the distribution so that $\mathbb{E}[X_1] = 0$ and $\text{Var}[X_1] = 1$. Hence one has $\text{Var}[X_t] = t$. We take X and $X^{(i)}$, $i = 1, 2, \ldots, N$ independent and identically distributed Lévy processes.

In the generic 1-factor Lévy model the latent variable is represented as

$$A_i = X_\rho + X_{1-\rho}^{(i)}, \quad i = 1, \ldots, N \tag{9.10}$$

and each A_i has the same distribution function H_1. Note that for $i \neq j$, we have $\text{Corr}[A_i, A_j] = \rho$. The threshold implied from the CDS risk-neutral probability of defaults $p_i(t)$ is given by

$$K_i(t) = H_1^{[-1]}(p_i(t)). \tag{9.11}$$

Denote by $p_i(y; t)$ the conditional default probability of firm i given the value y for the systemic factor. From (9.10) we have

$$p_i(y; t) = H_{1-\rho}(K_i(t) - y). \tag{9.12}$$

9.2.5   The shifted Gamma model

The Gamma(a, b) distribution with parameters $a, b > 0$ is infinitely divisible. Its density function is given by

$$f(x; a, b) = \frac{b^a}{\Gamma(a)} x^{a-1} \exp(-xb), \tag{9.13}$$

for $x > 0$. The Gamma-process G_t is defined as the stochastic process which starts at zero and has stationary, independent Gamma-distributed increments. The time enters in the first parameter, that is G_t follows a Gamma(at, b) distribution. A shifted Gamma variate can be defined as

$$X_t = \mu t - G_t. \tag{9.14}$$

We set

$$b = \mu = \sqrt{a} \tag{9.15}$$

so that $X_t = \sqrt{a}t - G_t$ is normalized in the sense that $\mathbb{E}[X_1] = 0$ and $\text{Var}[X_1] = 1$ since Gamma distributions with $b = \sqrt{a}$ have variance 1. Both the cumulative distribution function $H_t(x; a)$ of X_t

$$H_t(x; a) = 1 - C_G(\sqrt{a}t - x; at, \sqrt{a}), \tag{9.16}$$

and its inverse $H_t^{[-1]}(y; a)$

$$H_t^{[-1]}(y; a) = \sqrt{a}t - C_G(1 - y; at, \sqrt{a}), \tag{9.17}$$

can easily be obtained from the Gamma cumulative distribution function C_G and its inverse $C_G^{[-1]}$. Gauss-Laguerre quadrature can be used to evaluate the integral in (9.3).

9.2.6   Numerical integration Lévy base correlation

We now turn to the evaluation of the integral I in (9.3)

$$I = \frac{b^a}{\Gamma(a)} \int_{-\infty}^{\mu} f(y)(\mu - y)^{a-1} \exp\left(-(\mu - y)b\right) \, dy \tag{9.18}$$

to compute the unconditional loss distribution. It is straightforward to apply Generalized Gauss Laguerre integration to the transformed integral

$$I = \frac{1}{\Gamma(a)} \int_{0}^{\infty} f(\mu - t/b)t^{a-1} \exp\left(-t\right) \, dt. \tag{9.19}$$

Generalized Gauss Laguerre quadrature is a numerical method to evaluate integrals of the form

$$\int_{0}^{\infty} f(x) \, dx, \tag{9.20}$$

where $f(x) = w(x)\,p(x)$ is the product of a weighting function $w(x)$ and a smooth function $p(x)$, in the sense of being well approximated by a polynomial. The weighting function is

$$w(x; s) = x^s \exp(-x), \tag{9.21}$$

where $s > -1$. Note that the classical Gauss Laguerre quadrature is the special case corresponding to $s = 0$.

Note that the market factor X_ρ follows a shifted Gamma distribution with parameter $a\rho$, hence the Gauss Laguerre parameter is

$$s = a\rho - 1. \tag{9.22}$$

It is crucial to apply generalized Gauss Laguerre quadrature and hence have the weighting function depend on the correlation parameter ρ. This can easily be seen as follows. In classical Gauss Laguerre quadrature the weighting function is $w(x; 0) = \exp(-x)$ and hence the factor $x^{\rho-1}$ is part of the function which is assumed to be smooth, in the sense of being well approximated by a polynomial. This is particularly troublesome for small values of the argument $x \to 0$, and increasing the number of integration points will not help much, as the classical Gauss Laguerre quadrature is designed to address the integration over the infinite interval. The need for the generalized method can be seen in elementary tests such as computing the moments of the Gamma distribution.

The disadvantage of applying the generalized Gauss Laguerre quadrature is that the weighting function depends on the correlation parameter ρ. Hence we have to be able to accurately and efficiently compute the abscissas and weights. Two algorithms for the computation of abscissas and weights are presented in Appendix B.

The remainder of the discussion is specific for the Lévy base correlation case, in which we fix the parameters of the distribution to be all equal to one $b = \mu = \sqrt{a} = 1$.

A far better performing integration technique is obtained by splitting the integral into an infinite part, which can be evaluated analytically, and a finite part which remains to be treated numerically:

$$I = c(L) + \int_{L}^{\mu} . \tag{9.23}$$

We define this bound L as the minimum over all default thresholds for the individual names minus one. Hence we have

$$L = \min(R_i - 1), \tag{9.24}$$

where R_i is the default thresholds for the ith underlying entity.

$$Y_t^i = X_\rho^{(M)} + X_{1-\rho}^{(i)} \leq R_i \tag{9.25}$$

The idiosyncratic factor is bounded by one

$$X_{1-\rho}^{(i)} \sim (1 - \rho) - G_{1-\rho} \leq 1 - \rho \leq 1. \tag{9.26}$$

Consequently if the market factor is lower than this bound L

$$X_\rho^{(M)} \leq L = \min(R_i - 1), \tag{9.27}$$

all names are in default. Hence this first term contributes an amount equal to the cumulative distribution function $H_\rho(L)$ to the probability mass of the all default scenario.

The remaining integral over the finite interval $[L, \mu]$ can be evaluated using standard numerical integration techniques, based on the midpoint rule or on Simpson's rule. Alternatively, a probability density based integration scheme could be considered, giving equal probability weights to the different subintervals. In case an adaptive integration technique is undesirable, an upfront accuracy study needs to be performed to fix the number of evaluations.

9.3   IMPLIED COMPOUND AND BASE CORRELATION

Implied Compound Correlation (ICC) is the value ρ that, when input in (9.7) for Gaussian copula case or in (9.10) for the Lévy case, returns observed tranche market prices. An example is shown in Figure 9.1. It should be compared to implied volatility for options in the

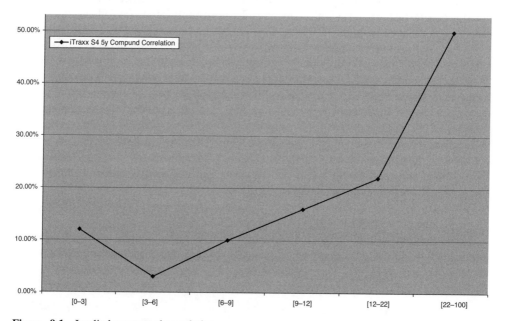

Figure 9.1   Implied compound correlation

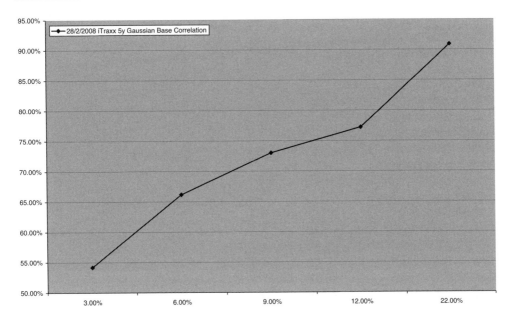

Figure 9.2 Gaussian copula base correlation

Black-Scholes framework. However, it was not equally successful and was replaced by base correlation.

Observe that implied compound correlation $\rho(A, D)$ is a function of both the attachment point A and the detachment point D. Hence it is a two-dimensional function. In the case of the iTraxx tranches a calibration results in six data points for this 2D function. After that one faces significant interpolation challenges for pricing tranchlets and bespoke portfolios. What should be the values to use for a [7%–8%] tranchlet on iTraxx or for a [15%–60%] tranche on a bespoke portfolio?

Moreover, ICC is not necessarily unique as there is no one-to-one relation between spread and ICC. So both a small and a large value may result from a calibration. This obviously leads to challenging questions: Which is the correct one? And, even more important, which value should be used?

Base correlation was introduced to overcome the challenges encountered with the use of implied compound correlation. *Base correlation* is the value ρ that correctly prices *base* or *equity tranches*, that is tranches having an attachment point at 0. Hence base correlation $\rho(D)$ is a one-dimensional function. Figure 9.2 shows a base correlation curve.

The expected loss on a tranche with a non-zero attachment point is computed as the difference between two base tranches as shown in (9.6). For the junior mezzanine tranche in iTraxx we have

$$\mathbb{EL}[3\%\text{–}6\%] = \mathbb{EL}[0\%\text{–}6\%; \rho_6] - \mathbb{EL}[0\%\text{–}3\%; \rho_3], \tag{9.28}$$

showing that the calibration of a base correlation curve will be a bootstrapping process.

Using the [0%–3%] tranche quote the base correlation ρ_3 at 3% can be determined. Using this value ρ_3 and the [3%–6%] tranche quote, the base correlation ρ_6 at 6% can be found. Proceeding this way, one determines the base correlation ρ_{22} at 22% from the [12%–22%] tranche, resulting in an implied spread for the [22%–100%] tranche. The loss on the total

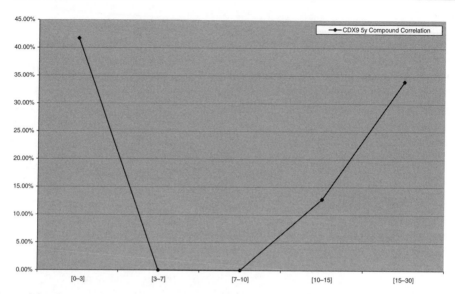

Figure 9.3   Compound correlation can hit 0% for mezzanine tranches

portfolio is determined by the recovery rates and spreads of the underlying names and does not depend on the correlation. Hence there is no base correlation value at 100% and it can certainly not be determined using a quote for the [22%–100%] tranche. A quote for the [22%–100%] tranche can be matched by implying a value for the base correlation at 22%, which can be different from the one obtained from the bootstrapping described above. The market quotes base correlation for equity tranches.

As it is a one-dimensional function base correlation is supposed to be better suited for interpolation than implied compound correlation. Recall that interpolation is required for tranchlet pricing and for pricing tranches of bespoke portfolios. However, prices depend heavily on interpolation techniques. Techniques used for implying the correlation of a bespoke tranche from the correlation on standardized credit indices are discussed in more detail in Chapter 12.

Calibrating correlation curves from market quotes is not always straightforward. Compound correlation can hit 0% for mezzanine tranches as shown in Figure 9.3.

Figure 9.4 shows that base correlation can hit 100% for senior tranches. This can be avoided by assuming lower recovery rates, since lowering the recovery rate shifts the base correlation curves down. However, this has a significant impact on bespoke tranche pricing through the correlation mapping techniques. Figure 9.5 shows the impact of the recovery rate assumption on the base correlation curves.

The impact of the recovery rate assumptions on the base correlation curves can be explained as follows. The basic CDS model with a single default intensity λ results in a cds quote c

$$c = (1 - R)\lambda, \qquad (9.29)$$

where R is the recovery rate. Hence if the assumed recovery rate goes down, the loss given default

$$\text{LGD} = 1 - R \qquad (9.30)$$

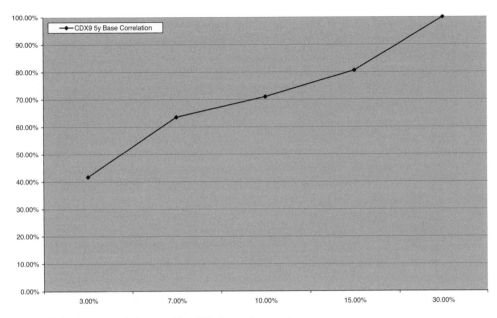

Figure 9.4   Base correlation can hit 100% for senior tranches

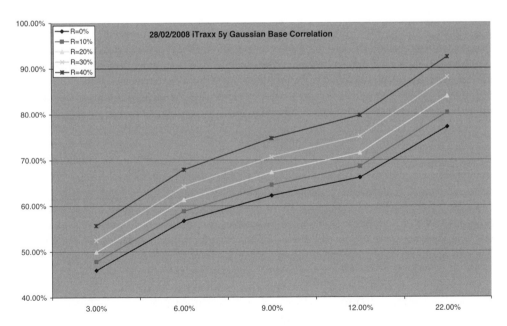

Figure 9.5   Gaussian BC curves recovery rates

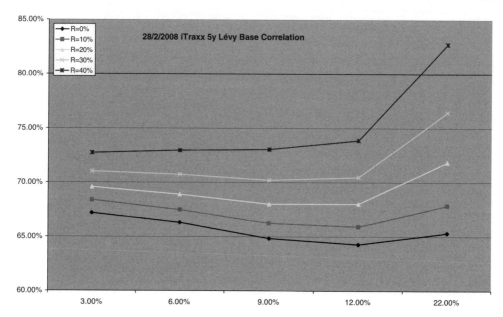

Figure 9.6   Lévy BC curves recovery rates

goes up and the default intensity

$$\lambda = \frac{c}{1 - R} \tag{9.31}$$

goes down, resulting in a lower probability of default, but with a higher loss given default. Consequently correlation values are lower for lower assumed recovery rates.

Figure 9.6 shows the impact of the recovery rate assumption on the Lévy base correlation curves. Note that in 2002 a typical value for the assumed recovery rate was $R = 20\%$. Moreover, a simple no arbitrage argument shows that if the [15%–30%] tranche is trading at 102 bp and the [30%–100%] tranche is trading at 58 bp the recovery rate cannot be higher than 30%.

We refer to McGinty et al. (2004) for additional literature on base correlation. Several authors have described 1-factor models using distributions other than the standard normal distribution, see e.g. Baxter (2006), Hooda (2006), Kalemanova et al. (2007) and Moosbrucker (2006). For more details we refer to our paper Garcia et al. (2009) and the references therein.

To the best of our knowledge Mandelbrot (1963) was the first who suggested the use of Lévy processes in financial modeling. He proposed to model the logarithm of the stock price process log S_t as a symmetric stable Lévy process and presented some statistical evidence for this approach. For more details on Lévy processes we refer to Bertoin (1996), Sato (2000) and Kyprianou (2006). For Lévy processes in finance we refer to Schoutens (2003) and to Cont and Tankov (2004).

Other approaches to compute the joint loss distribution exist. We refer to Moody's (Debuysscher et al., 2003) for models based on Fast Fourier Transform (FFT) and to Yang et al. (2006) for models based on the Saddle Point Approximation.

10

Historical Study of Lévy Base Correlation

Doubt is the father of invention.
Galileo Galilei

10.1 INTRODUCTION

In Chapter 9 we described the concepts of implied compound correlation and base correlation used in the market for pricing purposes. We have shown that Lévy base correlation could be used as an alternative to the Gaussian copula approach. We also refer to our paper (Garcia et al., 2009). In this brief chapter we go into more details on the approaches and show numerical results of tests using both approaches for pricing and hedging purposes.

The chapter is organized as follows. The historical study is outlined in Section 10.2. We look at base correlation in these two models in Section 10.3. First, we show the evolution over time and, second, we consider the behavior across maturity and look at the base correlation surface. In Section 10.4 we compare hedge parameters in the different models. We focus on the deltas of the tranches with respect to the index. This is also done across maturity. Finally our conclusions are presented in Section 10.5.

10.2 HISTORICAL STUDY

In this section we describe our historical study. The dataset used is the iTraxx Europe Main data from 20 April 2005 until 16 March 2007. We look at index and tranche spreads for the 5-, 7- and 10-year maturity contracts. Figure 10.1 shows the historical evolution of the spreads for the 5-year maturity.

The key parameters in both models are the base correlation curves. First, we show the evolution over time and, second, we consider the behavior across maturity and look at the base correlation surface. For trading purposes it is important to understand the hedge parameters in the two models. We present a comparison between the two models and focus on the deltas of the tranches with respect to the index.

10.3 BASE CORRELATION

10.3.1 Base correlation evolution over time

As mentioned above, both models are parameterized with a base correlation curve. We have compared the evolution over time of the base correlation curves in both models and found that their behavior is very similar.

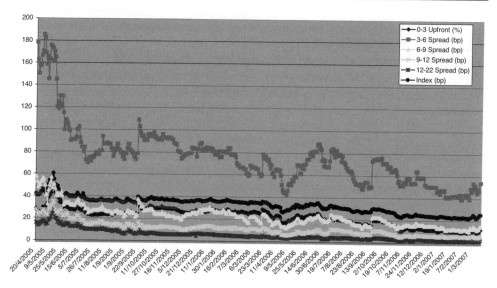

Figure 10.1 iTraxx Europe Main on-the-run 5-year spreads

The evolution over time for the 12–22 tranche for the Gaussian and Lévy base correlation models is shown in Figure 10.2. We present the results for the 12–22 tranche since this is the last one to be computed in the bootstrapping procedure, and consequently it is sensitive to all previous computations. Lévy base correlation and Gaussian base correlation clearly behave in the same way, just on a different scale.

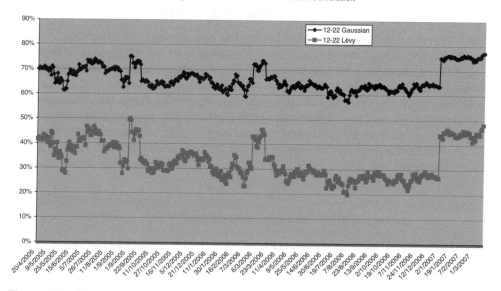

Figure 10.2 iTraxx Europe Main 5y Gaussian and Lévy Base Correlation for 12–22 tranche

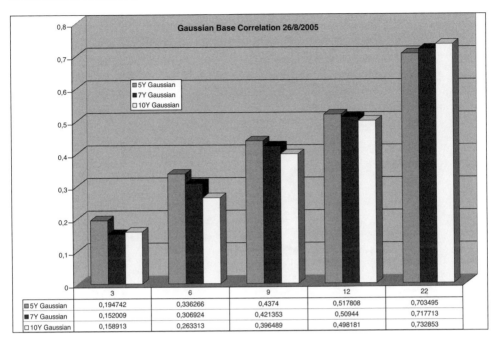

Figure 10.3   Gaussian copula base correlation

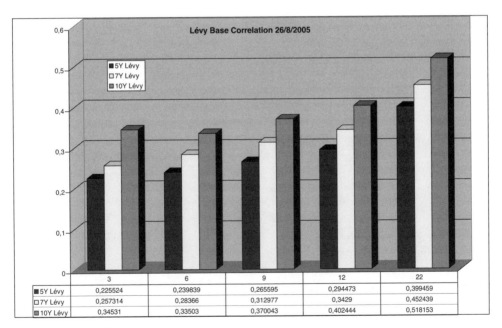

Figure 10.4   Lévy base correlation

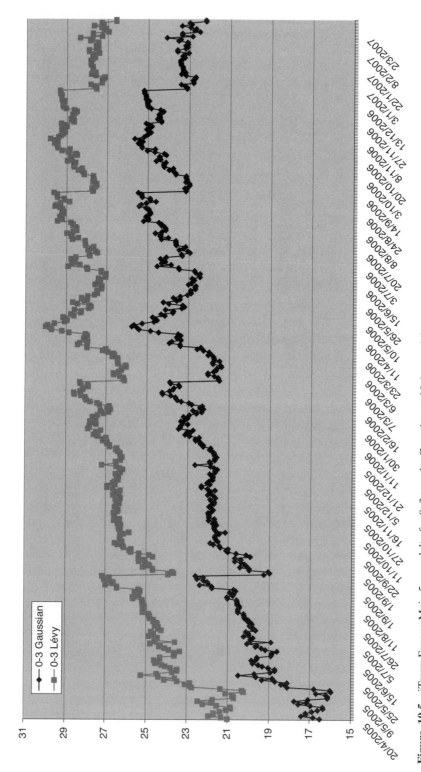

Figure 10.5 iTraxx Europe Main 5-year delta for 0–3 tranche Gaussian and Lévy model

10.3.2   Base correlation across maturity

We now turn to the base correlation surface, that is, we consider base correlation as a function of the attachment point and the maturity.

Figure 10.3 shows the Gaussian copula base correlation surface. For every maturity we observe the typical upward sloping curve at the standard attachment points. The behavior across maturity for a given attachment point is less uniform. This curve can be smiling, upward or downward sloping. Looking at these curves it should be clear that there is no widely accepted standard approach for interpolating a base correlation surface for a nonstandard attachment point or for a nonstandard maturity. Moreover, interpolation schemes may not be arbitrage-free. For a detailed discussion on a more efficient way to interpolate in the base correlation framework, we refer to our earlier paper (Garcia et al., 2008).

The Lévy base correlation surface is shown in Figure 10.4. Contrary to the Gaussian case, the behavior across maturity for a given attachment point is more uniform. There is an upward trend with maturity. We also see the typical upward sloping curve at the standard attachment points, except for the 10-year maturity, where we see a smile. In fact, this is expected and the explanation is as follows. In our earlier paper (Garcia et al., 2008), we have shown that both Gaussian and Lévy base correlation curves exhibit a smile for small attachment points. It is even more pronounced in the Lévy base correlation curve. On the other hand, it is well known that for the 10-year maturity contract the 3–6 tranche behaves as an equity tranche. On the 10-year maturity the 0–3 equity tranche is a deeper – in the sense of lower attachment points – equity tranche. Hence we expect it to have a larger base correlation value than the 3–6 tranche.

10.4   HEDGE PARAMETERS

The evolution over time for the delta of the 0–3 tranche with respect to the index for the Gaussian and Lévy base correlation models is shown in Figure 10.5. The values for this

Table 10.1   Regression of Lévy delta on Gaussian delta for the 5-year maturity tranches

Tr	$\beta_{Tr, T}$	Std Err	R^2
0–3	1.198891	0.001143	0.9996
3–6	0.761988	0.002592	0.9946
6–9	0.567959	0.001864	0.995
9–12	0.527024	0.004981	0.9601
12–22	0.49989	0.01036	0.8334

Table 10.2   Regression of Lévy delta on Gaussian delta for the 7-year maturity tranches

Tr	β	Std Err	R^2
0–3	1.25069	0.00104	0.9997
3–6	1.059253	0.004181	0.9928
6–9	0.638850	0.002096	0.995
9–12	0.567896	0.003036	0.9869
12–22	0.557808	0.009115	0.8893

Table 10.3   Regression of Lévy delta on Gaussian delta
for the 10-year maturity tranches

Tr	β	Std Err	R^2
0–3	1.182632	0.002417	0.9981
3–6	1.337550	0.002275	0.9987
6–9	0.895605	0.005092	0.9852
9–12	0.640572	0.001964	0.9956
12–22	0.622463	0.006962	0.9449

sensitivity parameter produced by the Gaussian and Lévy models clearly behave in the same way, just on a different scale. In order to quantify this similarity, a regression of the delta produced by the Lévy model on the delta produced by the Gaussian models is performed. This is done for all tranches and all maturities. The model is

$$\delta_{\mathrm{Tr},T}^{(L)} = \beta_{\mathrm{Tr},T}\delta_{\mathrm{Tr},T}^{(G)} \tag{10.1}$$

where $\delta_{\mathrm{Tr},T}^{(L)}$ is the delta of tranche Tr with respect to the underlying index, for a maturity T, produced by the Lévy model, and $\delta_{\mathrm{Tr},T}^{(G)}$ is the delta produced by the Gaussian model. We now turn to the quality of these regressions.

Table 10.1 shows the regression coefficient, the standard error and the coefficient of determination R^2 for each tranche for the 5-year maturity. The R^2 statistic confirms that the model (10.1) is a good fit. The regression results for the 7-year maturity are shown in Table 10.2. In this case the R^2 statistic also confirms that the model (10.1) is a good fit. Table 10.3 shows the regression results for the 10-year maturity. Also here the R^2 statistic confirms that the model (10.1) is a good fit.

These results show that, compared to the Gaussian model, the Lévy model produces a delta that is larger for the equity tranches and smaller for the senior tranches. Roughly speaking, we can say that the Lévy model delta is approximately 20% larger for the equity tranche and 40% smaller for the senior tranches. This result is to be compared to "statistical" deltas quoted by market participants which are typically 20% higher for the equity tranche.

10.5   CONCLUSIONS

We have compared the Gaussian copula and Lévy base correlation models. The results of a historical study of both models on the iTraxx Europe Main dataset have been presented. We have compared the evolution over time of the base correlation surfaces in both models and found that their behavior is very similar. Hedge parameters in the different models have also been studied. We have focused on the deltas of the tranches with respect to the index and found the values for this sensitivity parameter produced by the Gaussian and Lévy models clearly behave in the same way. This is illustrated by the fact that a regression of one on the other results in a very good fit. Roughly speaking, we can say that the Lévy model delta is approximately 20% larger for the equity tranche and 40% smaller for the senior tranches.

11

Base Expected Loss and Base
Correlation Smile

The surest way to corrupt a youth is to instruct him to hold in higher esteem those who think alike
than those who think differently.
Friedrich Nietzsche

11.1 INTRODUCTION

In Chapter 9 we described the concepts of implied compound correlation and base correlation (BC), highlighting the reasons for the market adoption of the latter. That is, *the pricing of tranches of the capital structure of a bespoke portfolio could not be done directly using compound correlation*. It also meant that the ability to price bespoke tranches was determinant for the creation and use by market participants of the concept of base correlation. By using equity or base tranches the price of a tranche [A–D] is calculated using the two equity tranches with A and D as detachment points. Moreover, the BC concept makes it quite straightforward to bootstrap between two standard attachment points for pricing bespoke tranches.

The methodology, however, has some weaknesses. First of all, it is very sensitive to the interpolation technique used. Even worse, the methodology may not be arbitrage-free. It does not provide any guidance on how to extrapolate the curve, especially below the 3% attachment point. Additionally, a fundamental reason for the existence of the standardized credit indices is their use in the *pricing discovery* process of bespoke tranches of credit portfolios. Although the base correlation concept solves the problem of pricing bespoke tranches it transfers to itself all the burden of pricing discovery. As we show below, base correlation is not an intuitive concept.

In this chapter we posit the concept of *base expected loss* as a much more *intuitive* concept than base correlation. We show that it addresses all the issues referred to in the last paragraph. We look at *base expected loss* at maturity both in the Gaussian copula and Lévy-based models. We first use the *base expected loss* concept for arbitrage-free pricing and we then integrate it within the base correlation methodology in non-Gaussian 1-factor models. By working with base expected loss, our goal is to develop an arbitrage-free correlation mapping technique independent of the pricing framework. It turns out that using a cubic spline interpolation with a monotonicity filter applied to it on the base expected loss produces very satisfactory results. There are good reasons to also use a non-Gaussian alternative model, such as having an alternative view on hedge parameters and analysis of sensitivities.

Earlier work on expected loss modeling has been done by Walker (2006), Livesey and Schloegl (2006), Torresetti et al. (2007) and Parcell and Wood (2007) amongst others. The approach we follow here is slightly different. First, we use it in the generic 1-factor Lévy framework and, second, we look at the expected loss at a certain point in time (in this case at maturity).

This chapter is organized as follows. Interpolation in the base correlation framework is discussed in Section 11.3. In Section 11.4 we define base expected loss, describe its properties and outline the upper and lower bounds it must satisfy. In Section 11.5 we discuss several interpolation techniques for base expected loss. Numerical results are given in Section 11.6. Finally our conclusions are presented in Section 11.7.

11.2   BASE CORRELATION AND EXPECTED LOSS: INTUITION

As mentioned before, the base correlation approach solved the problems of pricing nonstandard tranches of the capital structure. The concept, however, has at least two problems. First, it is linked with the fact that a 1-factor model is used for pricing different pieces of the capital structure. This point is depicted in more detail in Figure 11.1. In the figure we see that the expected loss of the [3%–6%] tranche is indeed equal to the expected loss of the [0%–6%] tranche, using correlation ρ_2, minus the expected loss of the [0%–3%] tranche using correlation ρ_1. There is, however, an incoherence in the approach: we assume that the tranche [0%–3%] in the tranche [0%–6%] will be evaluated using correlation ρ_2, while for the tranche [0%–3%] alone we have used correlation ρ_1. The problem is similar with the smile adjustment one makes when pricing options using Black-Scholes, where one has to use different volatilities for different maturities and strikes. It might be inherent to the use of a 1-factor model and the requirement of simplicity for pricing purposes.

The second problem, however, is intuition. We show in Figure 11.2 a time series of base correlation for the different tranches. From those curves it is extremely difficult, if not impossible, to infer if a tranche is overbought or oversold. Unless one is a trader and has been looking to those curves day in day out, one has no way to infer extreme market movements in any of the tranches.

Compare it with the time series of expected loss depicted in Figure 11.3. In that figure we show how the total expected loss is distributed among the different tranches. Observe that, from that figure, it becomes clearer when tranches are overbought or oversold. Additionally, at points of extreme market disruptions the costs of the most senior tranche increase relatively to the equity tranche (see e.g., around 20/04/2005 when auto companies had been downgraded and 6/08/2007 at the first signals of the credit crunch).

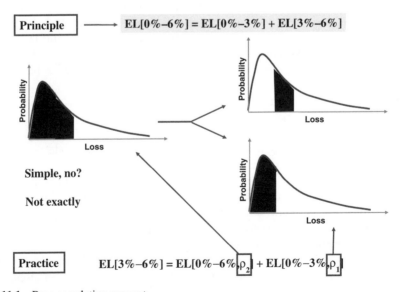

Figure 11.1   Base correlation concept

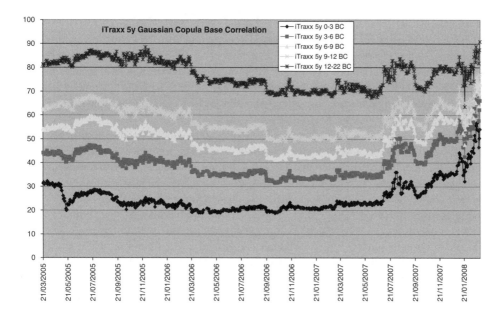

Figure 11.2   Gaussian copula base correlation history

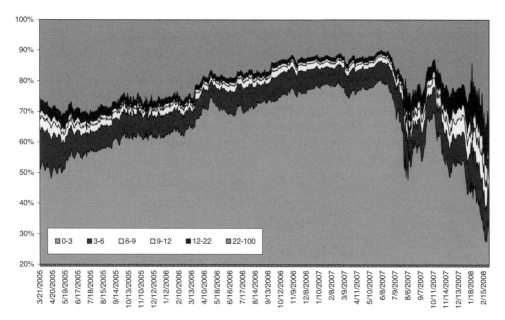

Figure 11.3   Distribution of the expected loss over the tranches as a percentage of the total expected loss (5-year iTraxx)

11.3   BASE CORRELATION AND INTERPOLATION

In Chapter 9 we presented the 1-factor Gaussian copula and the Lévy models using the so-called *recursion algorithm* developed by Andersen et al. (2003). In order to price bespoke tranches, nonstandard tranches or tranches of an older series, one may have to interpolate or extrapolate the base correlation curve of the current series. Although the techniques discussed here are general enough to apply to any liquid credit index, in what follows we will be referring to the European corporate index (iTraxx).

The easiest interpolation method to set up is piece-wise linear interpolation between 3% and 22%. Extrapolation outside this interval may result in either negative values or in values larger than 1. Applying a floor at 0 and a cap at 1 introduces sudden and troublesome changes in the derivative of the base correlation curve. Prescribing values at 0% or 100% is just an arbitrary choice. Market practitioners used to pricing bespoke CDO deals are well aware that sudden changes in the derivative of the base correlation curve may result in equally sudden changes in the fair spreads of tranchlets and, even worse, in model arbitrage.

In order to avoid sudden spread jumps that may lead to possible arbitrage opportunities, interpolation methods that produce continuous derivatives are preferred. To our knowledge the most widespread method used by practitioners is cubic spline interpolation. It has the advantage of producing continuous curves with continuous first and second derivatives. However, the extrapolation issues outside the 3%–22% region remain. Unfortunately, even smooth base correlation curves may be arbitrageable and it is impossible to guarantee absence of arbitrage unless all tranchlet prices are checked. It is clear that interpolating base correlation curves has some disadvantages.

11.4   BASE EXPECTED LOSS

We define base expected loss $l(x)$ as the expected loss of an equity tranche at maturity

$$l(x) = \mathbb{E}[\text{Loss}(0, x, \rho_x, T)]. \qquad (11.1)$$

This quantity is readily available in the base correlation framework. Note that this definition is different from what Parcell and Wood (2007) define as discounted base expected loss, which is the present value of the contingent leg. The ideas presented below apply to both approaches. In this chapter we consider the variant which does not depend on the discount curve – that is, the expected loss at maturity. This quantity appears, for example, in a structured credit product involving the equity tranche known as zero coupon equity. In order to avoid model arbitrage the base expected loss curve should obey two important conditions. First, base expected loss $l(x)$ is a nondecreasing function of the attachment point x, as its derivative corresponds to a probability:

$$\frac{\partial}{\partial x} l(x) = \mathbb{P}[\text{Loss} \geq x] \geq 0. \qquad (11.2)$$

Second, base expected loss $l(x)$ cannot be positively convex, as its second derivative is minus the density of the loss distribution:

$$\frac{\partial^2}{\partial x^2} l(x) = -f_{\text{Loss}}(x) \leq 0. \qquad (11.3)$$

Similar properties on expected loss-related quantities have been described in different formulations in the references mentioned above. There is another aspect to producing arbitrage-free interpolations – that is, the losses cannot decrease over time. We do not consider these temporal arbitrages, since our focus is on arbitrage-free pricing of nonstandard tranches.

One of the advantages of this loss-based approach is that boundary values are available. Clearly we have that $l(0) = 0$ and $l(1) = \mathbb{E}[\text{Loss}(0, 100\%, T)]$ is the expected loss on the underlying pool, independent of correlation, determined only by spreads and recovery rates. From the bootstrapping of implied base correlation points, we get the base expected losses for the standard attachment points. Starting from these values and the properties (11.2) and (11.3), we can construct an upper and a lower bound for base expected loss interpolations. Those bounds are extremely useful in determining nonarbitrageable trading strategies. We emphasize that any base expected loss curve, satisfying both (11.2) and (11.3), is arbitrage-free and vice versa and that curves can lie in the bounds but fail to be valid.

Figure 11.4 shows the construction of the bounds on the base expected loss. Convexity arguments can be used to show that the lower bound is the curve, obtained by piecewise linear interpolation of the base expected losses of the standard attachments points. This is the thick solid line. For the upper bounds there are several candidates. Clearly, base expected loss is bounded by the size of the tranche $l(x) \leq x$ and by the expected loss on the complete pool of underlying obligors $l(x) \leq l(1)$. The thin solid line shows this bound. Suppose $0 \leq p < q \leq 1$ and p and q are consecutive standard attachment points, that is there is no standard attachment

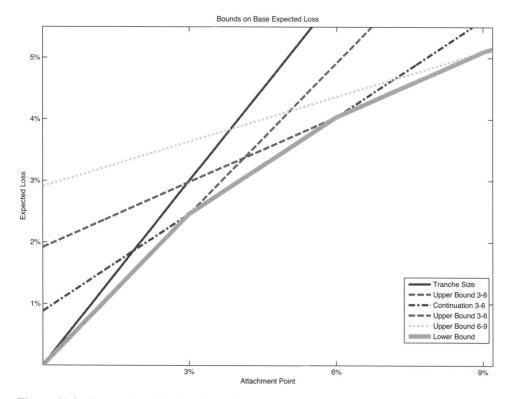

Figure 11.4   Construction of the bounds on the base expected loss on 1 April 2008

point between p and q. Convexity arguments can be used to show that the prolongation to the right of the straight line through the points $(p, l(p))$ and $(q, l(q))$ is an upper bound on $l(x)$ for $x \geq q$ and analogously the prolongation to the left is an upper bound on $l(x)$ for $x \leq p$. The dash dotted line is the prolongation of the lower bound for the [3%–6%] tranche. It is an upper bound for the [0%–3%] and [6%–9%] tranches. The dashed lines show the upper bounds for the [3%–6%] tranche as prolongations of the lower bounds on [0%–3%] and [6%–9%] tranches. The upper bound is, of course, the minimum of all applicable upper bounds. Note that the lower bound satisfies (11.3) but the upper bound does not; it is the envelope of a set of functions that do. Thus the upper bound is not a feasible base expected loss curve. An example of the violation of (11.3) can be seen at the 3% attachment point. The slope of the dash-dotted and dashed parts of the curve violate the convexity condition.

It should be intuitively clear that interpolating on the loss distribution instead of interpolating directly on the base correlation curve is advantageous as the former is the real quantity of interest. It is also straightforward to use the expected loss curve to impose boundary conditions to construct an arbitrage-free model. In our approach, the base correlation curve is implied from the expected loss curve and not the other way around.

11.5   INTERPOLATION

Besides being monotone and negatively convex, we want the interpolated base expected loss curve to be smooth, so cubic spline interpolation is certainly a candidate to be considered. Unfortunately, a cubic spline interpolant can exhibit oscillations, thus violating the monotonicity constraint (11.2). However, this does not rule out cubic interpolation for the base expected loss curve. The idea is to give up on the constraint imposing continuity of the second derivative, and impose other constraints related to monotonicity and convexity. In the next section, we show the effect of the interpolation schemes for the loss distribution on the base correlation curve.

Our preferred interpolation scheme is to use cubic splines and apply the monotonicity filter as described by Dougherty et al. (1989) to it. This approach has the advantage of leaving the interpolating spline unchanged when it is monotonic, resulting in a very smooth interpolant. A second interpolation approach is as outlined by Fritsch and Carlson (1980). On each subinterval a cubic interpolant is used and continuity of the first derivative is imposed. The slopes at the data points are chosen to preserve the shape of the data and to respect monotonicity. The second derivative is not necessarily continuous, as it may jump at the control points.

Next we discuss some interpolation techniques that can be applied but whose performance in terms of producing a smooth curve may not be as good as that of the two methods mentioned above. As mentioned in the previous section, piecewise linear interpolation on the base expected losses is the lower bound for any interpolated base expected loss curve. It is an acceptable method in the sense that it satisfies all the constraints. However, we want a smooth base expected loss curve with a continuous derivative, since the derivative of the base expected loss curve is related to the probability distribution of the losses. As can be seen from (11.3) convexity constraints prescribe that this derivative be nonincreasing. Another approach is the monotonic interpolation introduced by Steffen (1990). Contrary to spline interpolation this method has the advantage of being local. Since a third order polynomial is being used and monotonicity is enforced, convexity cannot be guaranteed. Some results for this interpolation scheme are given by Parcell and Wood (2007), in which they also present a piecewise quadratic interpolation method, augmented with an heuristic and an iteration scheme to enforce the monotonicity and convexity constraints. Note that piecewise quadratic interpolation for base expected loss translates into piecewise constant interpolation for the density of the loss distribution, which is a rather crude approximation.

11.6 NUMERICAL RESULTS

In this section we present numerical results using both the Gaussian copula and the Lévy shifted gamma models for iTraxx Europe Main. The market data is taken on 22 June 2007 and on 1 April 2008. These two dates permit us to compare how the models behave both in an environment of tight spreads and in a stressed environment. Unless mentioned explicitly, the June 2007 data set is used. We look at the 10-year contract. This particular contract has been chosen because both the [0%–3%] and [3%–6%] behave as equity tranches, allowing us to show interesting and insightful results. The expected loss on the complete pool is independent of the model used to price the tranches. Both the Lévy and the Gaussian copula models are calibrated to the same observed tranche spreads.

Figure 11.4 shows the base expected loss curve for the Gaussian copula on 1 April 2008, and Figure 11.5 shows this curve for 22 June 2007. We calibrate the model to the observed

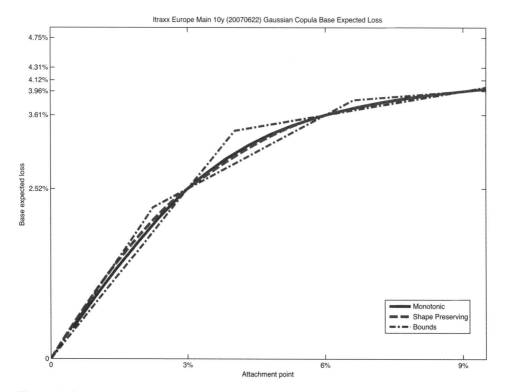

Figure 11.5 Gaussian copula base expected loss. The dash/dotted lines show the upper and lower bounds. The solid line shows the monotonic cubic spline interpolation and the dashed line shows the shape preserving cubic interpolation

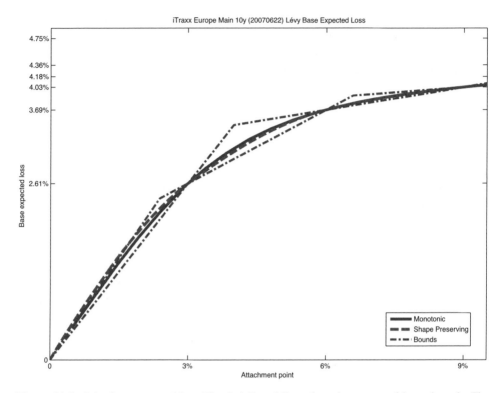

Figure 11.6 Lévy base expected loss. The dash/dotted lines show the upper and lower bounds. The solid line shows the monotonic cubic spline interpolation and the dashed line shows the shape preserving cubic interpolation

market tranche spreads and we get the base correlation and base expected loss values for the standard attachment points. For the base expected loss we also have the boundary values at 0% and at 100%. Starting from these values and the properties (11.2) and (11.3), we construct the upper and the lower bounds for base expected loss interpolations as described in Section 11.4. The dash-dotted lines show these bounds. It is clear that these bounds interpolate in the bootstrapped values. The solid line shows the cubic spline interpolation with application of the monotonicity filter as described in Section 11.5. Finally, the dashed line shows the shape preserving cubic interpolation. Note that for small values of the attachment point, the shape preserving interpolation methodology violates the upper bound. Both interpolation schemes as depicted by the solid and dashed lines satisfy the convexity constraint (11.3).

In Figure 11.6 we show the base expected loss curves for the Lévy model. Note that, as before, the shape preserving cubic interpolation violates the upper bound for small values of the attachment point. Both interpolations satisfy the convexity constraint (11.3). Comparing this figure to Figure 11.5, we see some differences between the Lévy and the Gaussian copula models. For the 0–3% tranche the Gaussian copula model gives a base expected loss at maturity of 2.52%, while the Lévy model gives a base expected loss at maturity of

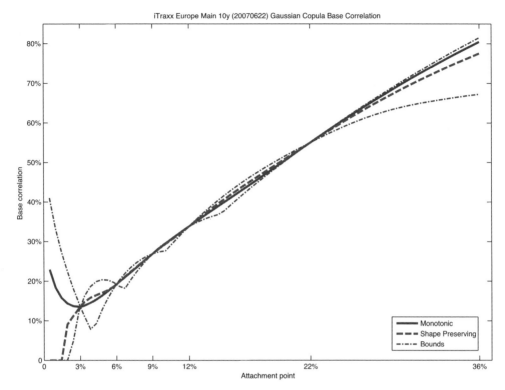

Figure 11.7 Gaussian copula base correlation. The dash/dotted lines show curves implied from the upper and lower sounds on base expected loss. The solid lines show the curve for monotonic cubic spline interpolation and the dashed line shows the shape preserving cubic interpolation

2.61%. As both models have been calibrated to the same observed market tranche spreads the difference between the models is clearly in the distribution of the expected losses over the tranches.

The Gaussian copula base correlation curves are shown in Figure 11.7. First of all, we have base correlation values for the standard attachment points as a result of the calibration to the observed market tranche spreads. We are not interpolating base correlation directly. As explained above, we have bounds on base expected loss and we interpolate the base expected loss curve. For a given attachment point and corresponding base expected loss value, we solve for the corresponding base correlation value. As there is a one-to-one relationship between base expected loss and base correlation, the bounds on the former imply bounds on the latter. These are shown as the dash-dotted lines. Recall that the upper bound on base expected loss is not a feasible base expected loss curve. Consequently, the implied base correlation curve is probably not arbitrage-free. The calibration for base correlation is also done when shape preserving cubic interpolation is carried out on the base expected loss curve. This results in the dashed line. Observe that for very small baskets idiosyncratic risk can be dominant, explaining why base correlation can go to zero. Finally, the solid line shows the implied base correlation curve when cubic spline interpolation with application of the

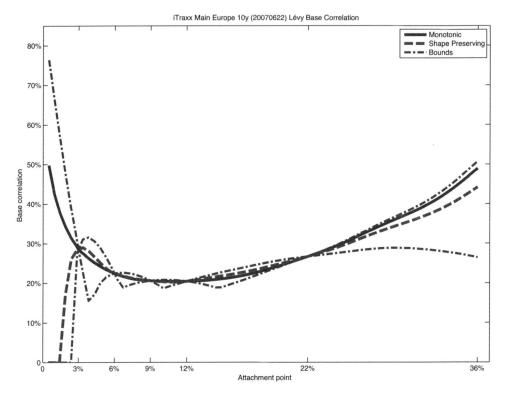

Figure 11.8 Lévy base correlation. The dash/dotted lines show curves implied from the upper and lower bounds on base expected loss. The solid line shows the curve for monotonic cubic spline interpolation and the dashed line shows the shape preserving cubic interpolation

monotonicity filter is done on the base expected loss curve. This results in a base correlation smile.

The Lévy base correlation curves are shown in Figure 11.8. Here also the base correlation hits zero when shape preserving cubic interpolation is done on the base expected loss curve. Comparing this figure to Figure 11.7, we see some differences between the Lévy and the Gaussian copula models. Lévy base correlation is somewhat flatter above 3% and can become quite large for very small attachment points. Gaussian copula base correlation is much steeper above 3% and also smiles below 3%, but to a lesser extent than Lévy base correlation.

Figure 11.9 shows the Gaussian copula base correlation on 1 April 2008. The dash-dotted lines show curves implied from the upper and lower bounds on base expected loss. The solid line shows the curve for monotonic cubic spline interpolation. Comparing this figure to Figure 11.7 we can see the differences in the base correlation curves in an environment of tight spreads and in a stressed environment. Figure 11.10 shows these results for the Lévy base correlation on 1 April 2008 and can be compared to Figure 11.8 showing similar curves in an environment of tight spreads.

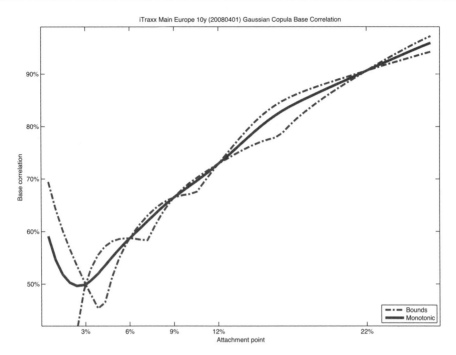

Figure 11.9 Gaussian copula base correlation on 1 April 2008. The dash/dotted lines show curves implied from the upper and lower bounds on base expected loss. The solid line shows the curve for monotonic cubic spline interpolation

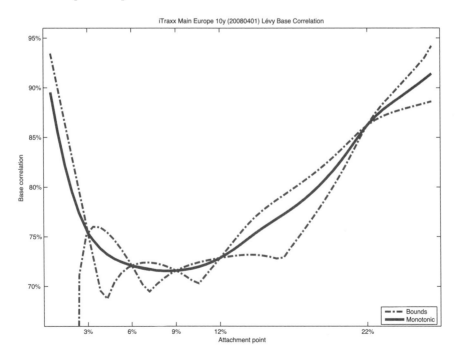

Figure 11.10 Lévy base correlation on 1 April 2008. The dash/dotted lines show curves implied from the upper and lower bounds on base expected loss. The solid line shows the curve for monotonic cubic spline interpolation

11.7   CONCLUSIONS

In this chapter we have investigated base expected loss and stated the monotonicity and convexity constraints it needs to obey. Based on these constraints we derived upper and lower bounds needed by an interpolation scheme for base expected loss in order to avoid model arbitrage. We studied the effect of interpolating base expected loss curves both in the Gaussian copula and in the Lévy 1-factor models for CDO tranche valuation, both in an environment of tight spreads and in a stressed environment. The one-to-one relationship between base expected loss and base correlation was used to derive the implied base correlation curves in both models. The best results have been obtained using a cubic spline interpolation with a monotonicity filter applied to it on the base expected loss curves.

We would like to mention three important results of this study. First, the implied base correlation curves show a smile, both for the Gaussian copula and the Lévy 1-factor model. In the Gaussian case the base correlation smile is less pronounced in the [0–3%] range and is more pronounced in the senior tranches. In the Lévy model, on the other hand, the base correlation smile is more pronounced in the [0–3%] range and is less pronounced in the senior tranches. Second, we show a practical algorithm to evaluate spreads for tranchlets outside the [3%–22%] range, since this is a well-behaved interpolation in the base expected loss framework instead of a dangerous extrapolation in the base correlation framework. Finally, our trading-driven pricing methodology based on the concept of expected loss and on interpolation on that curve is much more intuitive than a methodology based on interpolating base correlations curves directly.

Base Correlation Mapping

A goal without a plan is just a wish.
Antoine de Saint-Exupery

12.1 INTRODUCTION

In Chapter 9 we introduced the recursive approach for pricing synthetic CDO tranches developed by Andersen et al. (2003). We have seen that for pricing the tranches the exogenous correlation plays a crucial role. We showed that the market adopted first the concept of *implied compound correlation* and that a crucial problem of this approach resided in its unsuitability for interpolation when pricing nonstandard tranches. The concept of *base correlation* (BC) introduced by McGinty et al. (2004) solved the problems that implied compound correlation could not. We saw that in the base correlation methodology only equity or base tranches (with attachment point 0) are considered. The price of a tranche [A–D] is calculated using the two equity tranches with A and D as detachment points. Additionally, we showed the algorithm using both the Gaussian and Lévy frameworks. The BC concept became widely used and is supposed to be suitable for interpolation both for nonstandardized tranches and for bespoke portfolios.

In Chapter 10 we have shown results of historical tests involving Gaussian and Lévy base correlation. Problems of the base correlation approach have been addressed in Chapter 11. By comparing Figures 11.2 and 11.3 we have shown that the concept of expected loss is much more appealing to intuition than the concept of base correlation. In that chapter we presented the concept of base expected loss as a solution to many of the weaknesses existent in the base correlation approach. As already mentioned in Chapter 9, an important use for the standardized credit indices is to bring liquidity to the underlying class of instruments. That is, in the language of central bankers the indices serve as key mechanisms for the pricing discovery process of bespoke tranches. Additionally, as will be described in Part IV, the indices are supposed to be used for dynamic portfolio management of a credit portfolio, in this way serving as a key support for the securitization business model of financial institutions. The indices are the ideal instruments not only for hedging but also for the mark to market of bespoke credit portfolios (see Tett and Larsen, 2008, for an example during the credit crunch). In this chapter we extend the base expected loss at maturity framework to the pricing of tranches of nonstandard (or bespoke) portfolios. As with the management of equity portfolios where one needs to determine the appropriate volatility parameter in the case of a credit portfolio, one needs to determine the appropriate *correlation* for the bespoke portfolio. The technique of projecting the capital structure of a bespoke portfolio on the capital structure of a credit index for pricing purposes is known in the literature as *correlation mapping* (CM). Correlation mapping techniques have already been treated in the practitioner literature (see Baheti and Morgan, 2007). We complement the referred study in three important ways. First, we show results of the CM techniques using an arbitrage, free interpolation approach based on expected loss, which is independent of the model framework used. Second, we use it not only within the traditional

Gaussian approach but also within the Lévy-based framework. Third, the tests are done using realistic data for the iTraxx and CDX indices.

The remainder of this chapter is organized as follows. In Section 12.2 we define alternative correlation mapping techniques commonly used among practitioners. Numerical results are given in Section 12.3. Finally our conclusions are presented in Section 12.4.

12.2   CORRELATION MAPPING FOR BESPOKE PORTFOLIOS

The current market approaches for pricing bespoke tranches are known as *correlation mapping* methodologies and are based on the assumption of a quantity supposed to be market invariant. The idea of correlation mapping is depicted in Figure 12.1 in which the unknown loss distribution is mapped into the loss distributions of standardized credit indices. The main objective of the technique is to infer from the standardized credit indices the appropriate correlation parameters to be used for pricing bespoke portfolios.

The techniques in this section are based on the existence of so-called *market invariants* – that is, variables supposed not to vary when one goes from one portfolio to another. That is, the concept in a nutshell consists of assuming market invariants which are used to imply from the correlation curve of the *liquid* standardized credit indices the correlation to be input into the standard model to price bespoke tranches. There are several approaches used by market practitioners for correlation mapping purposes and in this section we will be describing just some of them. It is important to note that there is no such a thing as one unique approach and

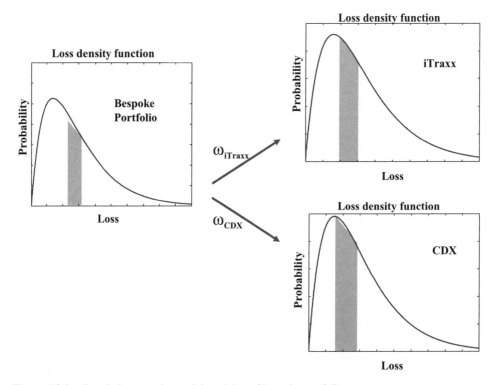

Figure 12.1   Correlation mapping and the pricing of bespoke portfolios

the process of correlation mapping is much more an *art* than a science. The approaches we will be testing in this chapter are the following:

- *No mapping.* This is the simplest possible approach and the base correlation for a certain attachment point on the bespoke portfolio is equal to the correlation for the same attachment point in the index portfolio:

$$\rho_{\text{Bespoke}}(A) = \rho_{\text{Index}}(A) \tag{12.1}$$

  It assumes that equity base correlation is invariant to the portfolio characteristics. This rather naive method assumes that correlation depends only on the *attachment point* of the capital structure and *not* on the credit quality of the underlying portfolio. Comparisons with this approach show how prices differ due to differences in the underlying portfolios.
- *Discounted moneyness matching.* In this approach one assumes that the attachment point as a fraction of the portfolio expected loss is an invariant measure to determine the cost of risk. The ratio between attachment point and portfolio expected loss is called moneyness in the market and the correlation for the attachment point A is given by:

$$\rho_{\text{Bespoke}}(A) = \rho_{\text{Index}} \left(A \frac{\mathbb{E}[\text{Loss}_{\text{Bespoke}}(0, 100\%)]}{\mathbb{E}[\text{Loss}_{\text{Index}}(0, 100\%)]} \right) \tag{12.2}$$

  It is a widely-used methodology in the market. If the bespoke and the index portfolios have the same expected losses then it will give the same results as no mapping. The main advantage of this approach is simplicity. One big disadvantage is that it does not take into account the dispersion of spreads in the portfolio. As the expected loss on the whole index does not depend on correlation it is discussable why the correlation at different attachment points should be completely determined by the expected loss on the whole index.
- *Moneyness at maturity.* This is very similar to the approach described in (12.2), the only difference being that there is no impact of the discount curve:

$$\rho_{\text{Bespoke}}(A) = \rho_{\text{Index}} \left(A \frac{\mathbb{E}[\text{Loss}_{\text{Bespoke}}^{mat}(0, 100\%)]}{\mathbb{E}[\text{Loss}_{\text{Index}}^{mat}(0, 100\%)]} \right) \tag{12.3}$$

- *Probability matching.* In this case the invariant is the probability of loss of an equity tranche at maturity. One searches for the attachment point in the index such that the cumulative loss probability at maturity equals the one of the attachment point in the bespoke portfolio:

$$\mathbb{P}[\text{Loss}_{\text{Bespoke}}^{mat} \leq A_{\text{Bespoke}}] = \mathbb{P}[\text{Loss}_{\text{Index}}^{mat} \leq A_{\text{Index}}] \tag{12.4}$$

and

$$\rho_{\text{Bespoke}}(A_{\text{Bespoke}}) = \rho_{\text{Index}}(A_{\text{Index}}). \tag{12.5}$$

Observe that changes in correlation do not affect the portfolio expected loss but the form of portfolio loss distribution. One advantage is that the approach takes into account the dispersion of the spread within the portfolio. The discrete nature of the portfolio means that the approach is inherently discontinuous and one needs to use interpolation techniques to smooth out the discontinuities. The mapping might fail if the quality of the bespoke portfolio is much worse than the one of the index. We think that any mapping technique that tries to map the capital structures of two very different portfolios will be prone to errors.

- *Base spread matching*. In this approach the invariant is the spread of the base tranche:

$$\text{Spread}_{\text{Bespoke}}(A_{\text{Bespoke}}, \rho_{\text{Index}}) = \text{Spread}_{\text{Index}}(A_{\text{Index}}, \rho_{\text{Index}}). \tag{12.6}$$

This approach takes into account the dispersion. A second advantage is simplicity. There are, however, three immediate disadvantages to this approach. First, it does not take into account either the size of the portfolio or its duration. Second, one might not find appropriate tranches on the index that would match the spreads in the bespoke. Two examples are the following: the bespoke portfolio has very low spreads and one needs to price a very senior tranche; the tranches of the bespoke portfolio are too wide and one needs to price a low mezzanine tranche. Third, it does not take into account the size of the tranche.

- *Base spread weighted by tranche size*. In this approach the invariant is the base spread taking into account the base tranche size:

$$\text{Spread}_{\text{Bespoke}}(A_{\text{Bespoke}}, \rho_{\text{Index}})A_{\text{Bespoke}} = \text{Spread}_{\text{Index}}(A_{\text{Index}}, \rho_{\text{Index}})A_{\text{Index}}. \tag{12.7}$$

The methodology recognizes the importance of the tranche size for the mapping technique. However, it does not take the duration of the contract into account.

- *Base expected loss at maturity matching*. In this approach one uses the *base expected loss at maturity* (as described in Chapter 11), as an invariant between the two portfolios:

$$\frac{\text{BEL}_{\text{Bespoke}}(A_{\text{Bespoke}}, \rho_{\text{Index}})}{\mathbb{E}[L_{\text{Bespoke}}]} = \frac{\text{BEL}_{\text{Index}}(A_{\text{Index}}, \rho_{\text{Index}})}{\mathbb{E}[L_{\text{Index}}]}. \tag{12.8}$$

One of its biggest advantage is its intuitiveness as one is dealing directly with the concept of expected loss. It takes spread, tranche size and duration into account.

- *Discounted base expected loss matching*. This is analogous with the one in (12.8) but the mapping is done using the discounted expected loss at time zero – that is, the discount curve impacts the mapping algorithm:

$$\frac{\text{BEL}_{\text{Bespoke}}(A_{\text{Bespoke}}, \rho_{\text{Index}}, 0)}{\mathbb{E}[L_{\text{Bespoke}}]} = \frac{\text{BEL}_{\text{Index}}(A_{\text{Index}}, \rho_{\text{Index}}, 0)}{\mathbb{E}[L_{\text{Index}}]}. \tag{12.9}$$

12.3 NUMERICAL RESULTS

In this section we show the results of the correlation mapping techniques presented in Section 12.2 for both the Gaussian copula and Lévy framework.

For illustration and testing purposes we use the CDX.NA.IG as the bespoke portfolio that is mapped into the iTraxx index on 1 April 2008. Tables 12.1 and 12.2 show detailed results using the base expected loss at maturity and discounted base expected loss, supposed to be more powerful due to the relation with nonarbitrage conditions, for both the Gaussian copula and Lévy base correlation methodologies. The results are shown in terms of risk duration (RD), base spread, base risk duration (BRD), discounted base expected loss (DBEL), base expected loss at maturity (BELT) and base correlation (BC). The observed market quotes for the CDX index without any mapping are shown as reference results.

Comparing the spreads after mapping with the reference spreads we see that for the Gaussian copula the mapping underprices all but the [15%–30%] tranche. Additionally, the differences can be quite large. In the case of Lévy, on the other hand, underpricing occurs for two tranches ([3%–7%] and [15%–30%]) and the differences with respect to the references are smaller than with the Gaussian copula.

Table 12.1 Gaussian copula base correlation mapping for CDX.NA.IG on 1 April 2008

Tr	Spread	RD	Base spread	BRD	DBEL	BELT %	BC
			Reference Results				
0–3	59.875%	3.417	2252	3.417	2.309	2.544	47.63
3–7	682.5	6.294	792	7.260	4.027	4.584	60.16
7–10	416	7.108	606	8.116	4.914	5.659	65.12
10–15	234	7.757	469	8.284	5.822	6.791	75.34
15–30	101	8.218	284	8.383	7.132	8.479	99.99
			Base Expected Loss Maturity Mapping				
0–3	57.98%	3.525	2145	3.525	2.268	2.503	50.12
3–7	654	6.362	770	7.299	3.934	4.480	62.97
7–10	332	7.381	570	8.197	4.670	5.379	71.02
10–15	185	7.946	432	8.347	5.407	6.311	84.21
15–30	143	8.059	286	8.303	7.132	8.479	99.65
			Discounted Base Expected Loss Mapping				
0–3	57.68%	3.543	2128	3.543	2.262	2.496	50.53
3–7	640	6.403	761	7.322	3.901	4.444	63.98
7–10	329	7.386	565	8.199	4.631	5.333	71.98
10–15	188	7.934	430	8.343	5.377	6.276	84.83
15–30	145	8.049	286	8.298	7.132	8.479	99.70

Table 12.2 Lévy base correlation mapping for CDX.NA.IG on 1 April 2008

Tr	Spread	RD	Base spread	BRD	DBEL	BELT %	BC
			Reference Results				
0–3	59.875%	3.667	2133	3.667	2.346	2.645	73.47
3–7	682.5	6.318	800	7.273	4.071	4.705	70.96
7–10	416	7.098	611	8.112	4.957	5.778	69.35
10–15	234	7.697	473	8.264	5.857	6.880	72.14
15–30	101	8.171	283	8.359	7.095	8.407	97.68
			Base Expected Loss Maturity Mapping				
0–3	58.28%	3.749	2055	3.749	2.311	2.607	74.79
3–7	690	6.290	796	7.258	4.046	4.676	71.51
7–10	337	7.341	585	8.185	4.790	5.579	72.77
10–15	188	7.854	443	8.316	5.530	6.486	79.52
15–30	124	8.075	282	8.311	7.032	8.323	99.37
			Discounted Base Expected Loss Mapping				
0–3	58.57%	3.734	2068	3.734	2.317	2.614	74.56
3–7	685	6.303	795	7.265	4.045	4.674	71.53
7–10	333	7.357	584	8.190	4.780	5.567	72.99
10–15	182	7.880	440	8.325	5.498	6.450	80.35
15–30	127	8.062	282	8.305	7.032	8.323	99.37

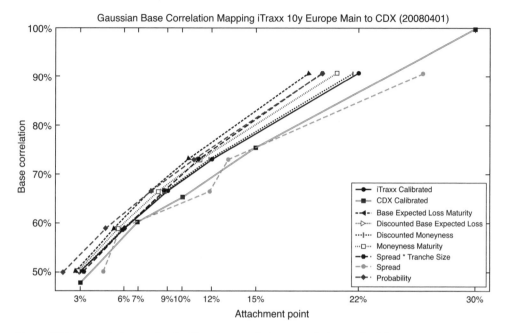

Figure 12.2   Correlations under the Gaussian copula base correlation methodology

Figures 12.2 and 12.3 respectively show the Gaussian copula and the Lévy base correlation curves obtained with different mapping techniques. The figures also show the calibrated base correlation curves for iTraxx (the reference index) and CDX (the real curve). Observe that the correlation curves located at the left (right) of the real CDX curve are underpricing (overpricing) equity tranches while overpricing (underpricing) the senior tranches. For the Gaussian copula approach the discounted moneyness curve closely follows the real curve. Under the probability approach the generated curve crosses the real curve indicating overvaluation for equity and super senior tranches while potential undervaluation of mezzanine. Observe that all methodologies, with the exception of the spread approach, generated convex curves and, additionally, there is no smile effect. For the Lévy base correlation approach, on the other hand, there is a smile. Additionally, the crossing of the different curves with the real one happened under all the methodologies.

The expected loss curves and the corresponding base correlation curves for the base expected loss at maturity and the discounted base expected loss are shown in more detail respectively in Figures 12.4 and 12.5. As expected, the higher the attachment point the higher the difference between the two approaches. As explained in more detail in Chapter 11, the interpolation scheme uses cubic splines with the monotonicity filter described in Dougherty et al. (1989) applied to it. Observe that for both frameworks the technique preserves the monotonicity and convexity constraints necessary to the absence of arbitrage.

Due to their importance for nonarbitrage conditions, Figures 12.5 and 12.6 depict in more detail the differences between the Gaussian copula and the Lévy base correlation curves obtained with the discounted base expected loss and the base expected loss at maturity.

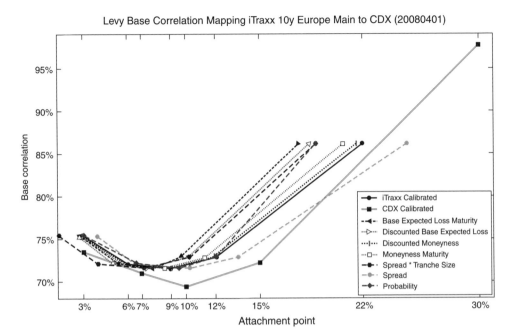

Figure 12.3   Correlations under the Lévy base correlation methodology

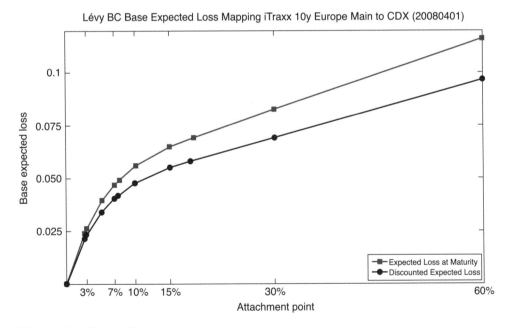

Figure 12.4   Expected loss

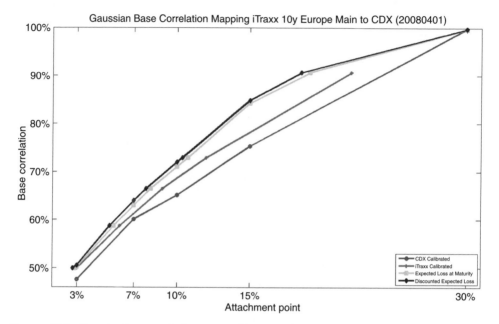

Figure 12.5   Gaussian base correlation expected loss mapping

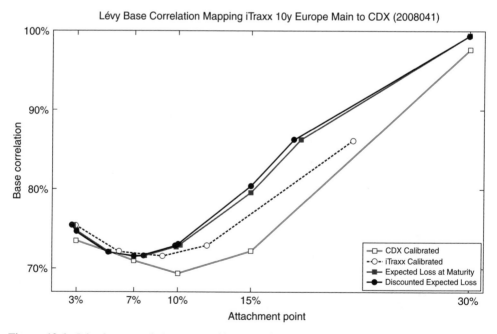

Figure 12.6   Lévy base correlation expected loss mapping

12.4   FINAL COMMENTS

The credit crunch that began in June 2007 has highlighted the importance of the standardized credit indices for hedging and pricing purposes of portfolios of credit instruments held by financial institutions. In this chapter, we have compared the results of several correlation mapping techniques under both the standard Gaussian copula and Lévy base correlation frameworks. For the mapping methodologies we have used some traditional techniques such as (discounted) moneyness and probability matching, some of their variants such as moneyness at maturity and approaches based on no arbitrage opportunities – that is, the base expected loss approaches described in Chapter 11. For academic purposes, the CDX index portfolio has been used as a proxy for a bespoke portfolio, as the quotes are well known, while the iTraxx portfolio is the index of reference into which the bespoke portfolio is mapped. Results have been shown in terms of mapped correlation curves for all methodologies.

In general we observed quite striking differences between Gaussian copula and Lévy-based approaches. Moreover, prices can be quite sensitive to the correlation mapping technique used. This is indeed a current key feature of the credit markets: the pricing of bespoke tranches is still much more an *art* than a science. As will be discussed later on in this book, we expect that once the standardized credit indices become well understood and largely used for dynamic credit portfolio management purposes, the techniques for correlation mapping will become much more standardized than is currently the case. In the next chapters, we will move forward to understand why those indices and the techniques discussed here are key for the evolution of the financial system.

13

Correlation from Collateral to Tranches

When the rich wage war it's the poor who die.
Jean-Paul Sartre

13.1 INTRODUCTION

In this chapter we show how variations on the correlation among the underlying collateral of an asset backed security (ABS) impacts the correlation among the tranches in a portfolio of ABSs. We also give evidence of the dependency on the time frame. This chapter should be read in conjunction with the framework described in Chapter 23 and in our earlier paper (Garcia et al., 2007) as a solution for the securitization business model of a financial institution.

This chapter is complementary to Chapters 22 and 23 in two ways. First, it shows how changes in correlation of the collateral underlying an ABS affects the correlation between ABS tranches. Second, it shows that this correlation changes with the investment horizon. The chapter brings support to the idea that the lowest possible cost of capital is associated with a short-term holding period, and as such the securities should be put on trading books and have their values monitored via the standardized credit indices. In the absence of time series of expected loss of ABS tranches we use a Monte Carlo simulation based on the widespread copula algorithm to generate data for the collateral and, consequently, the prices of the tranches.

The remainder of the chapter is organized as follows. In Section 13.2 we review the generic 1-factor model used for valuation of CDO tranches. The algorithm based on Monte Carlo simulation and importance sampling is presented in Section 13.3. In Section 13.4 results are given for the Gaussian copula tranche loss correlations, while Section 13.5 has the results for the Lévy copula and Section 13.6 has the results for the Marshall-Olkin copula. The conclusions are presented in Section 13.7.

13.2 GENERIC 1-FACTOR MODEL

We use the framework described in Section 9.2. The probability of default is implied from the CDS market as described in Section 4.4. Assume a portfolio of N firms is considered.

In an MC simulation random numbers are generated for the market factor and for the idiosyncratic factors. These random variates are plugged in (9.7) to generate the latent variable A_i.

Given the survival probability distribution implied from CDS quotes, the default time τ_i is found by inverting (4.1), that is, by solving for t for a given probability p. In the special case of a constant intensity $\lambda_i(u) = \lambda_i$ we have

$$\tau_i = \frac{-1}{\lambda_i} \log p. \qquad (13.1)$$

The generated default time τ_i for all underlying entities is compared to the maturity T of the contract to determine whether or not the contract suffers a loss. For each realization in the MC simulation the losses and their timings are determined and the losses on the tranches can be evaluated.

13.3　MONTE CARLO SIMULATION AND IMPORTANCE SAMPLING

The bible for Monte Carlo (MC) methods is the famous book by Glasserman (2004). For importance sampling applied to portfolios of credit risky assets we refer to Glasserman and Li (2003) and to Morokoff (2004).

In the MC simulation a random sample is drawn from the multivariate standard normal distribution with prescribed correlation matrix C. We apply importance sampling by scaling up the component along the dimension that has the largest impact on the portfolio losses. This is the eigenvector corresponding to the largest eigenvalue of the correlation matrix C. Denote by Q the orthogonal matrix whose columns are the orthonormal eigenvectors of C, and by Θ the diagonal matrix of eigenvalues, sorted such that $\theta_1 \geq \theta_2 \geq \ldots \geq \theta_N \geq 0$. Then we have the eigenvalue decomposition $C = Q \Theta Q^T$. Let q_1 be the first column of Q, corresponding to the largest eigenvalue so that

$$Cq_1 = \theta_1 q_1. \tag{13.2}$$

The scaled-up sample e can be computed efficiently:

$$e = (\alpha - 1)\left(q_1^T \tilde{e}\right) q_1 + \tilde{e}, \tag{13.3}$$

where α is the scale factor and $\tilde{e}$ is the original sample drawn from the multivariate standard normal distribution with prescribed correlation matrix C. The corresponding weight is

$$w(e) = \alpha \exp\left(-(\alpha^2 - 1)\frac{(q_1^T \tilde{e})^2}{2\theta_1}\right). \tag{13.4}$$

The special case of a 1-factor model for N names is very easy. The correlation matrix is

$$C = \begin{pmatrix} 1 & \rho & \cdots & \rho \\ \rho & 1 & \ddots & \vdots \\ \vdots & \ddots & \ddots & \rho \\ \rho & \cdots & \rho & 1 \end{pmatrix}. \tag{13.5}$$

It is straightforward to show that the largest eigenvalue is

$$\theta_1 = 1 + (N - 1)\rho \tag{13.6}$$

with the corresponding eigenvector

$$q_1 = \frac{o_1}{\|o_1\|}, \tag{13.7}$$

where $o_1 = (1 \quad 1 \quad \ldots \quad 1)^T$ is the vector containing all ones.

13.4 GAUSSIAN COPULA TRANCHE LOSS CORRELATIONS

Two baskets of 125 equally weighted names are considered, with a fixed recovery rate of $R = 40\%$. For simplicity the CDS quotes were distributed as follows: 20% at 50 bp; 20% at 100bp; 20% at 150 bp; 20% at 200 bp; and 20% at 250 bp. Additionally, the interest rate curve is assumed to be flat at $r = 4\%$ and the maturity is $T = 5$ year. We considered tranches that match the attachment and detachment points of the iTraxx standardized index: $[0 - 3]$ (A), $[3 - 6]$ (B), $[6 - 9]$ (C), $[9 - 12]$ (D), $[12 - 22]$ (E) and $[22 - 100]$ (F). We refer to tranche A as the equity tranche and to tranche F as the super senior tranche.

The correlation between the different tranches for a maturity of five years and 5%, 10% and 20% asset correlations are shown in Table 13.1. Regarding systemic risk we observe that a senior tranche is not a diversification of another senior tranche. The results show that correlations between senior tranches are higher and increase faster than between a junior and a senior tranche. In particular the correlation between two different super senior tranches increases dramatically with increasing asset correlation.

Table 13.2 shows the tranche correlations for the *one year maturity* contracts. Comparing these to the values in Table 13.1, we see that all the correlations are lower, except for the equity tranches which are dominated by idiosyncratic risk. Observe that the *decrease* in correlation between super senior tranches is significant.

The tranche correlation values for the three, seven and ten year maturities are shown in Table 13.3. We see that *increasing the maturity increases the correlation*. Table 13.4 shows the impact of 20%, 40% and 60% of overlap between the underlying collateral in the two portfolios for a maturity of five years and 10% asset correlation. Clearly the correlation between tranches increases dramatically with increasing overlap between the two portfolios.

Table 13.1 Five-year loss correlations as a function of the asset correlation ρ_a

ρ_t	A	B	C	D	E	F	A	B	C	D	E	F	A	B	C	D	E	F
A	41	43	32	20	10	1	59	55	39	26	15	3	75	65	47	35	22	8
B	43	57	50	32	15	1	55	71	62	43	24	4	65	82	72	55	36	12
C	32	50	61	50	27	2	39	62	74	63	38	7	47	72	83	75	51	18
D	20	32	50	57	42	3	26	43	63	72	55	11	35	55	75	83	67	24
E	10	15	27	42	53	11	15	24	38	55	74	30	22	36	51	67	87	48
F	1	1	2	3	11	27	3	4	7	11	30	62	8	12	18	24	48	84
			$\rho_a = 5\%$						$\rho_a = 10\%$						$\rho_a = 20\%$			

Table 13.2 One-year loss correlations as a function of the asset correlation ρ_a

ρ_t	A	B	C	D	E	F	A	B	C	D	E	F	A	B	C	D	E	F
A	44	28	7	1	0	0	60	40	16	6	2	0	74	53	29	16	8	1
B	28	37	18	5	1	0	40	58	39	17	6	0	53	75	58	36	18	3
C	7	18	22	12	4	0	16	39	50	35	15	1	29	58	72	59	33	6
D	1	5	12	14	8	0	6	17	35	44	30	2	16	36	59	70	52	10
E	0	1	4	8	10	1	2	6	15	30	44	9	8	18	33	52	74	31
F	0	0	0	0	1	3	0	0	1	2	9	31	1	3	6	10	31	69
			$\rho_a = 5\%$						$\rho_a = 10\%$						$\rho_a = 20\%$			

Table 13.3 Loss correlations as a function of the maturity for $\rho_a = 10\%$

ρ_t	A	B	C	D	E	F	A	B	C	D	E	F	A	B	C	D	E	F
A	62	52	31	17	8	1	59	59	48	37	25	7	65	66	63	57	46	18
B	52	70	57	35	16	2	59	71	64	49	30	8	66	71	68	58	43	16
C	31	57	69	55	30	3	48	64	75	67	44	11	63	68	75	70	50	18
D	17	35	55	64	47	6	37	49	67	75	60	16	57	58	70	77	64	23
E	8	16	30	47	66	22	25	30	44	60	80	38	46	43	50	64	83	46
F	1	2	3	6	22	52	7	8	11	16	38	69	18	16	18	23	46	76
			$T = 3$						$T = 7$						$T = 10$			

Table 13.4 Five-year loss correlations as a function of the overlap Ω for $\rho_a = 10\%$

ρ_t	A	B	C	D	E	F	A	B	C	D	E	F	A	B	C	D	E	F
A	65	58	40	26	15	3	73	61	40	26	15	3	81	64	41	27	15	3
B	58	76	64	44	24	4	61	81	67	44	24	4	64	87	69	45	24	4
C	40	64	78	66	39	7	40	67	82	69	39	7	41	69	87	71	40	7
D	26	44	66	76	58	11	26	44	69	81	59	11	27	45	71	86	61	11
E	15	24	39	58	79	31	15	24	39	59	84	31	15	24	40	61	89	33
F	3	4	7	11	31	68	3	4	7	11	31	73	3	4	7	11	33	81
			$\Omega = 20\%$						$\Omega = 40\%$						$\Omega = 60\%$			

13.5 LÉVY COPULA TRANCHE LOSS CORRELATIONS

All tranche loss correlations in the previous section are based on a Gaussian copula correlation model. We now turn to a copula based on a distribution with a heavier tail, in casu the unit variance Gamma $(a, \sqrt{a})$ distribution. The heavy tail property of the Gamma distribution is illustrated in Table 13.5. The measure ν is defined as the 99.97% quantile minus the expected value. The excess kurtosis $\kappa = 6/a$ of the Gamma distribution is inversely proportional to the shape parameter a. Hence *decreasing the shape parameter a* makes the *tail heavier*.

Departing from the Gaussian framework brings up the issue of which measures of association to use. An in-depth discussion of this topic is beyond the scope of this chapter and we refer to Frees and Valdez (1998) and Nelsen (1999) for details. Essentially these measures try to capture whether the probability of having large values for both random variables is high or low. We restrict ourselves to the following three measures. The classical linear or *Pearson correlation coefficient*

$$\rho(X_1, X_2) = \frac{\text{Cov}(X_1, X_2)}{\sqrt{\text{Var}(X_1)}\sqrt{\text{Var}(X_2)}} \tag{13.8}$$

is a measure of *linear* dependence. It is essentially the covariance

$$\text{Cov}(X_1, X_2) = \mathbb{E}\left[(X_1 - \mu_1)(X_2 - \mu_2)\right] \tag{13.9}$$

scaled by the square root of the variances $\text{Var}(X_1) = \text{Cov}(X_1, X_1)$. The expected values are denoted by $\mu_1 = \mathbb{E}X_1$ and $\mu_2 = \mathbb{E}X_2$.

Table 13.5   Unit variance Gamma versus standard normal distribution

a	0.1	1	10	N
ν	13.5025	7.1117	4.5972	3.4316
κ	60	6	0.6	0

Spearman's rho is a normalized correlation coefficient. It is the correlation coefficient after a transformation with the cumulative distribution function (CDF) of the random variable has been applied.

$$\rho^S(X_1, X_2) = \rho(U_1, U_2), \tag{13.10}$$

where $U_1 = F_1(X_1)$ and $U_2 = F_2(X_2)$ with F_1 and F_2 the cumulative distribution functions of X_1 and X_2 respectively. Hence *Spearman's rho* measures the *rank* correlation.

Finally, dependence in the *tail* or the *extreme values* is measured by the *indices of tail dependency*. The upper tail dependence ξ_u can be interpreted as the following conditional probability:

$$\xi_u = \lim_{p \to 1^-} \mathbb{P}[U_1 > p \,|\, U_2 > p] = \lim_{p \to 1^-} \mathbb{P}[U_2 > p \,|\, U_1 > p] \tag{13.11}$$

and similar for lower tail dependence ξ_l.

Table 13.6 shows the impact of replacing the Gaussian copula with the Lévy copula for a maturity of five years and 10% asset correlation. All correlation values shown so far are classical linear Pearson correlation coefficients. The Spearman's rank correlation values for the same case are shown in Table 13.7.

Table 13.6   Five-year loss correlations as a function of the parameter a for $\rho_a = 10\%$

ρ_t	A	B	C	D	E	F	A	B	C	D	E	F	A	B	C	D	E	F
A	1	1	4	9	11	11	6	7	15	21	19	13	18	27	31	26	18	8
B	1	2	5	11	12	11	7	10	18	23	18	11	27	42	49	38	24	9
C	4	5	12	31	33	28	15	18	39	51	41	24	31	49	69	65	44	17
D	9	11	31	78	87	71	21	23	51	81	74	45	26	38	65	78	66	26
E	11	12	33	87	99	86	19	18	41	74	95	71	18	24	44	66	89	52
F	11	11	28	71	86	100	13	11	24	45	71	99	8	9	17	26	52	95
			$a = 0.1$						$a = 1$						$a = 10$			

Table 13.7   Five-year loss Spearman correlations as a function of the parameter a for $\rho_a = 10\%$

ρ_t^S	A	B	C	D	E	F	A	B	C	D	E	F	A	B	C	D	E	F
A	3	3	4	8	15	15	15	18	19	28	31	22	47	53	54	52	43	21
B	3	5	5	11	20	20	18	22	24	33	34	22	53	59	61	57	45	21
C	4	5	7	14	24	23	19	24	26	37	36	24	54	61	64	62	49	23
D	8	11	14	28	50	46	28	33	37	56	61	41	52	57	62	71	64	31
E	15	20	24	50	96	88	31	34	36	61	83	63	43	45	49	64	75	44
F	15	20	23	46	88	99	22	22	24	41	63	92	21	21	23	31	44	79
			$a = 0.1$						$a = 1$						$a = 10$			

13.6   MARSHALL-OLKIN COPULA TRANCHE LOSS CORRELATIONS

Copula methods model dependence between probabilities. The dependence between the default times is indirect since these are obtained by inverting the survival probability distribution (4.1). However the strongest dependence between probabilities may not be the strongest dependence between default times. As an example, consider the case of perfect positive dependence among the probabilities. In this case, all the probabilities p in (13.1) are equal. However, the default times τ_i differ from each other since the default intensities λ_i can be different. The worst possible dependence for default times is when all default times are equal. The Marshall-Olkin copula introduces a dependence that can make all default times equal.

Let us consider the survival probability of firms who are subject to an idiosyncratic and a systemic shock common to all firms. The shocks are assumed to follow independent Poisson processes. The idiosyncratic shock intensity is λ_i for firm i and the systemic shock intensity is λ_s. The individual survival probability (4.1) for firm i becomes:

$$P_i(t) = \mathbb{P}(\min(\tau_i, \tau_s) > t) = \exp\left(-(\lambda_i + \lambda_s)t\right). \tag{13.12}$$

The characteristic ratio η_i is defined as the ratio of the systemic shock intensity to the sum of the intensities of the shocks to which firm i is subject:

$$\eta_i = \frac{\lambda_s}{\lambda_i + \lambda_s}. \tag{13.13}$$

Working out the joint survival probability of two firms:

$$P(x, y) = \mathbb{P}\left[\min(\tau_1, \tau_s) > x, \min(\tau_2, \tau_s) > y\right]$$
$$= \min\left([P_1(x)]^{1-\eta_1}[P_2(y)], [P_1(x)][P_2(y)]^{1-\eta_2}\right) \tag{13.14}$$

we arrive at the Marshall-Olkin survival copula:

$$\bar{C}(u, v) = \min\left(u^{1-\eta_1}v, uv^{1-\eta_2}\right). \tag{13.15}$$

The Marshall-Olkin copula has upper tail dependence:

$$\xi_u = \min_i \eta_i \tag{13.16}$$

while the Gaussian copula has no tail dependence unless the correlation coefficient $\rho = 1$ is one. The introduction of a common systemic shock creates a heavy tail dependence.

Table 13.8   Five-year loss correlations as a function of the systemic default intensity λ_s

ρ_t	A	B	C	D	E	F	A	B	C	D	E	F	A	B	C	D	E	F
A	0	0	0	0	1	1	0	0	0	1	2	2	2	2	3	7	8	8
B	0	0	0	0	1	1	0	0	1	3	4	4	2	2	5	12	14	14
C	0	0	0	0	4	4	0	1	1	6	13	13	3	5	14	32	37	37
D	0	0	0	2	16	16	1	3	6	24	48	48	7	12	32	75	86	87
E	1	1	4	16	96	98	2	4	13	48	100	100	8	14	37	86	100	100
F	1	1	4	16	98	100	2	4	13	48	100	100	8	14	37	87	100	100
			$\lambda_s = 1$ bp						$\lambda_s = 10$ bp						$\lambda_s = 100$ bp			

Table 13.9 Five-year loss Spearman correlations as a function of the systemic default intensity λ_s

ρ_t^S	A	B	C	D	E	F	A	B	C	D	E	F	A	B	C	D	E	F
A	0	0	0	0	1	1	1	0	0	1	2	2	3	3	3	5	9	9
B	0	0	0	0	1	2	0	1	1	2	6	7	3	7	8	12	22	23
C	0	0	0	0	2	3	0	1	1	2	10	11	3	8	12	19	34	35
D	0	0	0	0	3	6	1	2	2	4	17	20	5	12	19	30	54	55
E	1	1	2	3	18	43	2	6	10	17	72	85	9	22	34	54	96	98
F	1	2	3	6	43	100	2	7	11	20	85	100	9	23	35	55	98	100
	$\lambda_s = 1$ bp						$\lambda_s = 10$ bp						$\lambda_s = 100$ bp					

Table 13.8 shows five year loss correlations as a function of the systemic default intensity λ_s. The corresponding Spearman correlations are shown in Table 13.9. Note that the dependence comes from the introduction of a common systemic shock and that the latent variable correlation model (9.7) is not used here. This gives a very clear message that *super senior tranches are dominated by systemic risk* and consequently *do not diversify* each other. This is illustrated nicely in this simple model in which all shocks are independent and the common shock knocks out the whole portfolio. An obvious extension could be to combine the latent variable correlation model (9.7) with the Marshall-Olkin copula.

13.7 CONCLUSIONS

We have presented numerical evidence showing that the correlation between the different tranches in a portfolio can change significantly as a function of the underlying collateral correlation, the overlap between different pools of underlying collateral and the maturity of the deal or the time it is held in the portfolio. A first conclusion is that super senior tranches are dominated by systemic risk and are not an effective diversification for each other. This is already visible in results obtained with the Gaussian copula and moving to distributions with heavier tails and copulas with tail dependence amplifies these effects. Another important conclusion is that keeping the cost of capital of a securitization instrument fixed may certainly misprice it. Moreover, the cost of capital for an instrument should be portfolio dependent! The results have several important consequences, discussed in more detail in Chapter 23.

14

Cash Flow CDOs

Ignorance is not knowing something, stupidity is not admitting your ignorance.
Daniel Turov

14.1 INTRODUCTION

This chapter starts with a short explanation of what collateralized debt instruments are and how investors might use them, mainly focusing on the rating of simple cash flow CDO using the *binomial expansion technique* (BET), originally developed by Moody's. We give detailed descriptions of the waterfall and the BET. We then test how the model parameters affect the rating of the different tranches of a real cash flow CDO contract.

We cover the historical purpose of describing in detail the use of the BET approach to rate a cash flow CDO. Although the technique is quite old and usually deemed outdated, anecdotal evidence shows that many companies still use it, and that it may have been one of the causes behind the fall of a very large American insurance company dealing with a portfolio of CDOs. Moreover, the *diversity score* (DS), a key concept underlying the model, is still very much at the forefront of many portfolio managers' minds, making it useful to describe the underpinning of the BET framework. The model is shown in an algorithmic way, making it easy to be reproduced in academia. Additionally, the chapter provides data and a structure in which the parameters of the model are changed, showing how they impact the rating of the different tranches. By describing the algorithm in a detailed fashion it becomes very clear that there is *no way one can have access to the correlation parameter* that would describe the dependence relation between the collateral portfolio. That is, the model is completely unsuited for any development in the direction of using the standardized credit indices for dynamic credit portfolio management.

The remainder of this chapter is structured as follows. In Section 14.2 we give a brief summary of a cash flow CDO focusing on the description of the waterfall of a typical CDO contract. In Section 14.3 we give a detailed description of the BET methodology. In Section 14.4 we present a contract and its waterfall and the results of the stress tests made showing the sensitivity to the different parameters used in the BET. We present some quotes taken from two SEC filings by AIG discussing the usage of BET in Section 14.5. We conclude in Section 14.6.

14.2 THE WATERFALL OF A CASH FLOW CDO

As described in more detail in Chapter 7, there are two types of CDOs depending on the way the collateral pool is managed: cash flow and market value. In a cash flow CDO the manager is not supposed to engage in actively trading the assets held as collateral and there are very strict rules on buying and selling those assets. Any payment uncertainties in a cash flow CDO are related to the number and the timing of defaults. In this chapter we will be dealing with cash flow CDOs only.

Table 14.1 Tranches in a typical cash flow CDO

Classes	Subclasses	Interest
A	A1A	Fixed
	A1B	Fixed
	A2	Float
B	B1	Fixed
	B2	Float
C	C1	Fixed
	C2	Float
D	D1	Fixed
	D2	Float
E	E	

Each CDO has a prospectus containing the legal terms of the contract. A key part of the prospectus of a cash flow CDO is the *waterfall* or the *indenture*. It specifies how the cash coming from the collateral is allocated to the different note holders. We describe how a typical cash flow transaction is structured.

The notes to be issued by the SPV are tranched into different rating classes. The rating of each class is determined by the seniority of the note in the schedule of receiving principal and interest payments. We show in Table 14.1 a typical note structure. An example of a waterfall is shown in Figures 14.1 and 14.2. Note, however, that a waterfall can vary in very many ways. The senior tranche is generally the largest, while the mezzanine tranche typically comprises 5% to 15% and the thickness of the equity tranche is most often somewhere between 2% and 15%.

The senior tranches, the A notes, are the first in line to receive coupon payments, after the payment of fees. The mezzanine notes, B and C, receive their coupons only if after the interest payments on the senior notes have been made sufficient protection for these notes remains, that is, if the senior overcollateralization (O/C) and interest coverage (I/C) tests pass. The most subordinated note is called the equity tranche or the first loss piece, tranche E in Table 14.1. The equity holders will receive the so-called excess spread – that is, what is left after the payment of all the fees and interest to the more senior notes. Normally, a large or the whole part of the equity piece is held by the originator of the CDO. The redemption of the notes follows the same order of seniority: first, the most senior notes get redeemed, next the mezzanine notes and, at the end – if anything remains – the equity notes. Sometimes a structure can have junior notes, the D notes, between the mezzanine notes and the equity piece.

14.3 BET METHODOLOGY

In this section we give a brief description of the BET algorithm. We refer to Cifuentes and O'Connor (1996) for a first reference on BET. The BET methodology is based on the concept of *diversity score* (DS) and is an application of the binomial formula to a simplified version of the portfolio. The basic idea behind the methodology is to map the portfolio of heterogeneous correlated securities with distinct probabilities of defaults into a portfolio of homogeneous independent securities, each having the same probability of default. The second portfolio is said to be the idealized portfolio. Once the DS and the relevant probability of default are determined, the binomial formula is used to give first approximations for the default scenarios.

The first step is the calculation of the DS of the collateral portfolio. We describe the original algorithm for the DS. It does not explicitly account for correlation. An alternative approach is described in Cifuentes et al. (1998). The goal of the DS measure is to redefine the pool of correlated heterogeneous assets into a pool of DS independent homogeneous assets. Lower diversification implies higher concentration and lower DS. Diversification is measured on two levels: first at issuer level by dividing every issuer's exposure by the average issuer exposure and capping the resulting ratio to one. This gives the *Equivalent Unit Score (EUS)* per issuer. Increasing the number of issuers with exposures larger than the average decreases the EUS of the issuers. Diversification is also measured at the industry level by summing first all EUS of all issuers in a certain industry, called *Aggregate Industry Equivalent Unit Score* (AIEUS), and then scaling down the AIEUS into an industry diversity score whereby the bigger AIEUS are scaled down more. For example, if AIEUS(industry$_i$) = 1 then DS(industry$_i$) = 1; if AIEUS(industry$_j$) = 20 then DS(industry$_j$) = 5. The DS of the pool is equal to the sum of all industry DS. Increasing the average number of issuers per industry increases industry concentration and decreases the DS.

The second step consists of determining the expected cash flows from the collateral for each possible number of homogeneous bonds defaulting. Several assumptions need to be made:

1. *The principal payments from the collateral.* All homogeneous bonds are assumed to have the same maturity that is derived from the *weighted average life* (WAL) of the collateral pool. Alternatively, one could also take into account the expected principal redemption schedule of the collateral pool.
2. *The interest payments from the collateral.* All homogeneous bonds are assumed to have the same coupon, equal to the *weighted average coupon* (WAC) of the collateral pool.
3. *The weighted average recovery rate* (WAR) *in case of default.* A standard approach uses one predetermined rate, say 30%. Alternatively, one may also use a recovery rate that takes into account the types of exposures – that is, secured, unsecured, subordinate, bonds or loans – of the collateral pool. Another common approach is to generate the recovery from a beta distribution.

   Assume that N_T is the total notional of the collateral portfolio. The notional involved in the case of j defaults is given by

$$D_j = j \, \frac{N_T}{\text{DS}} \tag{14.1}$$

   and the loss on D_j is given by:

$$\text{Loss}_j = D_j \, (1 - \text{WAR}). \tag{14.2}$$

4. *The distribution of the losses in time.* A standard approach assumes six default scenarios:
   - 50%, 10%, 10%, 10%, 10%, 10%
   - 10%, 50%, 10%, 10%, 10%, 10%
   - 10%, 10%, 50%, 10%, 10%, 10%
   - 10%, 10%, 10%, 50%, 10%, 10%
   - 10%, 10%, 10%, 10%, 50%, 10%
   - 10%, 10%, 10%, 10%, 10%, 50%

   In each of the scenarios above, the losses are distributed over six years. In the first scenario, for example, 50% is lost in the first year and 10% in the remaining years. In the second scenario, 10% of the losses occur in the first year, 50% in the second year and 10% in the remaining years, and analogously for the remaining scenarios. With the scenarios above one can determine the amount of money left in the collateral.

In the third step, one goes through the waterfall and determines the amounts that each note holder will receive and how large the present value of their losses is in each of the collateral cash flow scenarios generated in step 2. In order to count for interest rate risk, a common market practice is to make parallel shifts on the levels of the yield curve. Here, we will be considering three possible scenarios: flat, up by 1% and up by 2%.

In the fourth step one uses the *weighted average rating factor* (WARF) and the *weighted average life* (WAL) of the collateral pool to determine the probability of default p of one idealized bond. With this probability and the binomial formula, one can calculate the default probability of each of the collateral cash flow scenarios generated in step 2 – that is from 0 up to DS idealized bonds. Assume, for example, that in one scenario we have $n \leq$ DS defaults. The probability P_n of n defaults is given by:

$$P_n = \binom{DS}{n} p^n (1-p)^{DS-n}. \tag{14.3}$$

The impact on the senior tranches depends on the tail of the loss distribution of the collateral portfolio. In order to emulate a fatter tail it is a common market practice to stress the probabilities in (14.3) by multiplying the probability of default p and the recovery rates by a stress factor: >1 for defaults, <1 for recoveries. The size of the stress factor depends on target rating. Increasing the target rating increases the default stress factor, and lowers the recovery rate stress factor. Suppose, for example, that one is targeting a note to have AA rating. The probability p, to be used in (14.3), and the recovery rate would be multiplied by 1.4 and 0.67 respectively (see Table 14.9 for details).

The fifth step consists of bringing together the results for the different default scenarios of step 3 with the probabilities for each of those scenarios calculated in step 4. This leads to a loss distribution and an expected loss for every scenario.

In the sixth step the expected loss obtained in step 5 is compared with a *target* loss – that is, the idealized loss for a bond with the maturity equal to the average life of the tranche and a rating equal to the target rating. The rating assigned to the tranche is equal to the highest rating for which the tranche passes the test. The algorithm above is conceived to determine a rating of a tranche and not to determine either its price or the market expected loss.

14.4   RESULTS

We will divide this section in two subsections. In Section 14.4.1 we give a detailed description of the CDO contract being rated and in Section 14.4.2 we give the results of the tests made in the contract.

14.4.1   Contract description

The data given here is for a structure that has already started. We have used a real contract in which we have changed the collateral amounts.

In what follows the expected loss (EL) will be evaluated using the following formula:

$$\mathbb{EL} = \sum_i c_i d_i \tag{14.4}$$

Table 14.2 Tranche notes of the CDO structure

Notes	Notional	Coupon Type	Coupon Spread (%)
A	167,494,728	Floating	0.65
B	37,000,000	Floating	1.0
C	42,623,383	Fixed	8.625
D1	8,005,709	Fixed	11.875
D2	17,632,067	Fixed	12.57
E	28,009,384	Fixed	3.0

where c_i is the loss allocated at a particular point in time t, and $d_i = \exp(-(r+s)\,t)$ is the corresponding risky discount factor, with r and s the risk-free and the spread rates respectively.

For our case the notes A (see Table 14.2), will be discounted at Libor + 0.65 while the notes D1 will discounted at 11.875%. This means that notes with the same seniority might have different expected losses (see, e.g., the results for notes D1 and D2 in Section 14.4.2). The notes issued in the structure with the current amount still outstanding are also shown in Table 14.2.

The fees to be paid in the structure are described in Table 14.3, and the hedges present in the structure are shown in Table 14.4.

Table 14.3 Fees to be paid during the lifetime of the CDO

Notes	Fixed Amount	Fixed Rate (%)	Calculation Basis
Adm. expenses flt	–	0.0175	Collateral balance
Adm. expenses fxd	40,000	–	–
Snr. coll. mgmt. fee	–	0.05	Collateral balance
Sub col. mgmt fee	–	0.45	Collateral balance

Table 14.4 Hedge fees to be paid during the lifetime of the CDO. All the contracts are payers. The instrument in the first line is a swap and the remainder are caps

Notional	Strike (%)	Start date	Expiry date
269,000,000	6.265	23/04/1999	23/05/2004
269,000,000	6.25	23/11/2004	23/11/2004
266,210,587	6.25	23/05/2005	23/05/2005
245,597,044	6.25	23/11/2005	23/11/2005
227,863,689	6.25	23/05/2006	23/05/2006
182,836,154	6.25	23/11/2006	23/11/2006
162,161,261	6.25	23/05/2007	23/05/2007
137,639,658	6.25	23/11/2007	23/11/2007
105,362,505	6.25	23/05/2008	23/05/2008
60,947,263	6.25	23/11/2008	23/11/2008
45,039,112	6.25	23/05/2009	23/05/2009
29,500,000	6.25	23/11/2009	23/11/2009
28,929,107	6.25	23/05/2010	23/05/2010
27,041,995	6.25	23/11/2010	23/11/2010
26,475,951	6.25	23/05/2011	23/05/2011

Table 14.5   Ratios used for the OC ratio tests

Class	Trigger
A/B	1.2
C	1.07
D	1.03

The ratios used for the OC ratio tests are shown in Table 14.5. Observe that, although we have kept the trigger of the tests as being described by ratios, it is also common that besides ratios there might be amounts involved, especially for the senior tranches.

The OC test for the A/B tranche is:

$$OC_{A,B} = \frac{NumeratorOC}{\sum\limits_{i} PrinicipalNote(i)}, \tag{14.5}$$

for the C tranche it is:

$$OC_{C} = \frac{NumeratorOC}{\sum\limits_{i} PrinicipalNote(i)}, \tag{14.6}$$

and for the D tranche it is:

$$OC_{D} = \frac{NumeratorOC}{\sum\limits_{i} PrinicipalNote(i)} \tag{14.7}$$

where the numerator is:

$$NumeratorOC = ColBalance + ColPrincipal - MarketValuesCurrentDefaults \tag{14.8}$$

and ColBalance means the total notional amount of the performing collateral bonds.

The values for the IC ratio tests are shown in Table 14.6.

The IC test for the A/B tranche is;

$$IC_{A/B} = \frac{NumeratorIC}{\sum\limits_{i} (Interest(i) + DeferredInterest(i))}, \tag{14.9}$$

Table 14.6   Ratios used for the IC ratio tests

Class	Trigger
A/B	1.2
C	1.07
D	1.03

Table 14.7   Collateral characteristics

Collateral Amount	257,136,962
DS	34
WARF	2081 (B1)
WAL	5.00
WAC	8.87%
Payment Freq.	Semi-Ann.
Fixed Rate(%)	100
Interest Acc.	8,437,169
Principal Acc.	4,499,582

for the C tranche it is:

$$IC_C = \frac{\text{NumeratorIC}}{\sum\limits_{i}^{A,B,C} (\text{Interest}(i) + \text{DeferredInterest}(i))}, \tag{14.10}$$

and for the D tranche it is

$$IC_D = \frac{\text{NumeratorIC}}{\sum\limits_{i}^{A,B,C,D} (\text{Interest}(i) + \text{DeferredInterest}(i))} \tag{14.11}$$

where the numerator is

$$\text{NumeratorIC} = \text{CollateralInterest}(i) + \text{Fees}. \tag{14.12}$$

The characteristics of the pool data are given in Tables 14.7 and 14.8 and the waterfall structure of the contract is shown in Figures 14.1 and 14.2.

Table 14.9 shows the stress factors used for the probabilities of default and for the recovery rates. Note that higher stress factors need to be used for higher ratings. The yield curve used shown in Table 14.10.

14.4.2   Tests and results

In our results we will show how the rating and the EL, evaluated as in (14.4), are affected under different parametrizations. Our basic scenario, by which we will compare the results on

Table 14.8   Distribution of bonds in the pool (all the bonds are fixed rate)

Rating	Amount	Rating	Amount
Baa2	3	B1	11
Baa3	3	B2	11
Ba1	12	B3	6
Ba2	3	Caa1	4
Ba3	5	–	–

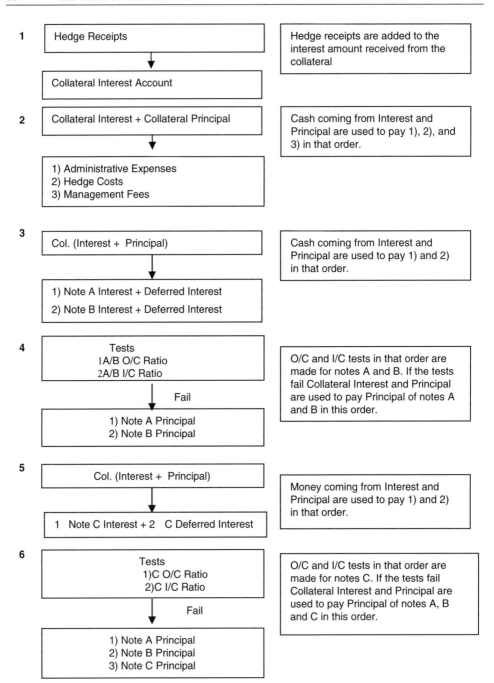

Figure 14.1 Typical waterfall structure

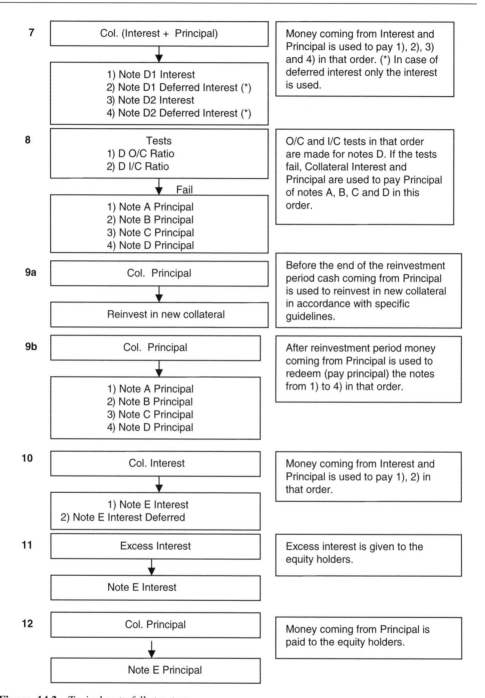

7

Col. (Interest + Principal)

1) Note D1 Interest
2) Note D1 Deferred Interest (*)
3) Note D2 Interest
4) Note D2 Deferred Interest (*)

Money coming from Interest and
Principal is used to pay 1), 2), 3)
and 4) in that order. (*) In case of
deferred interest only the interest
is used.

8

Tests
1) D O/C Ratio
2) D I/C Ratio

Fail

1) Note A Principal
2) Note B Principal
3) Note C Principal
4) Note D Principal

O/C and I/C tests in that order
are made for notes D. If the tests
fail, Collateral Interest and
Principal are used to pay Principal
of notes A, B, C and D in this
order.

9a

Col. Principal

Reinvest in new collateral

Before the end of the reinvestment
period cash coming from Principal
is used to reinvest in new collateral
in accordance with specific
guidelines.

9b

Col. Principal

1) Note A Principal
2) Note B Principal
3) Note C Principal
4) Note D Principal

After reinvestment period money
coming from Principal is used to
redeem (pay principal) the notes
from 1) to 4) in that order.

10

Col. Interest

1) Note E Interest
2) Note E Interest Deferred

Money coming from Interest and
Principal is used to pay 1), 2) in
that order.

11

Excess Interest

Note E Interest

Excess interest is given to the
equity holders.

12

Col. Principal

Note E Principal

Money coming from Principal is
paid to the equity holders.

Figure 14.2   Typical waterfall structure

the variations of the parameters, is the following:

1. flat yield curve;
2. 50% recovery rate;
3. assume that at the end of the CDO the collateral is completely liquidated.

The rating of a tranche will be the one for which it first passes all the default scenarios shown in (4). In what follows, unless otherwise mentioned, the EL shown in the tables will be the 50%-10%-10%-10%-10%-10% scenario.

Parallel shifts on the interest rate curve

The impact of the discount curve is shown by how parallel shifts in the curve can affect the rating and, as such, the EL of the tranche. This is shown in Table 14.11. Generally speaking – and depending on the hedges in the structure, that is swaps and caps – the impact of moves on the yield curve can be quite considerable. Observe that all the bonds in the collateral are fixed rate while the lower tranches are fixed and the upper floating. This means that if rates go up more interest is paid to the upper tranches with less for the lower tranches. Additionally, the hedges via the caps and the swaps (see Table 14.4), are such to limit the impact of increases in interest rates. As a result, the impact of increasing interest rates is more pronounced on lower tranches in the capital structure. This is indeed what we see in Table 14.11 where we show the results of shifts in the interest rates from -1% up to 2% in steps of 1%.

Due to the structure of CDO contracts, however, depending on the outstanding collateral, moves on the yield curve can certainly act as a step function on the EL of a senior tranche.

Impact of changes on the recovery rate

The impact of the recovery rate (RR) on the EL of the structure for the case of the basic scenario is shown in Table 14.12. Results are given for the following three cases of RRs: 30%, 50%, the basic scenario and 70%. Lowering RR increases losses in the event of default. The impact is higher on the junior tranches.

Impact of changes on the diversity score

Changing the DS is equivalent to changing the correlation of the collateral pool. In general, increasing correlation should impact the higher tranches negatively and the very low ones positively. It is well known that high correlation creates extreme scenarios such as every name going in default or no name defaulting.

Table 14.13 shows the impact of varying the DS by about 10% up and down. Observe that the changes are not sufficient to affect the A and B notes. For the C up to D2 notes the decline in correlation has diminished the losses while for the E notes it has caused an increase. One should be aware of the fact that the sensitivity to changes will certainly depend on the state of the collateral.

Impact of overcollateralization

Variations on the collateral pool affect the rating of a tranche significantly. With higher amounts of collateral, more cash becomes available to the notes. Hence a noticeable improvement of the

Table 14.9   Stress factors used for the default probabilities and for the recovery rates for each target rating

Rating	Default Probability	Recovery Rate
AAA	1.50	0.67
AA	1.40	0.67
A	1.31	0.73
BBB	1.23	0.81
BB	1.15	0.89
B	1.00	0.98
CCC	1.00	1.00

Table 14.10   Yield curve

Time	Rate (%)	Time	Rate (%)
1 W	0.021	2 Y	1.454
1 M	0.091	3 Y	2.073
2 M	0.182	4 Y	2.660
3 M	0.272	5 Y	3.079
6 M	0.545	7 Y	3.759
9 M	0.817	10 Y	4.393
1 Y	1.089	15 Y	4.988

Table 14.11   Impact of changes in the discount curve on the rating and EL for the different tranches

Tranche	IR − 1%		IR		IR + 1%		IR + 2%	
	Rating	EL	Rating	EL	Rating	EL	Rating	EL
A	Aaa	0	Aaa	0	Aaa	0	Aaa	0
B	Aaa	0	Aaa	0	Aaa	0	Aaa	0
C	Aa3	0.06	A1	0.07	A3	0.27	Baa1	0.28
D1	Baa1	0.34	Baa3	1.49	Ba1	0.25	B1	3.17
D2	Ba3	5.48	B1	5.78	B3	16.29	Caa2	32.93
E	Caa3	65.56	D	84.45	D	95.56	D	98.04

Table 14.12   Impact of changing the recovery rate assumptions

Tranche	30%		50%		70%	
	Rating	EL	Rating	EL	Rating	EL
A	Aaa	0	Aaa	0	Aaa	0
B	Aaa	0	Aaa	0	Aaa	0
C	Baa1	0.26	A1	0.07	Aa1	0.01
D1	Ba2	4.60	Baa3	1.49	A3	0.35
D2	Caa1	18.07	B1	5.78	Ba1	2.68
E	D	91.59	D	84.45	D	70.55

Table 14.13 Impact of the diversity score on the rating for the case of flat yield curve and RR at 50%

Tranche	30		34		38	
	Rating	EL	Rating	EL	Rating	EL
A	Aaa	0	Aaa	0	Aaa	0
B	Aaa	0	Aaa	0	Aaa	0
C	A1	0.10	A1	0.07	A1	0.04
D1	Baa3	1.86	Baa3	1.49	Baa2	1.12
D2	B1	6.59	B1	5.78	B1	5.01
E	D	83.66	D	84.45	D	85.30

ratings of all the tranches can be expected, as can be seen in the column +10% in Table 14.14. The falling in the collateral will additionally trigger failures of O/C and I/C tests, causing early redemptions of the senior notes. In general, then, one can see that the impacts are higher for the lower tranches than for the senior ones. This is indeed what is seen in Table 14.14.

Impact of changes on the average rating of the collateral portfolio

Changes in the ratings of the collateral pool affect the WARF of the pool and the probability of default of the idealized bond. Higher probabilities of default imply higher expected losses and lower ratings. Obviously, the junior tranches are the first to be impacted. This is confirmed by the results in Table 14.15.

Table 14.14 Impact of variations in the collateral pool

Tranche	−20%		−10%		0%		+10%	
	Rating	EL	Rating	EL	Rating	EL	Rating	EL
A	Aaa	0	Aaa	0	Aaa	0	Aaa	0
B	A2	0.25	Aaa	0	Aaa	0	Aaa	0
C	Caa3	37.35	Ba1	1.57	A1	0.07	Aa3	0
D1	D	100	Caa2	24.52	Baa3	1.49	Baa1	0.02
D2	D	100	D	81.33	B1	5.78	Ba3	0.13
E	D	100	D	100	D	84.45	B2	12.26

Table 14.15 Impact of downgrading the collateral by one notch

Tranche	−2 notches		−1 notch		0	
	Rating	EL	Rating	EL	Rating	EL
A	Aaa	0	Aaa	0	Aaa	0
B	Aaa	0	Aaa	0	Aaa	0
C	Baa2	0.55	Baa1	0.16	A1	0.07
D1	Ba3	6.57	Ba1	2.58	Baa3	1.49
D2	Caa1	22.82	B3	15.02	B1	5.78
E	D	95.70	D	92.44	D	84.45

Table 14.16   Impact of variations in the WAL of the collateral

	7.00		6.00		5.00		4.00	
Tr	Rating	EL	Rating	EL	Rating	EL	Rating	EL
A	Aaa	0	Aaa	0	Aaa	0	Aaa	0
B	Aaa	0	Aaa	0	Aaa	0	Aaa	0
C	A3	0.46	A3	0.31	A1	0.07	Aa2	0.03
D1	Ba1	3.26	Ba1	1.53	Baa3	1.49	Baa1	0.32
D2	B1	10.91	B1	9.98	B1	5.78	B1	2.80
E	D	88.28	D	87.89	D	84.45	D	81.07

Impact of changes on the WAL of the collateral pool

The weighted average life of the collateral is five years. The WAL is used in the BET method to determine the PD of the independent bond. The PD is a function of the WARF and the WAL. A higher WAL results in a higher PD and, hence, in higher EL. The results are shown in the Table 14.16.

14.5 AIG AND BET

We end this chapter with some quotes taken from two SEC filings by American International Group, Inc. ("AIG"), discussing the usage of BET. AIG Financial Products Corp. and AIG Trading Group Inc., including their respective subsidiaries (collectively, AIGFP), were using BET to value super senior credit default swaps as can be read in the form 10-Q for the quarterly period ended 30 September 2007, filed by AIG (AIG, 2007).

> AIGFP values its super senior credit default swaps using internal methodologies that utilize available market observable information and incorporate management estimates and judgments when information is not available. It also employs the Binomial Expansion Technique (BET) model where appropriate to help estimate the fair value of these derivatives. The BET model utilizes credit spreads for the collateral pool obtained from an independent source. The model also utilizes diversity scores, weighted average lives, recovery rates and discount rates.

At 30 September 2007, the notional amount of the credit derivative portfolio was USD 513 billion, of which USD 78 billion was multisector CDO. Approximately USD 63 billion of the multisector CDO pools includes some exposure to US subprime mortgages.

In the form 8-K, dated 11 February 2008 filed by AIG (AIG, 2008), the methodology and the data inputs used to determine the value of the super senior CDS portfolio of AIGFP are clarified. Several valuations are given along with a brief outline of the methodology used. BET with generic spreads was used for the valuation of 30 September 2007:

> Calculated using BET methodology with generic credit spreads on asset-backed securities provided by a third party.

For the next valuation of 31 October 2007, some information from the ABX indices was added:

> Calculated using BET methodology with generic credit spreads on asset-backed securities provided by a third party and adjusted using inputs derived by management from observed changes in the relevant ABX indices. Calculation on this basis at November 30, 2007 would have resulted

in a gross cumulative decline in valuation of USD 2.551 billion, a benefit of USD 863 million from cash flow diversion features and a cumulative decline in valuation net of cash flow diversion features of USD 1.687 billion.

Cash bond prices were used for the 30 November 2007 valuation:

> Calculated using BET methodology with cash bond prices provided by the managers of the underlying CDO collateral pools, or, where not provided by the managers, prices derived from a price matrix based on cash bond prices that were provided.

The form 8-K also shows the warning by the independent auditors, talking about a *material weakness*:

> AIG has been advised by its independent auditors, PricewaterhouseCoopers LLC, that they have concluded that at December 31, 2007, AIG had a material weakness in its internal control over financial reporting and oversight relating to the fair value valuation of the AIGFP super senior credit default swap portfolio. AIG's assessment of its internal controls relating to the fair value valuation of the AIGFP super senior credit default swap portfolio is ongoing, but AIG believes that it currently has in place the necessary compensating controls and procedures to appropriately determine the fair value of AIGFP's super senior credit default swap portfolio for purposes of AIG's year-end financial statements.

On 3 March 2009, Federal Reserve Chairman Ben Bernanke said AIG exploited a huge gap in the regulatory system:

> AIG exploited a huge gap in the regulatory system; there was no oversight of the financial products division. This was a hedge fund basically that was attached to a large and stable insurance company, made huge numbers of irresponsible bets, took huge losses.

14.6 CONCLUSIONS

In this chapter we have described the BET methodology and have shown how changes in several parameters of the model impact the rating and expected loss for the different tranches of a cash flow CDO. The parameters we have varied are: the interest rate curve, the recovery rates, the diversity score of the collateral portfolio, the overcollateralization, the average rating of the collateral and the maturities of the collateral. In general, the junior tranches are more sensitive to changes.

Generally speaking, the strength of the BET model resides in its simplicity. The problem is that simplicity comes at a cost. The concept of correlation is hidden in the calculation of the DS. As already mentioned in Section 14.3 there are two approaches for calculating the DS. In this chapter we have used the simplest of them, as is standard in the market for the sort of CDO analyzed here. Moreover, for the case of CDOs on more complex collateral, composed, for example, of ABS/MBS notes, one will need a more sophisticated formulation (of DS) that takes into account parameters such as correlation among the underlying assets (see e.g. Witt (2004)) for more details. Observe that by letting correlation as an implicit parameter it becomes quite dangerous to use this model together with any mapping technique into standardized credit indices.

A second aspect of the BET model is that it does not provide the timing of the defaults as is the case in more traditional models. This means that the process of rating a note using BET becomes a much more arbitrary process than one would like. In our case, for example, we have given to a note the rating for which the note survives every default scenario assuming the interest rate curve stays unchanged. A more conservative analyst could request the rating for which the note passes the same default scenarios but assuming a $+1\%$, or even a $+2\%$ shift in the interest rate curve. Hence the rating process is rather subjective.

AIG has provided an interesting illustration of the use of the BET model as shown in their SEC filings. It is a huge surprise that this model is still in use by some practitioners, given its obvious flaws.

Structured Credit Products:
CPPI and CPDO

The reasonable man adapts himself to the world; the unreasonable one persists in trying to adapt the world to himself. Therefore, all progress depends on the unreasonable man.

Bernard Shaw

15.1 INTRODUCTION

Two recent innovative structured credit products are credit *Constant Proportion Portfolio Insurance* (CPPI) and credit *Constant Proportion Debt Obligation* (CPDO). The invested capital is put in a risk-free bond and a position is taken on credit derivatives. In a CPPI the principal is guaranteed at maturity and the goal is to maximize the portfolio value. In a CPDO the target is a significant excess return over the risk-free rate, subject to the constraint of being highly rated.

Essential to the pricing of CPPI and CPDO is the determination by the structurer of the so-called *gap risk* – that is, the risk of the portfolio value falling below some low barrier, the *bond floor* for a CPPI and the *cash-out barrier* for a CPDO. Due to the leveraged nature of the investment and to possible jumps in the spreads, one may lose more than the amount allocated to the risky part. In this chapter we present two simple Monte Carlo-based approaches to determine the risks on CPPI and CPDO structures. In the first algorithm, the spread dynamic is generated using the usual Gaussian framework, and in the second we use a Lévy-based process. We show that when using the Gaussian framework and not accounting for the possibilities of jumps, an enormous model risk is incurred when evaluating the gap risk for both structures. The studies reported here have been used in practice to generate red flags to the ratings of CPDOs in April 2007 when the structure was quite fashionable, as shown in our paper (Garcia et al., 2008).

The remainder of the chapter is structured as follows. The multivariate variance gamma (MVG) model is introduced in Section 15.2. In Section 15.3 we show how to price swaptions in this model. The calibration is described in Section 15.4. In Sections 15.5 and 15.6 we show the results for CPPI and CPDO. The conclusions are presented in Section 15.7.

15.2 MULTIVARIATE VG MODELING

A variance gamma (VG) process can be constructed by time changing a Brownian motion (BM), with a subordinator G_t following a Gamma$(t/v, 1/v)$ distribution so that $\mathbb{E}[G_t] = t$. We take N correlated Brownian motions $W^{(i)}$ independent of the gamma process G_t and set:

$$X_t^{(i)} = \theta_i G_t + \sigma_i W_{G_t}^{(i)}. \tag{15.1}$$

Note that the $X_t^{(i)}$ process is in general not symmetric; it is symmetric only if $\theta_i = 0$. The correlation between two processes $(i \neq j)$ is:

$$\rho_{ij} = \frac{\theta_i \theta_j v + \sigma_i \sigma_j \rho_{ij}^W}{\sqrt{\sigma_i^2 + \theta_i^2 v}\sqrt{\sigma_j^2 + \theta_j^2 v}}, \tag{15.2}$$

showing contributions both of the common time-change and of the correlation between the Brownian motions. We use exponential Lévy models for the spreads and set:

$$S_t^{(i)} = S_0^{(i)} \exp(\omega_i t + X_t^{(i)}), \tag{15.3}$$

where the risk neutral condition is satisfied by setting:

$$\omega_i = \frac{1}{v} \log\left(1 - \frac{1}{2}\sigma_i^2 v - \theta_i v\right). \tag{15.4}$$

We have made the simplifying assumptions of simulating a constant maturity spread and we approximate the corresponding risky annuity by a constant. This assumption makes the forward spread:

$$F_t^{(i)} = F_0^{(i)} \exp(\omega_i t + X_t^{(i)}), \tag{15.5}$$

a martingale under the measure associated with the risky annuity stream. We do not model the whole term structure and we focus on one maturity only. Note that defaults are not modeled explicitly in this framework. However, as indices are diversified pools, the effects of defaults are encompassed in the mark to market losses. Also default risk is assumed to be limited in these structures since the underlyings are always on-the-run investment grade indices, rolled every six months. The insights provided by using this simplified model outweigh the small approximation errors made in keeping the risky annuity constant. Observe that the CPPI and CPDO instruments are quite complex. The power of the algorithms presented here are computational efficiency, simplicity and their ability to capture the quite high level of model risk inherent in these structures.

15.3 SWAPTIONS ON CREDIT INDICES

A swaption is an option to buy or sell CDS protection at a fixed spread on a future date. With a *receiver* the investor has the right to sell protection and receive spread. Alternatively, with a *payer* the investor has the right to sell risk. The market standard for modeling credit spread options is based on Black's formula. Contrary to options on single name CDS, index options continue to exist even after credit events and are said to be *non-knockout*. The forward spread is adjusted to account for the non-knockout feature and this is done by adding the additional cost of protection during the lifetime of the option. We denote by T the option maturity and T^* is the index maturity.

The adjusted forward spread F balances the premium leg, given by $FA(T, T^*)$ and the present value of the protection leg, which consists of the front end protection from 0 to T, due to the non-knockout feature, and the regular CDS protection from T to T^*. Market conventions imply that the forward annuity $A(T, T^*)$ from the swaption maturity T to the index maturity T^* as of the trade day, is calculated using a flat credit curve set at the level of the standard knockout index forward spread. Front end protection is settled at option maturity T, hence it is valued as the present value of the losses between 0 and T, discounted at T.

We use swaption prices to determine the parameters of the VG process. With a slight adaptation to take annuities into account, the Carr-Madan formula (Carr and Madan, 1998) can be used to price payer and receiver swaptions. The formula for the payer reads:

$$
\text{Payer}(T, K) = A(T, T^*)\frac{\exp(-\alpha \log(K))}{\pi} \times \int_0^{+\infty} \frac{\exp(-iv \log(K))\phi(v - (\alpha + 1)i; T)}{\alpha^2 + \alpha - v^2 + i(2\alpha + 1)v}dv,
$$
(15.6)

where $\phi(u; T)$ is the characteristic function of the logarithm of the adjusted forward spread process at maturity, which is known analytically for VG.

15.4   MODEL CALIBRATION

The strategies addressed here involve taking positions in iTraxx Europe Main, DJ CDX.NA.IG and their HiVol subsets. We sell protection on the main index and, in the case of CPPI, buy protection on the HiVol subset to reduce volatility. In our examples, positions are taken on the 5-year on-the-run series. The effective maturity goes down from 5 years and 3 months when we enter into the position, to 4 years and 9 months when the position is unwound, i.e. when the trade is rolled into the next series. From this the approximation error on the risky annuity can be estimated.

The first calibration step is a joint calibration on swaptions of the individual indices determining the parameters v, θ_i and σ_i, $i = 1, \ldots, 4$. Note that this calibrates the *default adjusted forward spread* processes to the index option market. The data is taken on 2 April 2007!

The processes for the spreads are built as follows. We take the parameters v, θ_i and σ_i, obtained from the calibration on the swaptions, and plug in the correct initial values. The initial quotes (in bp) for the four indices are as follows: iTraxx Main at $S_0^{(\text{iTraxx})} = 24.625$, iTraxx HiVol at 48.75, CDX Main at 37.5 and CDX HiVol at 88.5. Note that the difference is in the initial values, that is the adjusted forward (in bp) was $F_0^{(\text{iTraxx})} = 27.4$ for iTraxx Main, 54.3 for iTraxx HiVol, 41.0 for CDX Main and 95 for CDX HiVol.

The second step is a correlation matching procedure. Table 15.1 shows the historic correlation matrix of the daily log returns based on observations from 21 June 2004 until 13 March 2007.

Figure 15.1 shows the results of the joint calibration on swaptions of the individual indices determining the parameters v, θ_i and σ_i, $i = 1, \ldots, 4$.

Table 15.1   Log-return correlation of iTraxx and CDX

	iTraxx Main	iTraxx HiVol	CDX Main	CDX HiVol
iTraxx	1.0000	0.9258	0.4719	0.3339
HiVol	0.9258	1.0000	0.4398	0.3281
CDX	0.4719	0.4398	1.0000	0.8580
HiVol	0.3339	0.3281	0.8580	1.0000

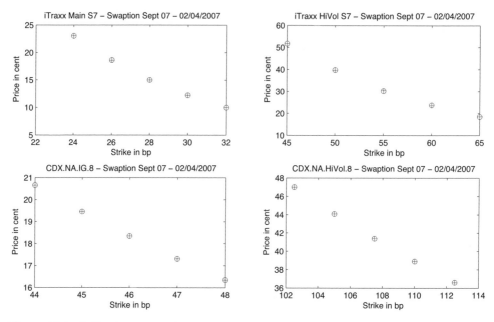

Figure 15.1   Calibration on swaptions

We match the historical correlations ρ_{ij} by setting the BM correlations ρ_{ij}^{W} equal to

$$\rho^{W} = \begin{bmatrix} 1.0000 & 0.9265 & 0.4935 & 0.3352 \\ 0.9265 & 1.0000 & 0.4470 & 0.3247 \\ 0.4935 & 0.4470 & 1.0000 & 0.8688 \\ 0.3352 & 0.3247 & 0.8688 & 1.0000 \end{bmatrix}.$$

(15.7)

A realization of the correlated VG spread paths is shown in Figure 15.2.

In summary, the model is calibrated to the options and to the index levels, with the prescribed correlation.

15.5   CPPI

CPPI was introduced by Black and Jones (1987) in an equity context. Credit CPPI is a strategy to create a capital protected and leveraged investment whose return depends on the performance of an underlying credit trading strategy.

We briefly outline the CPPI mechanism. Define the *bond floor* $B_t = \mathrm{PV}_t(B_T)$ as the time t value of the principal payment at maturity. The portfolio value V_t is the *net asset value* of the risk-free bond and the risky investment. The portfolio is marked to market (MtM) periodically. If the MtM is positive the risky exposure is increased, and decreased otherwise. We start with a portfolio of $B_T = 100$ and an investment horizon of $T = 6$ years. For simplicity we assume interest rates to be flat at 4%. We keep the *leverage factor* fixed at $m = 25$. The *cushion* $C_t = V_t - B_t$ is defined as the difference between the portfolio value and the bond floor. Multiplying the cushion with the leverage factor gives the *risky exposure* $E = mC_t$. The strategy is to sell protection on the 5-year on-the-run main indices for half of the risky exposure each, and to buy protection on the 5-year on-the-run HiVol subsets for $\zeta \frac{1}{2} \frac{30}{125}$ of the risky exposure. The

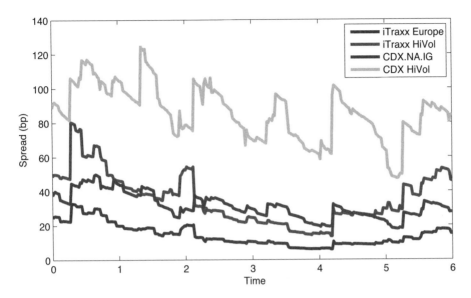

Figure 15.2 Correlated VG spread paths

portfolio is rebalanced on a regular basis until maturity or until we have a negative cushion at a rebalancing date. In the latter case all the positions are closed and the investor will receive the invested capital at maturity. The amount below the bond floor represents the loss incurred by the structurer of the deal and represents the gap risk (see Figure 15.3).

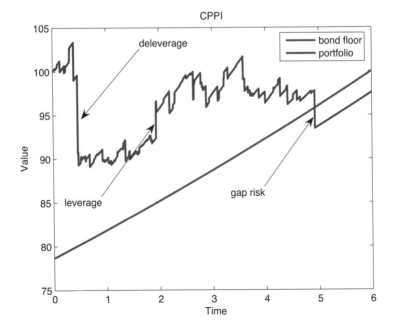

Figure 15.3 CPPI performance in the MVG model

Table 15.2   Effect of rebalancing on MVG gap risk

Rebalance	Risk	Frequency	Mean
2	0.1678	2.34 %	7.17
4	0.1673	2.43 %	6.88
12	0.0942	2.10 %	4.49
52	0.0847	2.10 %	4.04
252	0.0694	2.02 %	3.44

Table 15.3   Effect of rebalancing BM gap risk

Vol	Rebalance	Risk	Frequency	Mean
50 %	2	0.0180	0.73 %	2.50
50 %	4	0.0068	0.57 %	1.20
50 %	12	0.0005	0.18 %	0.27
50 %	52	0.0000	0.02 %	0.00
50 %	252	0.0000	0.00 %	0.00
75 %	2	0.2242	4.77 %	4.70
75 %	4	0.0849	3.99 %	2.13
75 %	12	0.0067	2.47 %	0.27
75 %	52	0.0001	1.02 %	0.01
75 %	252	0.0000	0.08 %	0.00

Due to the continuity of BM the gap risk under Black's model and continuous rebalancing is zero. A common trick to introduce gap risk in a BM setup is to change the rebalancing frequency. In Tables 15.2 and 15.3 we investigate the impact of the rebalancing frequency. The results are shown for a leveraging factor of $m = 25$ and no short positions ($\zeta = 0$). In these tables we show the impact of different rebalancing frequencies per year on the present value of the gap risk, the frequency of a gap occurrence and the mean size of the gap on condition there is a gap. As expected, increasing the rebalancing frequency decreases both the gap frequency and the size of the gap given there is a gap. This last effect is much more pronounced in the BM setting. The mean portfolio value did not change under different rebalancing frequencies.

The implied volatility observed on the swaption market was 50% to 55%. Assuming 50% volatility for the BM it is not possible to generate gap frequencies under the Brownian model of the same magnitude as in the MVG model. The only way to get gap risk of the same magnitude in BM was by increasing the volatility. We show results for the case of 75% volatility. By doing so we no longer match the implied volatility observed in the option market. Additionally, observe that even in this case the gap risk reduces significantly once the rebalancing frequency increases to more than twice per year.

In Table 15.4 we show the impact of the short positions on the gap risk, the return and its volatility. Observe that increasing the amount of shorts from 0% to 100% reduces the return volatility and the PV of the gap risk by almost 50% while reducing return by roughly 5% only. The impact of the leverage factor in the MVG model is shown in Table 15.5. An increase in the leverage increases the mean return and its volatility at the cost of a significant increase in gap risk. When spreads widen in a CPPI strategy, one has to close positions in order to avoid hitting the bond floor. Alternatively, if spreads tighten, prices go up and due to fixed leverage

Table 15.4   Effect of short positions on the CPPI strategy under MVG

ζ	Mean	Std	Pv gap	bp pa
0	139.1	11.0	0.0732	1.3720
50	135.7	8.5	0.0508	0.9531
100	132.2	6.7	0.0421	0.7892

Table 15.5   Effect of leverage factor under MVG

m	Mean	Std dev	Pv gap	bp pa
25	139.1	11.0	0.0732	1.3720
30	141.5	13.8	0.1249	2.3405
40	146.3	19.1	0.2171	4.0699
50	151.0	25.4	0.3609	6.7656

one has to buy more. Consequently, the capital guaranteed feature in a CPPI strategy implies that one buys at the high and sells at the low.

15.6   CPDO

The aim of the CPDO strategy is to obtain a fixed prescribed return during the whole investment horizon. Once the PV of the return up to maturity is reached the risky positions are closed; this is a *cash-in* event, and the investment is returned to the investor. If the portfolio underperforms one has to increase the leverage to keep up with a fixed return. If performance is extremely bad and falls below a certain low threshold we have a so called *cash-out* event – all the positions are closed and what remains is returned to the investor. An example of such a cash-out event is depicted in Figure 15.4.

A characteristic feature of a CPDO is that once one comes close to the target one deleverages. Alternatively, once losses are incurred one has to leverage more to cope with the fixed prescribed return. In a CPDO one buys at the low and sells at the high.

The CPDO strategy used in our study is as follows. We target an excess return of $\kappa = 200$ bps per annum above risk-free rate with a very high rating (AAA). For each evaluation date, we calculate the portfolio value V_t composed from the cash account, the fee income and the MtM of the positions and we compute the target T_t as the PV of all future coupons plus the notional at maturity ($T = 10$ years). Next, we check for cash-in ($V_t \geq T_t$) or cash-out ($V_t \leq V_0 C_o$) events. The cash-out level is $C_o = 15\%$. The shortfall $F_t = \alpha T_t - V_t$ is the difference between the (loaded) target and the present value of the portfolio. We assume a target loading factor of 5% ($\alpha = 1.05$). The present value of the risky income is estimated as $I_t = \beta S_t A_t$, where a risky income fraction $\beta = 0.75$ is used. This so-called *CPDO fudge factor* β is used by market practitioners to make sure that the expected cash-in time is earlier than the maturity of the instrument. Real CPDO deals had modifications of the basic schema that made them maximally leveraged (at least initially). The fudge factor is the simplest model capturing this. The value of 75% used here has been taken from a product presentation. Another structure had a factor which was a predetermined linear function that was pre-set at inception for the term of the transaction. An immediate consequence is that the structure is overcollateralized in coupons and as such can get very high ratings.

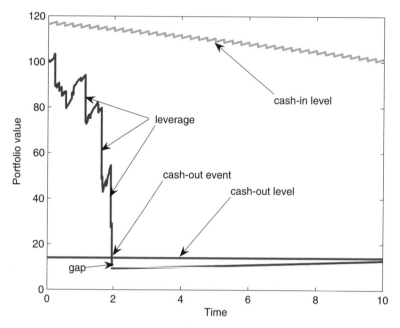

Figure 15.4   CPDO portfolio value evolution and cash-out event

Finally, we find the exposure as $E_t = \min\{F_t/I_t, MV_0\}$. Note that the leverage $m = E_t/V_0$ is capped at $M = 15$. We assume that new positions in the indices are taken every six months, thus minimizing the risk of a default on any of the underlying names of the index. The 10-year target cash-in probabilities for the different rating classes are as follows: 99.27% (AAA), 98.99% (AA+), 98.51% (AA), 98.12% (AA−), 97.71% (A+) and 97.27% (A). In Table 15.6 we show the results of the experiments for both MVG and BM. In the tables B_{35} and B_{50} represent BM with volatilities of 35% and 50% respectively.

The impact of the target spread is obvious: the higher the target the lower the cash-in probability. With fudge factor $\beta = 1$ the impact of the target is much more pronounced under MVG than under BM. Changing the fudge factor to $\beta = 0.75$ reduces the cash-in probability considerably. Under MVG one does not get the AAA rating. Under BM one gets AAA only if the volatility is reduced.

Table 15.6   Cash-in probabilities for the CPDO model

$\beta = 1$	MVG	B_{35}	B_{50}
100	99.75%	99.96%	99.87%
150	99.44%	99.93%	99.47%
200	98.86%	99.65%	99.30%
$\beta = 0.75$			
100	99.02%	99.79%	99.24%
150	97.86%	99.29%	98.35%
200	97.43%	98.53%	97.62%

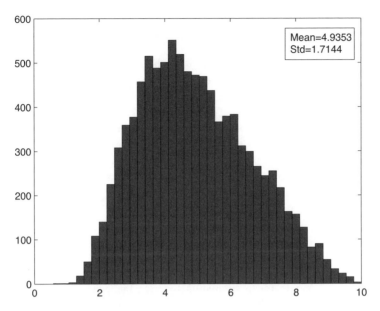

Figure 15.5   Cash-in time distribution for $\beta = 1.00$

Figure 15.5 shows the cash-in time distribution for the case of excess return of 150 bps for $\beta = 100\%$ under MVG and Figure 15.6 shows the cash-in time distribution for $\beta = 75\%$. Decreasing the fudge factor decreases the expected cash-in time. The reason for this is that a reduction in the fudge factor is compensated by a higher leverage of the position which leads to an earlier cash-in time.

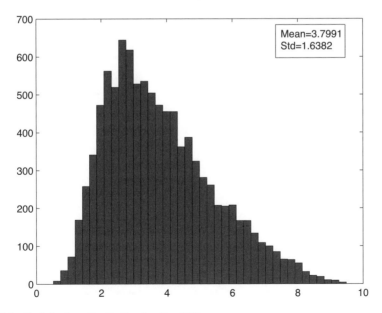

Figure 15.6   Cash-in time distribution for $\beta = 0.75$

The simulations were performed in April 2007. At that time we already questioned the AAA rating of CPDOs. Recently *IFR* magazine has published articles about troublesome CPDO rating (see IFR 2008a, 2008b).

On 6 November 2008 Standard & Poor's Ratings Services lowered and withdrew its ratings on five CPDOs (Castle Finance I Ltd. EUR 325 M Surf CPDO Notes Series 7, Chess II Ltd. EUR 100 M Surf CPDO FRN Series 25, Rembrandt New Zealand Trust No. 2006–1 NZD 70 Million FRN, Rembrandt Australia Trust No. 2006–2 AUD 50 M FRN, and Rembrandt Australia Trust No. 2006–3 AUD 40 M Community Income CPDO Notes). These rating actions follow widening and increasing volatility in CDS spreads, which have led the net asset value (NAV) of these CPDOs to fall below the 10% cash-out trigger. Once the NAV falls below 10%, the transaction is unwound. The low NAV on the transactions means that noteholders *suffer principal losses*, and therefore the ratings have been lowered to D.

15.7 CONCLUSION

We have introduced the Multivariate Variance Gamma (MVG) model for correlated credit spreads. The model is calibrated to the options and to the index levels, with the prescribed correlation. We used Monte Carlo simulation to price the gap risk on CPPI and CPDO strategies and to estimate the cash-in probability as a proxy for the rating of a CPDO. The gap risk calculated under MVG is significantly higher than under Brownian motion (BM), where it is zero in a continuous model. To get a comparable gap risk value under BM, an extremely low rebalancing frequency is required in addition to a volatility value that is much higher than observed in the options market.

The capital guaranteed feature in CPPI creates a buy at the high and sell at the low adverse effect. Once losses begin to occur one has to deleverage, decreasing the impact of possible jumps. The target return feature in CPDO results in buying at the low and selling at the high. Once losses begin to occur one has to leverage more to guarantee the targeted return, creating a very leveraged position, which significantly increases the risks. Consequently the exposure to model risk is higher for CPDOs than for CPPIs.

We found no justifications for the AAA rating of CPDOs even with favorable conditions, such as low spread levels and low implied volatilities, both for BM and MVG-based models in which costs are even not taken into account. The possibilities of jumps in the Lévy set up showed the enormous model risk that any user was running by using the standard Gaussian process.

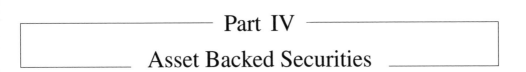

Part IV
Asset Backed Securities

16

ABCDS and PAUG

The big guys are the status quo, not the innovators.
Kenneth Fisher

16.1 INTRODUCTION

In Chapter 4 we discussed the synthetic single name CDS and described models to price it. We have outlined the importance of a CDS by itself and as an essential component of the corporate synthetic CDO asset class. We have also seen the fundamental role played by single name CDSs on the pricing algorithms for not only the corporate standardized credit indices but also for the bespoke corporate CDOs, via the correlation mapping techniques presented in Chapter 12.

In this chapter we describe the CDS of ABS, also known as ABCDS. The instrument has existed since at least 1998 and its purpose was to provide a synthetic form of assets for CDOs of ABSs. Those first ABS CDO transactions were balance sheet CDOs, and the protection buyers realized a reduction of regulatory capital costs. Other protection buyers were engaged on negative basis trade deals, in which the investor buys an ABS bond and an ABCDS, realizing a gain as the spread of the bond was higher than the premium paid on the CDS plus its cost of funding the ABS bond. As expected, the documentation was nonstandard and based on the templates for corporate CDSs. The growth of subprime mortgages and interest of investors, especially *hedge funds interested in taking a short position on subprime mortgages*, brought up the necessity of a specific dealer transaction template for the instrument that indeed became available by mid 2005. It is interesting to notice that, as we mention in Chapter 22, exactly at this time Schiller was reporting the existence of a housing bubble in the US.

Although we write about ABCDSs in general, we have written this chapter with ABCDSs of subprime mortgage backed securities in mind. In this book, the only index we price for CDOs of ABSs is the TABX.HE, the standardized credit tranches for subprime MBSs. That is, there might be aspects we comment in here that would not be relevant for an ABCDS of auto loans for example. The remainder of the chapter will be organized as follows. In Section 16.2 we address the differences between ABCDSs and the corporate CDSs, pointing out the difficulty of creating an ABCDS template that would be imported from the Corporate CDS template. In Section 16.3 we describe the *pay as you go* (PAUG) feature.

16.2 ABCDSs VERSUS CORPORATE CDSs

Just like the corporate CDS, an ABCDS is a credit default swap on an asset backed security. The two are quite distinct from each other. As outlined in Chapter 4, the reference obligation on a corporate CDS is just a reference, and the real focus is on a credit event on the underlying obligor. In an ABCDS, the reference obligation is a *specific* tranche of an ABS. The necessity for this is that each ABS has its own specific collateral, with its own characteristics, amortization schedules and maturities. Additionally, an ABS may issue notes of different rating classes, implying different risk profiles and tranche-specific ABCDSs.

A very important difference is the definition of a credit event. The failure to pay issues on the corporate side is quite clear and well defined. On an ABS, however, the matter is much less clear cut. Consider, for example, a senior note of an ABS. The events of failure-to-pay senior tranches are already taken into account in the documentation of the deals in a way that cash flow may certainly be deviated from subordinated tranches to pay senior tranches. Deferred interest is another example of possible ambiguous circumstances. Interest payments may be deferred where there is insufficient cash flow due to delinquency or defaults. Another cause of deferred interest occurs when possible caps in the underlying collateral generate insufficient interest to pay the interest to the ABS tranches. In that case, the interest is deferred until there is sufficient cash coming from the collateral to pay it. When there are collateral losses the ABS may trigger writedown of tranche principals. In that case, interest and principal payments are based on the lower figures. Sometimes, however, the situation improves and the writedown process is made reversible. Some ABSs, however, do not include the writedown process and the tranche principals are only considered in default at the maturity of the deal. The maturity of the deal is another difficulty. An ABS may be prepaid and the prepayment schedule affects its maturity. Hence there is no fixed maturity date for the collateral, which impacts the ABCDS maturity.

The difficulties underlying an ABCDS are inherent to the nature of the ABS product. Observe that any suspension in interest and principal payments may be small and reversible. Additional problems are the tranche sizes. In general, tranches below AA are quite small, implying that physical settlement may not be feasible unless the protection buyer owns the tranche as well.

Despite these problems, the first template used for ABCDS, during the period of 1998 to 2004, was based on the corporate CDS. The following credit events could trigger payments from the protection seller:

1. Failure to pay principal by the legal maturity of the deal.
2. Failure to pay interest or principal, when the possibility of paying it on a later date is not permitted in the terms of the ABS contract.
3. In case of a writedown, the failure to pay principal or interest clausulas are triggered if writedowns are not explicitly permitted in the terms of the contract.
4. Downgrade to Ca or below by Moody's, or to CCC – or below by S&P associated with a failure to pay interest of principal.
5. Downgrade to C by Moody's or to D by S&P.
6. Failure to pass overcollateralization tests. That is, when it becomes obvious that there would not be cash or interest enough to pay some senior tranches in the capital structure.

Where an ABS note permits interest and principal payments to be deferred, a rating agency downgrade would be necessary to trigger a credit event. Modeling deferred interest or principal and reversible writeups is an extremely complex task and one usually not done by the rating agencies – that is, the rating agencies model that the cash would eventually be there at some point in time without considering the precise timing of the payments. Hence the rating does accurately represent these possible credit events. The rating agencies also overlook the caps on the collateral. In the next section we discuss the *Pay as You Go (PAUG)* currently used by the industry.

16.3   ABCDS PAY AS YOU GO: PAUG

The PAUG template is much more flexible than the corporate ABCDS-inspired template. It has been designed in such a way that the ABCDS closely follows the cash events of the underlying ABS. It is much more recent and involves two possibilities: one in which the Pay As You Go feature is mixed with physical settlement, known as the *dealer template*; and the pure Pay As You Go framework, known as the *end user* template.

16.3.1   PAUG: dealer template

In the PAUG framework, if there is an interest shortfall the protection buyer receives from the protection seller the shortfall amount, and this happens even where interest has been deferred. If the ABS security pays the deferred interest later, then the protection buyer pays the amount back to the protection seller. Additionally this feature can be triggered many times during the lifetime of the ABCDS. In the PAUG template, those events and the amounts involved are formally known as *floating amount events* and *floating amounts* respectively. The reversed amounts that are paid back from the protection buyer to the protection seller are called *additional fixed amounts*. Note that the events do not trigger the undoing of the whole structure. The same did not happen with the template described in the last section. That is, in the template inspired by the corporate CDS market, only when a deferred interest event happens simultaneously with a large downgrade event would it trigger a credit event. Additionally, in this last case, the deferred interest is a minor event, given that one would be confronted with the unwinding of the whole structure. That is, one is confronted with either the hurdles of a physical settlement or a quite uncertain cash settlement that depends on the pooling process, having as underlying an illiquid structure.

The principal writedowns happen in the same fashion as with the above described deferred interest case. That is, any writedown is paid from the protection seller to the protection buyer, and the notional of the ABCDS is adjusted in accordance. In case there is a later reversal of writedowns the protection buyer pays the reversed amount back to the protection seller. The outstanding notional on the ABCDS is adjusted in accordance to the writedown amounts. Additionally, the template contemplates the possibility for many writedown events. An important catch, however, is that the protection buyer may *force* a physical settlement of the whole ABCDS in the case of a writedown event even if there has been no downgrade. In the case of the corporate ABCDS template, however, the reversible writedown process would either be ignored or would cause the unwind of the whole ABCDS *only in case of simultaneous large downgrade*.

With respect to the interest shortfall events this means, the PAUG template brings more flexibility by making the ABCDS follow more closely the cash events happening in the ABS instrument. With respect to the writedown events, however, the template brought to *the protection buyer* the *choice* of defining it as either a floating amount event or a credit event. In the first case there is the typical pay-as-you-go settlement, and in the second case physical settlement. And that even in the absence of a substantial downgrade. Additionally, the protection buyer does not need to own the underlying ABS.

The interest shortfall may have two causes. Either there is a default on the payment of interest or it comes from the fact that there is a cap on the underlying ABSs that limit the total amount of interest available from the pool. Observe that even if a pool is performing well there may be insufficient cash to be paid on interest because there might be contractual legal restrictions on the increase of the rates to be paid by the loans in the collateral. In the so-called *available funds cap* (AFC) there is a limit in the amount of interest to be paid by the ABS note. Given that there might be resets on the rates of the underlying collateral, the deferred interest may be paid on a later date. There are three different procedures in which the interest shortfall may be paid:

1. *No cap is applied.* In this case the protection seller pays the full amount of the interest shortfall. That is, LIBOR + Coupon Spread − CDS Spread.
2. *Variable cap.* In this case there is a cap on the amount to be paid by the protection seller. That is, the payment made is LIBOR + min(CDS Spread, Coupon Spread) − CDS Spread. That is, the maximum to be received by the protection buyer is LIBOR.
3. *Fixed cap.* In this case the protection seller does not need to pay any LIBOR and the fee is limited to the CDS spread. That is, the protection buyer reduces the amount to be paid to the protection seller by a value equal to the CDS fee.

In the case of failure to pay principal the protection buyer may interpret it either as a floating amount event or as a credit event. Those events happen most often either at maturity or when there are problems with the collateral of the portfolio. Both *distress rating downgrades* and *maturity extension* are pure credit events and are optional for the protection buyer. The loan modification issues during the credit crunch evidenced that the maturity of a deal can be extended.

Last but not least we discuss the step-up features. Modifying the prepayment assumptions changes the duration of an ABS. If prepayment decreases the duration will increase. In order to cope with changes in the expected maturity of a deal there are step-up features inside the ABS. In the PAUG template, a step-up on the ABS will be followed by a step-up in the fee of the ABCDS. However, the protection buyer has the option to cancel the contract, usually within five business days.

16.3.2   PAUG: end user template

This template has been very much influenced by monoline insurers, as they sell protection on AAA-rated ABS. There are some important differences between this template and the one described in the last section.

1. This template has no possibility for physical settlement. That is, in case of writedown there is a cash settlement.
2. There is no step-up cancelability option. That is, when the ABS underlying contract does not finish at the initial expected maturity with consequent step-up fee, the ABCDS buyer has to accept the increase in the premium.
3. Interest shortfalls that happen due to caps are not covered by the ABCDS.

16.4   CONCLUSION

In this chapter the different templates used for the ABCDS have been discussed in quite some detail. In the next chapters models to price a CDO of ABS are outlined. The purpose of this chapter is to develop an understanding of the advantages and the limitations of those models.

One Credit Event Models for CDOs of ABS

The difference between genius and stupidity is that genius has its limits.
Albert Einstein

17.1 INTRODUCTION

In this chapter we compare algorithms to price CDOs of ABSs using MC simulation under the Gaussian copula. This is done using the 1-factor market approach under two different correlation assumptions and a multifactor model using an approach similar to the one developed by Fitch (Zelter et al., 2007) for Structured Finance CDOs. Additionally, we give the impact of four different assumptions for the amortization profiles.

The chapter is organized as follows. In Section 17.2 we show the approach used to price an ABS bond, and different assumptions for the amortization parameter and how to use it to imply default probabilities. In Section 17.3 we analyze the impact of the different model parameters for ABS pricing. In Section 17.4 we give a brief description of the multifactor Gaussian copula approach inspired by the Fitch model. In Section 17.5 we show how to get default times from simulated returns. In Section 17.6 we show the results of the simulations for the pricing of different tranches of the CDO of ABS. We conclude in Section 17.7.

17.2 ABS BOND AND ABCDS

In this section we give valuation formulas for an ABS bond and its CDS. Observe that the main difference between an ABS with respect to a simpler corporate bond is that due to amortization and the real possibility of prepayments the outstanding notional is time-dependent. In what follows we will make some simplifying assumptions. First, we assume the amortized (ABS) bond is a floater paying a coupon C above LIBOR. Second, the amortization schedule is deterministic. Third, we apply a one default event model – that is, we assume the ABCDS behaves as a corporate bond, and that in the event of default the ABCDS stops existing and the protection seller receives the recovery (R) value of the ABS. Although this is current market practice we note that this is a very strong assumption.

In what follows we will assume four amortization profiles:

- Conditional Prepayment Rate (CPR)

$$n_t = (1 - c)^t \tag{17.1}$$

- Bullet

$$n_t = \begin{cases} 1 & t \leq T_b \\ 0 & t > T_b \end{cases} \tag{17.2}$$

- Linear

$$n_t = \begin{cases} 1 - \frac{t}{T_l} & t \le T_l \\ 0 & t > T_l \end{cases} \tag{17.3}$$

- Quadratic

$$n_t = \begin{cases} 1 - \left(\frac{t}{T_q}\right)^2 & t \le T_q \\ 0 & t > T_q \end{cases} \tag{17.4}$$

Consider there are N payment dates, n_i is the outstanding notional at payment date t_i, the average life A_L of the ABS is given by:

$$A_L = \sum_{i=2}^{N} (n_{i-1} - n_i) t_i \tag{17.5}$$

and we assume that $t_1 = 0.0$, $t_N = T$ (maturity of the ABS), $n_1 = 1.0$ and $n_N = 0.0$. A first step in the pricing algorithm of an ABS note is to calculate the amortized notional using a prepayment assumption. The prepayment parameter is calibrated in such a way that one recovers observed average life.

We assume the default process to follow a homogeneous Poisson process and as such for any $0 \le t \le T$ the risk-neutral survival probability $q(t_i)$ at time t_i and the default intensity λ, satisfy:

$$q_i = q(t_i) = \exp(-\lambda t_i). \tag{17.6}$$

We assume a risk-free discount rate (r) given by a flat interest rate curve:

$$d_i = d(t_i) = \exp(-r t_i) \tag{17.7}$$

The price of the amortized (ABS) bond B is computed as

$$B = \sum_{i=2}^{N} n_{i-1}(L_i + c)d(t_i)q(t_i)\Delta t_i + q(t_N)d(t_N)n_N$$
$$+ \sum_{i=2}^{N} (n_{i-1} - n_i) d(t_i)q(t_i) + R \sum_{i=2}^{N} n_{i-1}d(t_i)(q(t_{i-1}) - q(t_i)). \tag{17.8}$$

In these equations the summations run over the payment dates t_i and L_i is the LIBOR rate at time t_i. The recovery rate is R, and $\Delta t_i = t_i - t_{i-1}$ is the year fraction. In the present study for simplicity we considered $L_i = r$.

The *risky duration* D_R and the *expected loss* $\mathbb{E}L$ are important quantities which are computed as follows

$$D_R = \sum_{i=2}^{N} n_{i-1}d_i q_i (t_i - t_{i-1}) \tag{17.9}$$

$$\mathbb{E}L = (1 - R) \sum_{i=2}^{N} n_{i-1}d(t_i)(q(t_{i-1}) - q(t_i)) \tag{17.10}$$

The fair spread s on the deal is given by

$$s = \frac{\mathbb{E}L}{D_R} \tag{17.11}$$

In the next section we show the results of the algorithm used here and the sensitivities to the input parameters.

17.3   SINGLE NAME SENSITIVITY

In the first step of the pricing algorithm for the ABS bond we calibrate the appropriate parameters in the chosen prepayment assumption (see 17.2) to match the observed A_L as in (17.5). The output of this step is the amortized notional ($n_i's$ for $2 \leq i \leq N$). In the second step the price of the bond (17.8) is used to imply default probabilities, and in the case of a homogeneous Poisson process (17.6) this means a suitable intensity $lambda = \lambda$.

In the results shown in this section we assume the ABS has a coupon $c = 55$ bp and the interest rate flat at $r = 2.6881\%$. The average life A_L is 8 years, the bond price B is 80% and the maturity T is 30 years. We assume quarterly payments, $\Delta t = t_i - t_{i-1} = 0.25$, and hence $N = 121$. The four prepayment assumptions used in this study are shown in Figure 17.1.

In Figure 17.1 we show the variation of the outstanding notional with respect to the different amortization profiles assuming the same AL for all the amortization schedules. Observe that

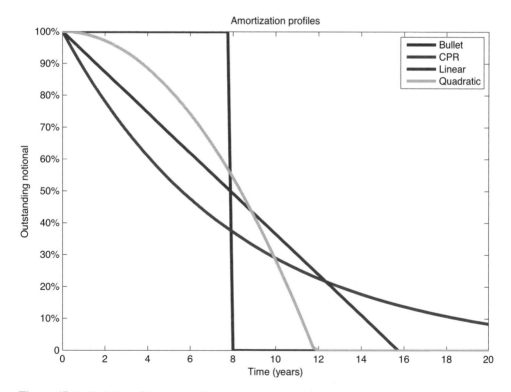

Figure 17.1 Variation of the outstanding notionals in time for the different amortization profiles

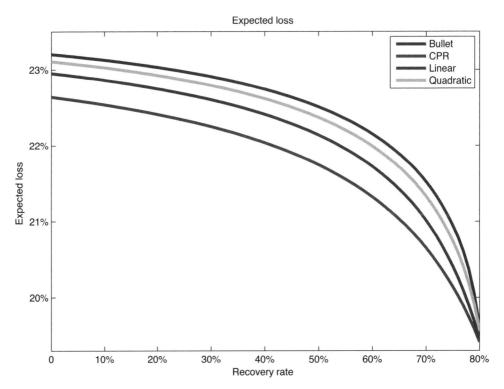

Figure 17.2 Expected loss with respect to recovery rate assumptions for the different amortization profiles

there is an order in terms of decreasing amortization speed going from *cpr* over *linear* and *quadratic* to finally *bullet*.

Figure 17.2 shows the impact of the recovery rate assumptions on the expected loss for the different amortization profiles. As expected for any amortization profile a higher recovery rate implies a lower expected loss. There is an upper bound on the input recovery rate in order to be compatible with the observed market price. For example, if the recovery rate is 90%, the price cannot be lower than 90 cents to the dollar.

Figure 17.3 shows the impact of the recovery rate assumptions on the fair spreads for the different amortization profiles. For a certain amortization profile a higher recovery rate assumption results in a higher spread.

Figure 17.4 shows the impact of the recovery rate assumptions on the risky duration for the different amortization profiles. Given an amortization profile a higher recovery rate assumption results in a higher spread and consequently a lower risky duration.

Figure 17.5 shows the impact on the default intensity with respect to recovery rate assumptions for the different amortization profiles. For a certain amortization profile a higher recovery rate assumption results in a higher default intensity. Observe that all these graphs show the order implied by the amortization profile, going from *cpr* over *linear* and *quadratic* to finally *bullet*.

The results of the pricing algorithm, matching the observed bond price and average life, with respect to different assumptions of prepayment functions are shown in Tables 17.1 and 17.2 for respectively 0% and 40% recovery rates. It serves as a more detailed summary of what has been observed in the figures.

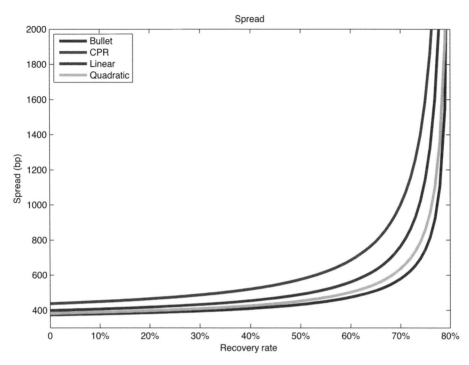

Figure 17.3 Fair spreads with respect to recovery rate assumptions for the different amortization profiles

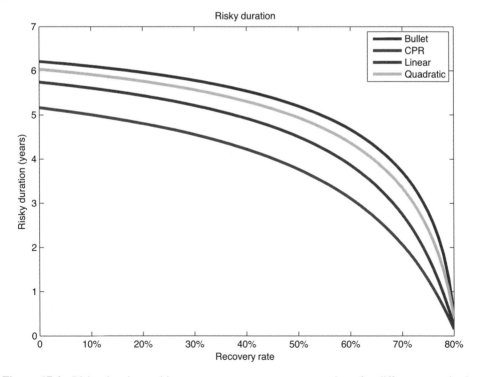

Figure 17.4 Risky durations with respect to recovery rate assumptions for different amortization profiles

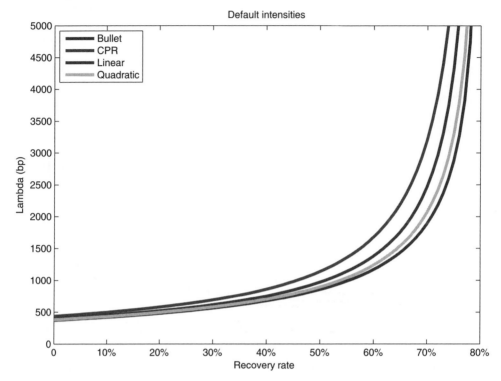

Figure 17.5   Default intensities

Table 17.1   ABS characteristics for different assumptions of prepayment and with recovery rate assumed zero ($R = 0$)

Amortization	$\mathbb{E}$Loss (%)	RD	λ (bp)	Spread (bp)
Bullet	23.2024	6.2093	371.9386	373.6732
CPR	22.6410	5.1644	436.0220	438.4071
Linear	22.9519	5.7429	397.6705	399.6538
Quadratic	23.1076	6.0328	381.2126	383.0350

Table 17.2   ABS characteristics for different assumptions of prepayment and with recovery rate set at 40% ($R = 40\%$)

Amortization	$\mathbb{E}$Loss (%)	RD	λ (bp)	Spread (bp)
Bullet	22.7432	5.5437	677.9809	410.2555
CPR	22.0384	4.2261	859.8282	521.4817
Linear	22.4113	4.9232	751.5958	455.2209
Quadratic	22.6180	5.3096	703.7445	425.9830

17.4   MULTIFACTOR CORRELATION MODEL

In *latent variable* models default occurs when a certain variable Y_i falls below a threshold K_i which is implied from CDS prices. The so-called *market* or *systemic* factor X_m and the *idiosyncratic* factor $X^{(i)}$ are random variables whose functional form depends on model assumptions.

In the generic 1-factor Gaussian model the latent variable is represented as

$$Y_i = \rho X_m + \sqrt{(1 - \rho^2)}\xi_i \qquad (17.12)$$

where X_m and ξ_i are the market and the idiosyncratic factors, independent and identically distributed variables. Both have the same distribution $N(0,1)$.

In our case, however, we extend the simple 1-factor model to a multifactor model and in this case the latent variable for a single entry is modeled as follows:

$$Y_i = \xi_g X_g + \xi_r X_r + \xi_s X_s + \xi_4 X_4 + \xi_5 X_5 + \xi_6 X_6 + \xi_7 X_7 + \xi_8 X_8 + \xi_i X_i, \qquad (17.13)$$

where all variates X are standard normal distributed. The coefficient $\xi_g = \sqrt{0.45}$ determines the global correlation. Other ξ coefficients are zero, except $\xi_r = \sqrt{0.10}$ for subprime RMBS or $\xi_s = \sqrt{0.10}$ for structured finance CDO and $\xi_4 = \sqrt{0.05}$ if the vintage is 2004, or $\xi_5 = \sqrt{0.10}$ if the vintage is 2005, or $\xi_6 = \sqrt{0.20}$ if the vintage is 2006, or $\xi_7 = \sqrt{0.20}$ if the vintage is 2007, or $\xi_8 = \sqrt{0.20}$ if the vintage is 2008.

The coefficient for the idiosyncratic remainder is

$$\xi_i = \sqrt{1 - \xi_g^2 - \xi_r^2 - \xi_s^2 - \xi_4^2 - \xi_5^2 - \xi_6^2 - \xi_7^2 - \xi_8^2}. \qquad (17.14)$$

This is the approach used by Fitch for their CDOs of ABSs *before* the credit crunch that began in June 2007. In this case the maximum correlation possible reaches 75%.

17.5   MONTE CARLO SIMULATION

Typically in an MC simulation one generates random numbers for the market and idiosyncratic factors that are plugged in (17.13) and (17.14) to generate the return Y_i. With the value of the default intensity (λ_i) implied from ABS bond prices (see (17.6) in Section 17.2) one determines the default time τ_i, as

$$\tau_i = \frac{-1}{\lambda_i} \log(1 - N(Y_i)), \qquad (17.15)$$

where $N(x)$ is the standard normal cumulative distribution. If the default time of a certain ABS in the portfolio is lower than its maturity date then the contract is terminated and the outstanding notional is substituted by its recovery value. The contract will go until maturity otherwise.

Each simulation consists of generating one set of systematic factors and as many idiosyncratic factors as the number of ABSs in the portfolio. The default times of all the underlying collateral are determined and one can determine the present value of loss side.

17.6   RESULTS

In this section we show the results of the MC simulation procedure both 1-factor and multifactor for the different tranches of a CDO of ABSs under different assumptions of amortization schedules and recovery rates. As already mentioned in Section 17.4, the multifactor simulation uses the correlation structure of Fitch for CDOs of structured finance, see Zelter et al. (2007), and for the 1-factor model we show the results using flat 75% and 90% correlations. The amortization assumptions are CPR, bullet, linear and quadratic and have been described in more detail in Section 17.2. The different recovery rate assumptions are 0%, 40%, 50%, 60% and 70%, flat for all ABSs, and Moody's rating agency recovery rate (with a few minor corrections if the bond prices turn out to be lower than the recovery rates) specific for each ABS in the collateral portfolio.

The results are shown in Tables 17.3 and 17.4 in terms of expected loss divided by tranche size. The tranches are [0, 0.10%], [0.10%, 3.10%], [3.10%, 10.0%] and [10.0%, 100.0%]. In the tables the tranches are represented by their attachment points. The tables are subdivided based on the amortization schedule used to generate the results. Table 17.3 has the results for the Bullet and CPR amortization schedules and Table 17.4 has the results for the Linear and Quadratic amortization schedules. The upper left subtable refers to the bullet, the lower left to the linear, the upper right to the CPR and the lower right to the quadratic amortization schedule. Each subtable belonging to a certain amortization schedule contains three other tables (upper, mid, down) characterized by the type of MC simulation made. The upper and mid tables refer

Table 17.3   Expected loss for the different tranches of a CDO of ABSs for different amortization profiles (bullet and CPR) and different recovery rates assumptions: 0%, 40%, 50%, 60%, 70% and the rating agency recovery rate

0.00%	0.10%	3.10%	10.00%	A	0.00%	0.10%	3.10%	10.00%
	$\rho = 90\%$					$\rho = 90\%$		
42.29%	35.00%	25.74%	8.45%	0	75.64%	49.90%	32.69%	7.10%
59.32%	47.70%	34.92%	7.17%	40%	89.05%	64.54%	42.01%	5.68%
66.78%	53.28%	38.77%	6.61%	50%	92.70%	70.40%	45.88%	5.14%
76.43%	60.72%	44.04%	5.83%	60%	95.90%	77.52%	50.82%	4.39%
90.56%	72.27%	51.42%	4.62%	70%	98.53%	86.61%	57.39%	3.40%
94.88%	74.39%	49.01%	4.61%	RA	98.66%	86.65%	54.89%	3.41%
	$\rho = 75\%$					$\rho = 75\%$		
58.13%	47.49%	32.34%	7.53%	0	84.29%	59.46%	37.86%	6.45%
73.58%	59.18%	40.41%	6.37%	40%	93.26%	71.94%	46.20%	5.15%
79.45%	64.04%	43.85%	5.88%	50%	95.40%	76.67%	49.85%	4.66%
86.21%	70.22%	48.50%	5.13%	60%	97.29%	82.48%	54.28%	3.96%
94.50%	79.28%	55.24%	4.09%	70%	98.87%	89.82%	60.55%	3.06%
96.66%	80.30%	53.21%	4.09%	RA	98.95%	89.74%	58.27%	3.08%
	3 Factors					3 Factors		
78.22%	63.87%	41.34%	6.26%	0	93.29%	72.82%	45.41%	5.38%
89.20%	73.72%	48.38%	5.20%	40%	97.08%	82.19%	53.13%	4.31%
92.31%	77.36%	51.33%	4.79%	50%	97.89%	85.49%	56.08%	3.86%
95.40%	81.85%	55.26%	4.22%	60%	98.60%	89.33%	60.01%	3.29%
98.14%	87.88%	61.01%	3.38%	70%	99.29%	93.82%	65.55%	2.49%
98.75%	88.41%	58.56%	3.40%	RA	99.39%	93.82%	62.65%	2.55%
	Bullet			AM		CPR		

Table 17.4 Expected loss for the different tranches of a CDO of ABSs for different amortization profiles (linear and quadratic) and different recovery rates assumptions: 0%, 40%, 50%, 60%, 70% and the rating agency recovery rate

0.00%	0.10%	3.10%	10.00%	A	0.00%	0.10%	3.10%	10.00%
	$\rho = 90\%$					$\rho = 90\%$		
58.92%	42.89%	29.90%	7.82%	0	51.27%	38.42%	27.43%	8.22%
76.10%	56.82%	39.10%	6.38%	40%	68.75%	51.59%	36.38%	6.81%
82.69%	62.98%	43.05%	5.75%	50%	75.64%	57.59%	40.43%	6.25%
90.09%	71.05%	48.20%	4.95%	60%	83.89%	65.15%	45.49%	5.44%
97.30%	81.97%	55.24%	3.83%	70%	94.71%	76.60%	52.71%	4.29%
98.11%	82.05%	52.33%	3.85%	RA	97.04%	77.75%	50.32%	4.33%
	$\rho = 75\%$					$\rho = 75\%$		
73.10%	53.95%	35.35%	7.05%	0	66.65%	50.37%	33.54%	7.34%
86.15%	66.28%	43.83%	5.65%	40%	80.98%	62.07%	41.55%	6.06%
90.29%	71.11%	47.25%	5.15%	50%	85.96%	67.16%	45.23%	5.57%
94.49%	77.62%	51.92%	4.44%	60%	91.15%	73.37%	49.60%	4.85%
98.25%	86.30%	58.63%	3.44%	70%	96.87%	82.23%	56.38%	3.85%
98.56%	86.26%	56.45%	3.46%	RA	97.90%	82.81%	54.36%	3.84%
	3 Factors					3 Factors		
88.16%	68.97%	43.59%	5.81%	0	84.40%	66.19%	42.10%	6.04%
94.97%	78.59%	51.10%	4.71%	40%	92.91%	75.97%	49.48%	5.01%
96.59%	82.22%	54.29%	4.28%	50%	95.08%	79.42%	52.34%	4.59%
97.97%	86.39%	58.13%	3.67%	60%	97.09%	83.86%	56.30%	4.00%
99.06%	91.85%	63.99%	2.85%	70%	98.75%	89.62%	62.15%	3.16%
99.21%	91.94%	61.45%	2.90%	RA	99.01%	89.98%	59.68%	3.21%
	Linear			AM		Quadratic		

to a 1-factor MC simulation with 90% and 75% flat correlations, while the lower refers to the multifactor MC using the Fitch correlation function.

Within the same amortization profile comparing the upper and mid tables for a given recovery rate the losses of the equity (senior) tranches decrease (increase) with higher flat correlation. For the case of the multifactor model the maximum value of the correlation is 75% indicating that, in general, the correlation level is lower than the 75% flat for the 1-factor model. This means that indeed for a given recovery rate the equity (senior) tranche will have higher (lower) losses than in the case of the 1-factor model. For a given amortization profile and within the same simulation approach we observe that as the bond prices are fixed, unless the recovery rate reaches a too high value incompatible with bond prices, we know that the total loss is independent of the recovery rate. It implies that increasing recovery rates will shift the losses from the senior tranches to the equity tranches.

As can be expected from Figure 17.1 the impact of the different amortization profiles on the expected loss of the tranches in increasing (decreasing) order of losses for the senior (equity) tranche is the following: CPR, linear, quadratic and bullet. Observe that the impact of the amortization profiles on the supersenior tranche is huge. As an example, using the rating agency recovery rate there is a decrease of 25% when one moves from bullet to CPR amortization assumption and the multifactor model. Observe that the nonarbitrage conditions are satisfied see Chapter 11 or Garcia and Goossens (2008) for details. In particular, note that the relative loss – that is, the loss divided by tranche size – decreases as one moves up the capital structure.

The impact of the amortization profile is large. As an example we compare the expected losses on the super senior tranche for the RA 3-factor model configuration. We find 3.40% for the bullet profile, 2.55% for the CPR profile, 2.90% for the linear profile and finally 3.21% for the quadratic amortization profile.

17.7   CONCLUSIONS

In this chapter we have outlined a traditional Gaussian copula-based simulation model to price tranches of a CDO of ABSs. For each individual ABS in the collateral the probability of default is implied from observed ABS bond price with a flat default intensity. Results have been shown for four different assumptions of amortization profiles that are each calibrated to market observed average lives of the ABSs. Detailed analysis has been done for the sensitivity of the expected loss, spreads, risky duration and default intensity for different assumptions of recovery rates and amortization profiles. Additionally, the same sort of detailed sensitivity studies has been done for the pricing of tranches of a CDO of ABSs.

18

More Standardized Credit Indices: ABX, TABX, CMBX, LCDX, LevX

Keep away from people who try to belittle your ambitions. Small people always do that, but the really great make you feel that you, too, can become great.

Mark Twain

18.1 INTRODUCTION

In Chapter 8 we gave a brief description of the corporate standardized credit indices. The corporate indices have brought liquidity to the underlying asset class besides serving the purpose of hedging corporate credit instruments. Many practitioners, for example, take the deterioration on the XOver spreads as an early signal of generalized market deterioration. In this chapter, we describe the ABX.HE index and its tranches TABX.HE, the standardized credit instruments for subprime home equity MBS. Similar to the corporate case the indices have been introduced to bring liquidity to the underlying asset class and to serve as a hedge for portfolios of subprime MBS.

In June 2007 the market was developing structured finance indices for many asset classes such as credit card receivables, auto loans and student loans. The idea has always been that the *innovation* behind the indices bring liquidity to the underlying asset class.

In Chapter 22 we show that these indices are important instruments for identifying the deterioration on the subprime MBS market. We think that after the normalization of the market those indices will serve as important mechanisms for the price discovery process for the underlying asset class.

The remainder of this chapter is organized as follows. In Section 18.2 we describe the ABX.HE indices and its tranches, TABX.HE. In Section 18.3 we go into less detail on LevX/LCDX and its underlying asset class. The CMBX and ECMBX indices are briefly outlined in Section 18.4. In Section 18.5 we show that these indices served as early indicators of what was to come.

18.2 ABX AND TABX

The indices serve several purposes. The hope has been that, analogous to what happened with the corporate credit indices iTraxx and CDX, the ABX.HE and TABX.HE indices would bring liquidity to the underlying asset class. With liquidity in place one would be able to extend to the MBS market the same sort of investment strategies that exist for the corporate market.

The indices can be used as benchmarks for MBS portfolio managers. The tranches in TABX.HE bring the opportunity to take views on the possible losses underlying the indices. One could also take an inter-asset class position by, for example, buying LevX and/or LCDX positions while selling ABX.HE and/or TABX.HE protection. As a matter of fact, we are aware that after the deterioration of the credit market in June 2007, market participants had taken positions in the LCDX index expecting similarities with the ABX.HE index. Knowledgeable investors could take a capital protected leveraged position in the indices via a CPPI strategy (see Chapter 15), using the indices as the asset class. Investors may take views on different vintages, e.g. selling protection on the 2005 vintage while buying protection on the 2007 vintage, through the different indices of ABX.HE. The indices also bring the possibility for *dispersion trades* – that is, buying protection on the index while selling protection on some individual references.

Two very important and interconnected uses of the indices are hedging and price discovery, both related to a *dynamic credit portfolio management* framework for financial institutions, which is treated in Chapter 23. For those purposes one needs standardized models to be used for evaluating sensitivities and standardized market techniques for *mapping* the expected loss of a bespoke portfolio on the expected loss of the indices. The first issue is addressed in Chapter 19 and the second in Chapter 12.

We limit ourselves here to the essentials required to understand the pricing approach presented in Chapter 19. For a practitioner-oriented approach to modeling mortgage defaults we refer to Hayre et al. (2008). For a more general and recent reference on mortgage and mortgage-backed securities we refer to Fabozzi et al. (2007), for a more specialized reference on subprime mortgage and mortgage-backed securities we refer to Goodman et al. (2008).

18.2.1   The ABX index

The ABX.HE is the standardized credit index for subprime home equity mortgages. It began trading on 19 January 2006. From its inception the purpose of the index has been to bring *liquidity*, *transparency*, standardization and market consensus for pricing purposes. Liquidity comes from the standardization of the necessary documentation, support from the dealer community, and the use of the index as a mechanism for pricing discovery and portfolio management of bespoke portfolios. The ISDA ABCDS documentation was completed in 2005 and one year later (January 2006) the ABX.HE index was launched. The absence of a standard pricing algorithm with transparent input parameters is very important for understanding the whole mechanism which led to the credit crunch that began in June 2007 and will be treated in more detail in Chapter 22.

The constituency of the ABX.HE series can be seen in Figure 18.1. The ABX.HE index has the following characteristics:

1. *Amount of issuances in the collateral.* The underlying collateral is built with a static pool of CDSs on subprime MBSs. Underlying each ABX.HE series are 20 CDSs on MBSs having the same rating. Until the 2007 credit crunch a new series was launched every six months. As a result of the credit crunch there were insufficient issuances to build the ABX.HE 08–1. Instead of changing the criteria to build a new index the issuers decided to postpone the creation of a new index until the markets' return.
2. *On the rating of the series.* For each series there are six ABX indices referencing PENAAA, AAA, AA, A, BBB and BBB-. As a consequence for any MBS to be included in the index it needs to have tranches with all the six ratings. For example, the ABX.HE AAA 06–1 has 20 CDSs on AAA subprime MBSs tranches originated in the second semester of 2005. Analogously the ABX.HE AA 07–2 has 20 CDSs on AA subprime MBSs originated in the first semester of 2007. So the MBSs referenced by the ABCDSs in the collateral of ABX.HE must be from within a six month period of the launch of the index. Unlike the iTraxx/CDX indices there is *no overlap* between any two consecutive ABX series.

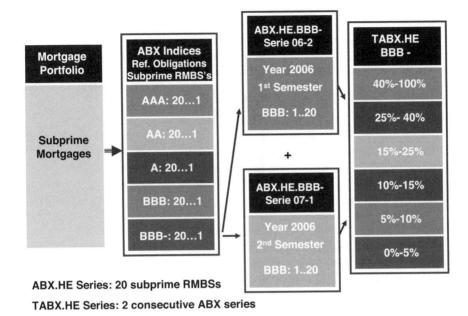

Figure 18.1   ABX.HE and TABX.HE BBB- standardized credit indices for the US home equity subprime MBS market

3. *Some characteristics of the collateral.*
   - The choice for the reference entities underlying the index is made by a dealer consortium that chooses 20 deals among the 25 largest subprime home equity issuers.
   - One originator cannot have more than four deals in one index.
   - A master servicer cannot have more than six deals.
   - The offering size of any deal cannot be lower than USD 500 million.
   - At least 90% of the assets in the deals needs to be 1st lien mortgage.
   - The WAFICO should be at least 660. (WAFICO stands for weighted average FICO score of the mortgage pool. Fair Isaacs and Company was among the first institution to generate credit scores for mortgages back in the 1950s. FICO scores range between 300 and 900. A FICO score of 660 or more is considered good and means one gets a lower rate and does not need high upfront payments. Among the factors affecting the FICO score of a mortgagor are: length of credit card history, employment history, number of credit cards in use, loan history, late or missed payments, underpayments or any possible negative credit information.
   - The floating interest rate should be with respect to one-month LIBOR.
   - The *weighted average life* (WAL) of the AA, A, BBB and BBB- should be at least 4 years, while for the AAA it should be at least 5 years.
   - It must be rated by both Moody's and S&P and the lesser of the rating will be used.
4. *Quotes.* Another difference with the corporate indices is that the ABX.HE is traded on price. Consequently, one cannot imply on the index the prepayment assumptions underlying the pricing algorithm. The implication for pricing purposes is treated in Chapter 19 on pricing TABX.HE tranches.

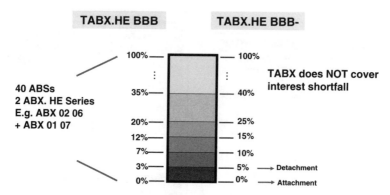

Figure 18.2   TABX.HE BBB and BBB- attachment and detachment points

5. *Credit events.* The contract follows ISDA *pay as you go (PAUG)* convention, treated in Chapter 16, with a fixed cap and cash-only settlement. The ABX.HE index protects against principal writedown and interest shortfall. As a result, the credit events for the ABX.HE index are reversible and are not binary as for the corporate indices.

18.2.2   TABX.HE: the tranches of ABX.HE

The TABX.HE is the standardized credit index for tranches of the ABX.HE index. It was launched in January 2007, about one year after the creation of the ABX indices. Some important points on the TABX.HE index are the following:

1. *Number of references.* The underlying TABX.HE references consist of 40 CDSs on sub-prime MBSs that are in two consecutive ABX.HE series.
2. *The series.* Currently there are two TABX.HE series: one is based on the ABX.HE.BBB and the other is based on the ABX.HE.BBB- series. The detailed form of the indices and their attachment and detachment points is shown in Figure 18.2.
3. *Payment frequency.* The tranche payments occur on a monthly basis.
4. *Legal aspects.*
   - Standardized TABX.HE tranches use ISDA PAUG convention with principal writedown and shortfall credit events.
   - Unlike ABX.HE, TABX.HE *does not cover interest shortfall.*
   - Credit events are reversible and prone to receive reimbursements.
   - Their legal maturity is equal to the maturity of the longest ABCDS in the pool.
5. *Amortization and defaults.* The prepayment of the collateral will first go to the most senior tranche and then go down the capital structure towards the equity tranche. For defaults, on the other hand, the order is reversed, from the equity tranche up towards the super senior tranche. The consequence is that the duration of the different tranches represents a balance between prepayment and defaults.
6. *Basis risk.* For the iTraxx/CDX indices the risk covered by the whole index is equal to the sum of the risk taken by the tranches. The fact the TABX tranches do not cover interest shortfall brings a *basis risk* with respect to the underlying indices. That is, the sum of the protection on the tranches will not be equal to the protection on the whole index.

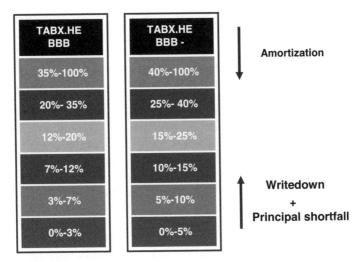

Figure 18.3 Amortization

The TABX.HE tranches bring the possibility of taking trading positions in the capital structure of the index collateral, e.g. long the tranche [5% − 10%] while short the tranche [10% − 15%].

A CDO of ABS can be compared to TABX.HE in order to highlight the standardization issues underlying the indices. In a CDO of ABS one may have tranches of different ratings, sectors and maturities. As we have seen in Chapter 14, many of the structures present a waterfall to divert cash, from both interest and principal, to the senior notes in case the performance of the collateral deteriorates. Additionally, CDO of ABS may be managed and they do not have standardized attachment and detachment points. The collateral portfolio does not need to have a fixed number of references, and exposure for each name does not need to be the same. ABX and TABX, on the other hand, are static indices, with tranches coming from the same rating with standard maturities, and the same exposure per collateral reference. Additionally, the indices do not have a waterfall and the priority of payments and losses is very simple; losses start to affect the lower tranches while incoming cash is paid to the higher tranches first as shown in Figure 18.3.

It should be clear that there is not yet a standardized market model for ABX/TABX. We discuss this point further in Chapter 19.

18.3 LEVX AND LCDX

In analogy with iTraxx and CDX for corporates, and ABX for the subprime for the MBS market, LCDX and LevX are the standardized credit indices for the leveraged loan market. The ISDA published the Syndicated Secured LCDS Standard Term Supplement on 8 June 2006. Nearly one year later, on 22 May 2007, the LCDX index was launched together with modifications on the ISDA standard. On 10 October 2007 the TLCDX was launched: the tranches on LCDX. On 30 July 2007 it was time to launch the European LCDS standard. On 20 September 2006 the LevX was launched as the standardized credit index for the European LBO market.

The iTraxx LevX is composed of a Senior Index with 75 equally-weighted LCDS for 1st Lien, and a Subordinated Index with 45 equally-weighted LCDS for 2nd/3rd Lien. The contracts are non-cancelable with semi-annual portfolio rolls, quarterly coupons and a 5-year maturity.

The LCDX is composed of 100 equally-weighted single name loan CDSs, called LCDSs. Both indices are traded over the counter and the same applies to the underlying LCDSs. There are two credit events that trigger a payout by the protection seller: bankruptcy and failure to pay an underlying loan after a grace period. As LCDSs have no restructuring clausula the same applies to the index. Once a credit event occurs and until the date it is settled the index may continue trading in two formats, with and without the defaulted reference.

The credit event may be settled in two ways: cash or physical delivery. In the case of physical settlement the deliverable obligations should be 1st Lien loans. The LCDSs underlying the index are on 1st Lien loans. Note that the lower the quality of the underlying loan the higher the risk of prepayment (duration reduction), and the lower could be the liquidity of the index, including revolvers and term loans. They must be syndicated secured loans and be listed on the Syndicated Secured Loan List used by dealer polls as references in the LCDS contracts. In physical settlement the protection seller receives the underlying loan and pays par. Although the method is standard it has a difficulty when the notional on the outstanding loan is not the same as in the LCDS. Moreover, not every counterparty on the index may be able to receive the underlying loan. Additionally, the position on the index may not match in one way or another the position on a loan. For LCDS cash settlements the classical mechanism is used – that is, the recovery price to be paid by the protection seller is determined in an auction process.

For more information on these indices we refer to MarkIt (www.markit.com).

18.4   CMBX AND ECMBX

The CMBX is the index for US commercial mortgage backed securities. The size of the market is significantly lower than the one for the ABX. The index consists of 25 commercial MBSs and, as with the ABX, there are six separate indices for each series: CMBX AAA, AA, A, BBB, BBB- and BB. It rolls twice a year on the 25 April and October. Unlike ABX.HE for which prices are quoted, spreads are quoted for this index.

The references obligations must be either debt or pass-through with a pool of fixed rated mortgages. The obligations must be secured and issued within the last two years. The offering size must be at least USD 700 million. A maximum of 40% of the obligations may come from one state, and only up to 60% of the same property type. The factor should be one. The AAA index references the bond from each deal that is composed of the most credit enhanced tranche, with the longest average life and it must reference publicly issued securities. The AA, A, BBB and BBB- may refer to publicly or privately issued securities. The securities must be rated by at least two of the three following rating agencies: Moody's, S&P and Fitch.

18.5   INDICES AS INDICATORS

Figure 18.4 shows the prices of the ABX.HE.BBB- indices for all four vintages: 6–1, 6–2, 7–1 and 7–2. Observe that the prices of the ABX.HE.BBB- indices were already falling in January and February 2007. They reached a local minimum of 77.81, 63.16 and 62.25 for the 6–1, 6–2 and 7–1 vintages respectively on 27 February 2007. That day is known as *the Chinese Correction* or *Black Tuesday In China* as the SSE Composite Index of the Shanghai Stock

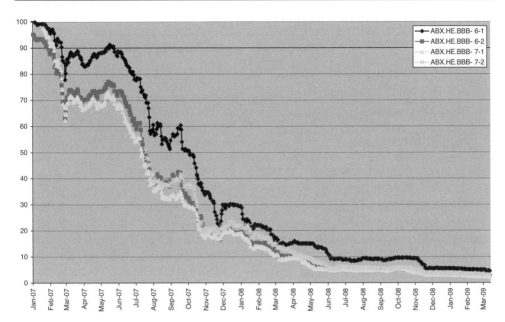

Figure 18.4   ABX.HE.BBB- prices

Exchange tumbled 9%, the largest drop in 10 years. That day marked a regime shift, which can also be seen in the VIX, that is the CBOE SPX volatility index.

The prices of the ABX.HE.AAA indices are shown in Figure 18.5 for all the four vintages. These indices showed only a negligible reaction to the Chinese Correction. They reacted half a year later, when it became completely systemic.

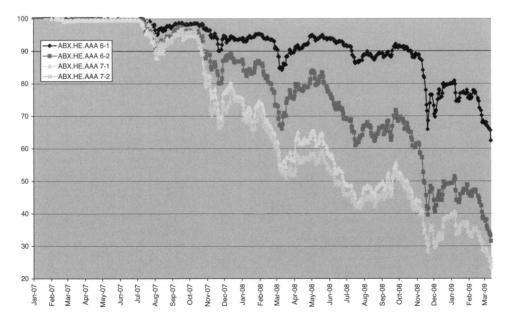

Figure 18.5   ABX.HE.AAA prices

Table 18.1   Delinquencies in ABX.HE pools (in %)

	06-1	06-2	07-1	07-2
30–59 days	5.56	6.14	6.03	7.17
60–89 days	3.24	3.54	3.95	4.54
90+ days	9.08	8.67	12.08	10.63
Bankruptcy	3.52	3.00	2.63	2.20
Foreclosure	16.17	19.39	17.89	17.93
REO	9.58	10.56	8.83	7.90
Total 60+	41.59	45.16	45.37	43.21

February 2007 data served as an early indicator for the deterioration. February 2009 data quantifies the decline. Table 18.1 shows the delinquencies in the ABX.HE pools for the February 2009 collection period. Across all vintages an astonishing 45% is 60 days delinquent or worse, with nearly 10% being real estate owned (REO) and approximately 18% being foreclosed. Table 18.2 shows the rating by Moody's and S&P of the ABX.HE 07–2 constituents. Some of those are even on watch negative. Stating that there have been some rating migrations is a euphemism.

Figure 18.6 shows the spreads of the CMBX.NA indices with the lowest rating in every series, that is BBB- for the 1-1 series and BB for the series 2-1, 3-1, 4-1 and 5-1. A detail of this graph, focusing on the BBB- 1-1 and BB 2-1 spreads in 2007, is shown in Figure 18.7. The BBB- 1–1 index nearly doubled and the BB 2-1 index jumped by little over 100 bp on 27 February 2007. Since then, these indices have been widening to a whopping several thousand basis points.

Table 18.2   ABX.HE 07-2 constituent ratings by Moody's and S&P

PENAAA		AAA		AA		A		BBB		BBB-	
Ca	B	Ca	B	C	CCC	C	CC	C	D		D
Caa2	AAA	Caa2	AAA	C	B	C	CCC	C	CCC	C	CCC
Ca	BB	Ca	B	C	CCC	C	CCC	C	CC	C	CC
Caa3	BBB	Ca	BB	C	CCC	C	CCC	C	CCC	C	CC
Ca	B+	Ca	B	C	CCC	C	CCC	C	D	C	D
Ca	AA	Ca	A	C	CCC	C	CCC	C	D	C	D
Caa2	BBB	Caa3	BB-	C	CCC	C	CCC	C	CCC	C	CC
Ca	AA	C	BB	C	CCC	C	CCC	C	D	C	D
Aa3	BBB	A2	BBB	Ba1	B-	Caa2	CCC	C	CCC	C	CCC
Ca	B-	Ca	B-	C	CCC	C	CCC	C	CC	C	CC
Ca	B	Ca	B	C	CCC	C	CCC	C	CC	C	CC
Caa1	BBB	Caa2	B	C	CCC	C	CCC	C	CCC	C	CC
B1	BBB	B2	BB	C	CCC	C	CCC	C	CCC	C	CCC
Ca	AAA	Ca	AAA	C	BBB	C	CCC	C	D	C	D
Caa2	B	Caa2	B	C	CCC	C	CCC	C	CC	C	CC
B2	AA	B3	BBB	C	CCC	C	CCC	C	CCC	C	CC
Caa3	BBB	Ca	B	C	CCC	C	CCC	C	CCC	C	D
Ba2	AAA	B2	AAA	C	B	C	CCC	C	CCC	C	CC
Caa1	BB	Caa2	BB	C	CCC	C	CCC	C	CCC	C	CC
Ca	B	Ca	B	C	CCC	C	CCC	C	D	C	D

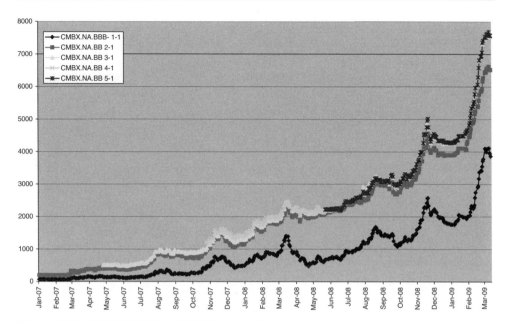

Figure 18.6 CMBX.NA BB and BBB- 1-1 spreads

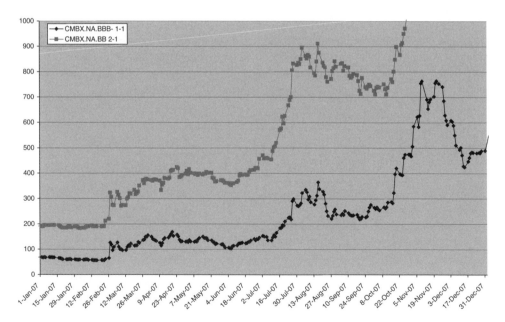

Figure 18.7 CMBX.NA BBB- 1-1 and BB 2-1 spreads in 2007

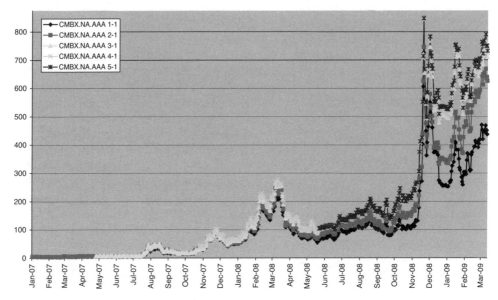

Figure 18.8 CMBX.NA AAA spreads

Figure 18.8 shows the spreads of the CMBX.NA.AAA indices for all the five series. Observe that these indices also had only a negligible reaction to the Chinese Correction. They reacted half a year later, when it became completely systemic.

The deterioration can be quantified by looking at the number of rating downgrades. Table 18.3 shows these numbers for the CMBX.NA indices for all the five series and the different ratings. Observe that there are 25 components in these indices, so the second and third series have seen 80% of the collateral being downgraded, except for the AAA rated deals. For the fourth and fifth series these percentages are 60% and 40% respectively.

Table 18.3   Rating downgrades in CMBX.NA

	1	2	3	4	5
AAA	0	0	0	0	0
AJ	1	19	19	15	9
AA	1	19	19	15	9
A	2	20	21	16	9
BBB	4	20	22	17	9
BBB-	7	21	22	17	10
BB		21	23	16	10

19

1-factor Models for the ABS Correlation Market Pricing TABX Tranches

Follow the course opposite to custom and you will almost always do well.
Jean-Jacques Rousseau

19.1 INTRODUCTION

In Chapter 8 we discussed the corporate standardized credit indices and in Chapters 9, 10 and 11 we discussed pricing issues of those instruments. In Chapter 18 we described more recent standardized credit indices with focus on ABX.HE and TABX.HE, the standardized credit indices for subprime MBSs.

When pricing TABX we are confronted with three sorts of difficulties. First, the instruments underlying the contract are CDSs on ABSs and, contrary to the corporate CDS case, their prices are not readily available. Second, a more fundamental issue is that the notional underlying the contract is amortizing. The amortization schedule depends on the assumptions of *prepayment* on the mortgage pool and one possible estimation of the prepayment is available on the remittance report of the underlying ABS. Third, market participants have not (yet) agreed on a standard algorithm to price these indices.

The purpose of this chapter is to adapt the recursive algorithm, described in Chapter 9, to price the TABX tranches by using both the Gaussian copula and the Lévy base correlation methods. Additionally, the proposed approach takes into account the amortization schedule to price TABX. We will assume the prepayments are as given in the remittance reports.

The remainder of this chapter is organized as follows. In Section 19.2 we review the generic 1-factor model for valuation of CDO tranches and define Lévy base correlation. Valuation formulas for both the ABS bond and the CDS on it are given in Section 19.3. In Section 19.4 we describe a simplified version of the model in order to explain the sensitivity to the input parameters. In Section 19.5 we show the results using the simplifications described in Section 19.4. Results related to prepayment assumptions and model calibration are given in Section 19.6. In Section 19.7 the implications of this pricing model are discussed. Finally, our conclusions are presented in Section 19.8.

19.2 GENERIC 1-FACTOR MODEL

We briefly review the framework described in Section 9.2. Consider a portfolio of N names and fix a time horizon T. It is standard market practice to assume the default process follows an inhomogeneous Poisson process and as such for any $0 \leq t \leq T$ the default times τ_i and default intensities $\lambda_i(t)$, $i = 1, \ldots, N$, satisfy

$$\mathbb{P}(\tau_i > t) = \exp\left(-\int_0^t \lambda_i(u)\mathrm{d}u\right) \tag{19.1}$$

where $\mathbb{P}$ is the risk-neutral probability measure. In a 1-factor model of portfolio defaults, a single systemic factor X is introduced, conditional upon which all default probabilities are independent. The single name survival probabilities $\mathbb{P}(\tau_i > t)$ are typically implied from the credit default swap (CDS) market. The fair spread of a CDS balances the present value (PV) of the contingent leg, that is the present value of losses in case of defaults, and the present value of the fee leg.

The key step in valuing CDO tranches is to compute the joint loss distribution. In the recursion algorithm one computes a discretized version of the conditional loss distribution by means of a simple recursion formula. The unconditional loss distribution is found by integrating over the market factor. Analogous to the CDS case, the fair spread of a CDO tranche balances the present value of the fee leg and the present value of the contingent leg. In the base correlation framework, the expected loss on a tranche [A–D] is computed as the difference of the expected loss of two equity tranches [0–D] and [0–A]:

$$EL[A-D] = \mathbb{E}L[0-D; \rho_D] - \mathbb{E}L[0-A; \rho_A]. \tag{19.2}$$

In *latent variable* models default occurs when a certain variable A_i falls below a threshold K_i which is implied from CDS prices. The so-called *market* or *systemic* factor X and the *idiosyncratic* factor $X^{(i)}$ are random variables whose functional form depends on model assumptions. In the generic 1-factor Lévy model the latent variable is represented as

$$A_i = X_\rho + X_{1-\rho}^{(i)}, \quad i = 1, \ldots, N, \tag{19.3}$$

where X and $X^{(i)}$ are independent and identically distributed variates and each A_i has the same (infinitely divisible) distribution function H_1. Note that for $i \neq j$, we have $\mathrm{Corr}[A_i, A_j] = \rho$. The threshold implied from the CDS risk-neutral probability of defaults is given by

$$K_i(t) = H_1^{[-1]}(p_i(t)). \tag{19.4}$$

The conditional default probability of firm i given the value y for the systemic factor is given by

$$p_i(y; t) = H_{1-\rho}(K_i(t) - y). \tag{19.5}$$

We consider two choices for the distributions of the latent variables. First, note that the classical Gaussian copula model is a special case of this generic 1-factor model, in which the normal distribution is used. Second, we use a shifted Gamma distribution and set $X_t = \sqrt{a}t - G_t$, in which G_t follows a Gamma $(at, \sqrt{a})$ distribution so that $\mathbb{E}[X_1] = 0$ and $\mathrm{Var}[X_1] = 1$. Both the cumulative distribution function $H_t(x; a)$ of X_t, and its inverse $H_t^{[-1]}(y; a)$, can easily be obtained from the Gamma cumulative distribution function and its inverse.

Lévy base correlation is defined as the base correlation in the shifted Gamma model with fixed $a = 1$. A comparison with the Gaussian base correlation can be found in Garcia and Goossens (2007). Arbitrage-free interpolation techniques for base correlation methods based on base expected loss have been described by Garcia and Goossens (2008).

19.3 AMORTIZING BOND AND CDS

The standard recursive approach using 1-factor Gaussian copula and Lévy has been discussed in Chapter 9. In this section we give valuation formulas for an ABS bond and its CDS. As mentioned earlier, the main difference with respect to the corporate case is that, due to amortization and prepayment, the notionals are time-dependent. Assume the amortized (ABS) bond is a floater paying a coupon C above Libor. Its value B is computed as

$$B = \sum_{i=1}^{n} N_i(L_i + C)d(t_i)P_S(t_i)\Delta t_i + P_S(t_n)d(t_n)N_n$$

$$+ \sum_{i=1}^{n-1} (N_i - N_{i+1})d(t_i)P_S(t_i) + R\sum_{i=1}^{n} N_i d(t_i)(P_S(t_{i-1}) - P_S(t_i)) \quad (19.6)$$

In these equations the summations run over the payment dates t_i. We denote by L_i, N_i, $P_S(t_i)$ and $d(t_i)$ the LIBOR rate, the notional, the survival probability and the risk-free discount factor respectively at time t_i. The recovery rate is R, and $\Delta t_i = t_i - t_{i-1}$ is the year fraction.

The value of the amortized CDS, paying a spread S on notionals N_i is computed as

$$C = (1 - R)\sum_{i=1}^{n} N_i d(t_i)(P_S(t_{i-1}) - P_S(t_i)) - S\sum_{i=1}^{n} N_i d(t_i)P_S(t_i)\Delta t_i. \quad (19.7)$$

The fair spread of a CDS balances the present value of the contingent leg, that is the present value of losses in case of defaults, and the present value of the fee leg.

19.4 A SIMPLE MODEL FOR AMORTIZATION AND PREPAYMENT

In this section we look at a simple model for amortization and prepayment and study the impact on survival probability, duration and expected loss for a fixed price of the amortizing bond.

We make the following assumptions. A simple day counter is used so that the payment times $t_i = i\Delta t$, are integer multiples of the constant year fraction Δt. The notionals at the payment times are given by

$$N_i = N(t_i) = \exp(-\lambda_{Not}i\,\Delta t) = n^i, \quad (19.8)$$

where λ_{Not} is the constant amortization factor, modeling *both the scheduled amortization as well as prepayments*. The discount factors are assumed to be given by

$$d(t_i) = \exp(-ri\,\Delta t) = d^i, \quad (19.9)$$

corresponding to a flat interest rate r. The default intensity λ_{Surv} is constant, so that the survival probability is given by

$$q(t_i) = \exp(-\lambda_{Surv}i\,\Delta t) = q^i. \quad (19.10)$$

We define the constant α as the product of these three factors

$$\alpha = dnq. \quad (19.11)$$

In this chapter we assume that the recovery rate $R = 0$ is zero. The price of the bond is

$$B = ((r + C)\Delta t + (1 - n))\frac{\alpha}{1 - \alpha}. \quad (19.12)$$

Figure 19.1 shows the survival probability versus the amortization after one year for a fixed bond price. The expected loss versus the amortization is shown in Figure 19.2. Finally,

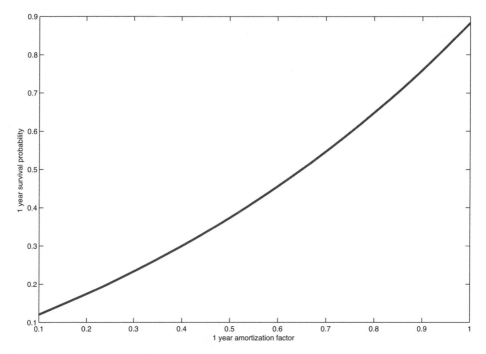

Figure 19.1   Survival probability versus prepayment for a fixed bond price

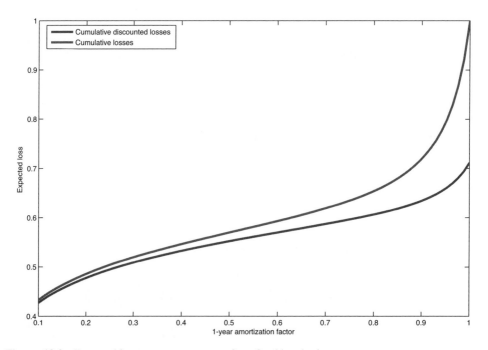

Figure 19.2   Expected loss versus prepayment for a fixed bond price

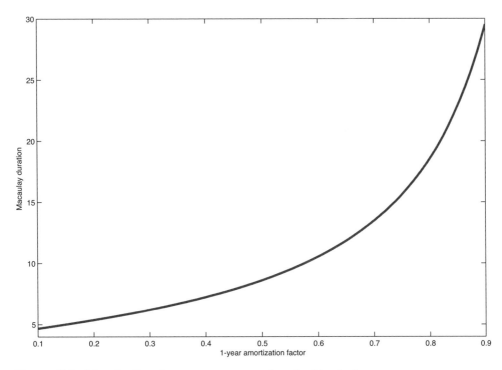

Figure 19.3 Macaulay Duration versus prepayment for a fixed bond price

Figure 19.3 shows the Macaulay Duration versus the amortization. The following parameters were used to generate the figures. The bond price was $B = 40\%$, the coupon was $C = 2\%$ above the interest rate $r = 5\%$, and the year fraction was taken to be $\Delta t = 1/12$, corresponding to monthly payments. We conclude that for a given *fixed* bond price, if amortization increases, the duration goes down, the expected loss goes down and the survival probability goes down.

Prepayment speeds are generally available for ABS instruments. An open question is whether the prepayment assumption available in remittance reports match those embedded in the prices of synthetic traded instruments. The rest of this chapter is devoted to this question.

19.5   ABX.HE CREDIT INDEX

The ABX.HE is the index for subprime home equity mortgages. A new series is supposed to be issued every six months. However, Markit has delayed the launch of the ABX.HE 08-01 series due to limited availability of candidate underlyings as a result of the credit crunch related to subprime home equity. Five ABX.HE indices have been created, corresponding to the ratings: AAA, AA, A, BBB and BBB-. The portfolio is static and consists of 20 CDSs on subprime MBS. Hence it is unfunded. TABX is the instrument for the tranches of ABX.HE, and it has only been defined for the BBB and BBB- rated indices, respectively TABX.HE.BBB and TABX.HE.BBB-. The collateral pool for the TABX series is composed of two successive ABX.HE pools, that is 40 CDSs on subprime MBSs. An important difference between ABX and TABX is that ABX covers interest shortfall, while TABX does not. Figure 18.1 shows an illustration of ABX and TABX. The naming convention is based on a reference to the vintage.

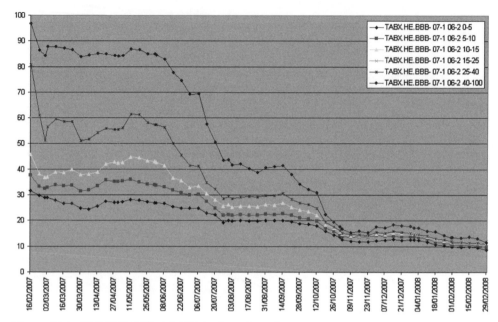

Figure 19.4   TABX.HE.BBB- 06-2 07-1 prices of tranches

ABX.HE 06-2 is the index referencing MBSs issued in the second semester of 2006 and
TABX-HE 07-1 06-2 BBB- refers to ABX.HE.BBB-07-1 and ABX.HE.BBB- 06-2. Figure
18.4 shows historical prices of the ABX.HE.BBB- indices for the series 06-1, 06-2, 07-1 and
07-2. Historical prices of tranches of TABX.HE.BBB- 06-2 07-1 are shown in Figure 19.4,
while Figure 19.5 shows historical prices of tranches of TABX.HE.BBB- 07-1 07-2.

Table 19.1 shows some indicative spreads versus ratings for various instruments. The key
point to note is that the synthetic ABX instruments were trading at distressed levels.

When pricing TABX we have run into several difficulties. The pricing algorithm needs
quotes of CDS on ABS as an input for the evaluation of default probabilities. A first difficulty
is that those quotes are not readily available. When quotes are available, it is only a single
quote, corresponding to the legal maturity. Hence we do not have a term structure of quotes
for different maturities. For this reason we have used bond prices of the underlying ABSs to
imply default probabilities.

A second difficulty is that there is *no market accepted standard approach* to determine the
prepayment for pricing purposes. The prepayment assumptions are key to the pricing algorithm
as will become clear. In this case we took prepayment assumptions from the remittance reports.
Additionally, we varied the prepayment assumptions to cope with much more stressed scenarios
that may be priced in by market participants.

A third difficulty is related to the order of the calibration process. Both a bottom up approach,
starting from the equity tranche and moving up the capital structure, or a top down approach,
starting from the super senior and moving down the capital structure, can be applied to calibrate
to the observed prices. At the time of pricing the senior tranches of TABX were the most liquid
ones. Hence these quotes are more reliable, making the top down approach seem the preferred
choice. For the corporate indices (iTraxx and CDX), however, the standard approach is bottom
up. We have applied both bottom up and top down calibration.

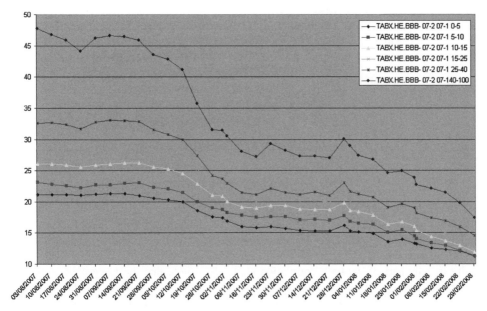

Figure 19.5   TABX.HE.BBB- 07-1 07-2 prices of tranches

Table 19.1   Typical spreads (in bp in summer 2007) versus ratings for different instruments

	06-1	06-2	07-1	07-2	CDS	Cash
AAA	53	103	116	164	n/a	48
AA	216	473	658	613	n/a	225
A	649	1323	1733	1655	700	800
BBB	1800	2490	2547	2406	900	900
BBB-	2510	3062	3007	2508	1200	1200

In the next section we give some results obtained with our pricing algorithm. We also discuss the implications for the securitization business model for banks and for the whole financial system in general.

19.6   PREPAYMENT AND MODEL CALIBRATION

In this section we present results using both the Gaussian copula and the Lévy base correlation method for TABX 06-02 07-01. The market data was taken on 10 August 2007 and is shown in Table 19.2. We have assumed that the prepayment speeds for the bond and the CDS on it are equal

$$\text{CPR}_{\text{CDS}} = \text{CPR}_{\text{Bond}} \qquad (19.13)$$

and that the same holds for the default intensities

$$\lambda_{\text{CDS}} = \lambda_{\text{Bond}}. \qquad (19.14)$$

Table 19.2   Prices of TABX-HE 07-1 06-2 BBB- and TABX-HE 07-2 07-1 BBB- tranches

07-1 spread	Aug 10 price	Oct 26 price	tranche	07-2 spread	Oct 26 price
500	20.05	14.46	0–5	500	17.57
500	22.36	15.85	5–10	500	18.96
500	25.77	17.19	10–15	500	21.09
500	28.77	18.17	15–25	500	23.10
267	29.11	17.67	25–40	500	24.20
72	41.99	19.38	40–100	410	31.50

Figure 19.6 shows the results of the base correlation for the bottom up approach. In this case the [0%–5%] tranche price determines $\rho(5\%)$, the base correlation parameter at the 5% attachment point, the [5%–10%] tranche price determines $\rho(10\%)$ and so on. Observe that the base correlation curves for both methods have the same shape. Both are decreasing with increasing attachment points, corresponding to tranches with equity behavior. This is the equity tranche part of the base correlation smile. Also note that the Lévy base correlation values are larger than the corresponding Gaussian base correlation values, which is consistent with our findings in our earlier paper (Garcia and Goossens, 2008). In the bottom up approach the [25%–40%] tranche price determines $\rho(40\%)$ and we are left with a big gap between the implied price and the observed price for the [40%–100%] tranche. It turns out that both methods fail to find a value for $\rho(40\%)$ which correctly prices the [40%–100%] tranche,

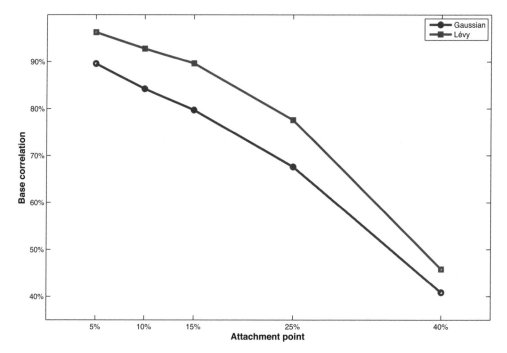

Figure 19.6   Gaussian and Lévy base correlation curves for the bottom up calibration, assuming prepayment speeds as given in remittance reports and default intensities implied from bond prices

given the assumed prepayment speeds and default intensities. We concluded that indeed the prepayment assumptions in the remittance reports do not correspond to the market expectations for prepayments as represented in the super senior part of TABX.

For the top down calibration, we have changed our assumptions. The prepayment speeds and default intensities were modified as follows. The prepayment speeds were assumed to be four times slower:

$$\text{CPR}_{\text{CDS}} = 0.25\text{CPR}_{\text{Bond}} \qquad (19.15)$$

and the default intensities have been doubled:

$$\lambda_{\text{CDS}} = 2\lambda_{\text{Bond}}. \qquad (19.16)$$

We have done this believing that indeed the synthetic instruments were already pricing lower prepayment speeds than reported in the remittance reports (see *IFR Magazine* 13 October 2007 (p. 41): "Lower prepayments are coming").

Figure 19.7 shows the base correlation curves for a top down calibration. Observe that the base correlation curves for both methods have the same shape. Both are increasing with increasing attachment points corresponding to senior tranches like behavior. This is the senior tranches part of the base correlation smile. Also note that the Lévy base correlation values are smaller than the corresponding Gaussian base correlation values, which is consistent with our findings in our earlier paper. Starting from the most liquid tranches one cannot find base correlation values that match the prices of the equity tranches.

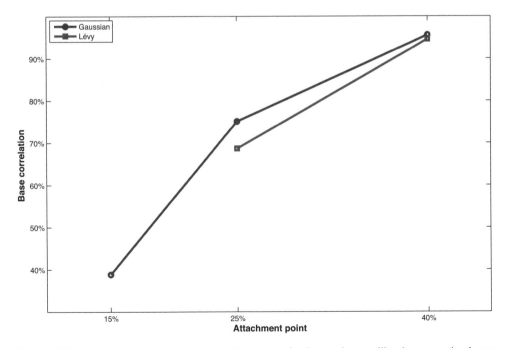

Figure 19.7 Gaussian and Lévy base correlation curves for the top down calibration, assuming lower prepayment speeds and higher default intensities

We can conclude that with a bottom up calibration a big gap between the implied price and the observed price for the most liquid super senior tranche is seen. Calibrating to the observed price for the super senior tranche is not possible with the initial assumptions, based on remittance reports and bond prices. If we assume lower prepayment speeds and higher default intensities, senior tranches can be matched. However, a top down approach with these modified assumptions cannot match the equity and junior mezzanine tranches.

19.7 PRICING MODEL IMPLICATIONS

There are two important points related to TABX tranche pricing: first, the absence of reliable CDS data; second, the prepayment speeds in the remittance reports are too high to generate the amount of losses implied in the tranche quotes.

Note that we are already assuming the recovery rate to be 0. Looking at the corporate indices, we have observed prices on the senior tranches that are too high to be handled by the standard Gaussian copula algorithm.

Pricing the CDX [15%–30%] senior tranche with a base correlation value equal to 100% resulted in a price gap, that is a calibration error, that cannot be neglected, at distressed times, at least with an assumed recovery rate of 40%. A possible solution being proposed by market participants nowadays, is to reduce the recovery rate from 40% to 30% or even 25%. In our TABX pricing here we are already past this point, as the recovery rate is assumed to be 0.

However, given the importance of the MBS market and the securitization activity, we think the market needs to come up with a simplified and uniform assumption for the prepayment, let us call it the *risk neutral prepayment assumption*, for pricing purposes that would bring more transparency to TABX tranches. We discuss this in more detail in what follows.

The recent creation of the standardized credit indices has brought an enormous amount of *technological innovation* to the credit market. Those instruments have helped to increase liquidity in at least two ways. First, on a deal by deal basis they have helped to advance the *price discovery* process of more illiquid bespoke deals. By increasing the transparency in the prices for the whole capital structure, the indices help market participants to have a view on prices for the capital structure of bespoke deals. Second, these liquid indices may be used as a portfolio management tool to completely or partly hedge a credit portfolio. This explains the strong growth those instruments experienced in the period from 2002 until 2007. Observe that in order to hedge or price portions of the capital structure of a credit corporate portfolio one uses the standardized corporate credit indices and their tranches, for which a well known and understood standard methodology is available. During the credit crunch there has been no major problem with CDO tranches of corporates whose indices are well understood and transparent.

A simple example of the mispricing of risk in the CDO of ABS asset class is the following. Table 19.3 shows the typical support levels and thicknesses to attain a certain rating for both an ABS and a CDO in the *pre-credit crunch era*. For the CDO the typical collateral comprised about 100 ABS notes mostly rated BBB and BBB- and about 5% to 10% rated BB. In order to get the AAA rating the tranche would need a subordination level of 20%. Figure 19.4 shows the historical prices of the tranches of TABX.HE.BBB- 06-2 07-1. Observe that the tranche [40%–100%], which has a subordination level of 40%, has been already trading at levels below 90% since March 2007. This means that although from a rating perspective as seen in Table 19.3 TABX.HE [40%–100%] would be rated AAA, the prices were implying a far lower rating. This is the core problem underlying the credit turmoil that began in 2007.

Table 19.3   Typical rating of subprime ABS and of a CDO capital structure

ABS			CDO		
Rating	Thickness	Support	Rating	Thickness	Support
AAA	80%	20%	AAA	80%	20%
AA	5%	15%	AA	10%	10%
A	6%	9%			
BBB+	2%	7%			
BBB	1%	6%	BBB	5%	5%
BBB-	1%	5%			
BB	1%	4%			
Equity	4%	0%	Equity	5%	0%

As discussed in the following chapters, one of the main reasons behind the credit crunch has been the mispricing of the risks of CDO of ABSs. In the case of a portfolio of ABSs, however, there is neither a standard model nor data available to price the standardized credit indices and their tranches. The importance of this point cannot be overstated. The size of the mortgage market is about USD 6–8 trillion. Moreover, the securitization activity has been a key driver for the spectacular increase in efficiency on the use of capital by large financial institutions. The problem with the CDO of ABSs is that the indices have not been transparent enough to offer the same insights as those offered by the corporate indices. In our opinion, transparency in terms of models, data and a standard risk-neutral prepayment assumption for pricing purposes are essential ingredients in the recipe for revitalizing this market.

19.8   CONCLUSIONS

In this chapter we have outlined 1-factor models for TABX tranche pricing. We have shown how to adapt the standard market approach to price TABX using both the Gaussian copula and the Lévy base correlation method. Several hurdles need to be taken before TABX can be priced transparently and hence used efficiently. First, there is only limited data available for the collateral, the CDS being particularly troublesome. Second, an assumption on prepayment is essential for pricing purposes. Using the values available in the remittance report of the underlying ABS, one will not be able to recover observed market prices for the most liquid super senior tranche. Given the size and importance of the securitization activity in general and of the MBS market in particular, we believe that market practitioners need to come up with much more transparency in dealing with the standardized credit indices and its tranches. Those indices are the natural instruments, not only essential for pricing purposes but also for managing a credit portfolio.

Bond Price Implied Spreads

There are two possible outcomes. If the result confirms the hypothesis, then you've made a
measurement. If the result is contrary to the hypothesis, then you've made a discovery.

Enrico Fermi

20.1 INTRODUCTION

Using a no-arbitrage argument the CDS spread implied by the bond's dirty price can be computed. We apply an existing technique for corporate bonds to our one event credit model for ABS. Contrary to a CDS on a corporate bond, a CDS on an ABS does not have the cheapest to deliver option.

A widely accepted definition of the basis is as follows. The basis is the difference between the CDS spread and the asset swap spread (ASW) of the bond referenced by the CDS. This basis should technically be zero by no-arbitrage arguments. In practice it can be nonzero due to several elements, which may include counterparty risk, funding costs and mismatch between ASW and CDS contracts.

Literature on the CDS spread and hence the basis implied from bond prices is available. We refer to Zhou (2008) and references therein for more details. The main assumptions are that the investor funds at LIBOR flat and that there is no counterparty risk. We assume that collateral is posted to mitigate counterparty risk so that counterparty risk does not need to be taken into account. An interesting experiment is to change the funding assumption and assume that the investor needs to fund at a certain margin above LIBOR. Note that CDS spreads are based on LIBOR, which is by definition the relevant curve for AA banks.

We focus here on negative basis trades related to securitization instruments. In this case a basis appears in several places. First between the underlying bonds and their CDSs in the collateral pool, and second between the bond and the CDS related to the tranche. The only observed value for the basis is the one related to the tranche on the settlement date of the trade – that is, for one single bond and not for the bonds in the underlying collateral pool.

20.2 BOND PRICE IMPLIED SPREADS

We consider negative basis trades – that is, both the bond and the corresponding CDS are bought. We observe the bond's dirty price p

$$p = 1 - D, \tag{20.1}$$

where D is the price discount. The bond pays a fixed coupon C. Given an assumed recovery rate R, buying a CDS for a notional of

$$N_{\text{CDS}} = 1 - \frac{D}{(1 - R)} \tag{20.2}$$

results in a default neutral trade. The CDS spread is denoted by S.

This position needs funding to buy the bond. This is done by taking on a loan for a notional of

$$N_{\text{Loan}} = p = 1 - D. \tag{20.3}$$

Initially we assume the funding can be done at LIBOR flat. We denote by $L(t, T)$ the T-maturity forward LIBOR seen at time t.

The cash flows are as follows. Initially there is no net cash flow as the $1-D$ for purchasing the bond is obtained from the loan. Every payment date a coupon C is received and the CDS payment of SN_{CDS} and the loan payment of LN_{Loan} need to be paid, resulting in a net cash flow to the investor of

$$c_{T_i} = \left(C - (1 - D)L(T_{i-1}, T_{i-1}) - \left(1 - \frac{D}{1-R}\right)S \right)\Delta t_i, \tag{20.4}$$

where $\Delta t_i = t_i - t_{i-1}$ is the time fraction and the payment times are denoted by t_i.

On default at time τ the investor receives the recovery rate R on the bond and the loss given default $(1 - D - R)$ from the counterparty of the CDS. On the other hand, the loan for $(1 - D)$ needs to be repaid and the accrued coupon payments need to be made on the CDS and the loan. Consequently, the investor is left to pay accrued CDS coupon and loan interest

$$c_{\tau,T_i} = - \left((1 - D)L(T_{i-1}, T_{i-1}) + \left(1 - \frac{D}{1-R}\right)S \right)(\tau - T_{i-1}) \tag{20.5}$$

where T_i is the payment date immediately preceding the default time τ.

At maturity, the bond pays 1 and the loan of $1 - D$ needs to be repayed, resulting in a net flow of

$$c_M = 1 - (1 - D) = D. \tag{20.6}$$

The expected present value of these cash flows (20.4), (20.5) and (20.6) is zero by no-arbitrage arguments. Hence we have that

$$\mathbb{E}\left[\sum_{i=2}^{N} \left(c_{T_i}d(T_i)\mathbf{1}_{\{\tau > T_i\}} + c_{\tau,T_i}d(\tau)\mathbf{1}_{\{T_{i-1} < \tau \leq T_i\}} \right) + Dd(T_N)\mathbf{1}_{\{\tau > T_N\}} \right] = 0, \tag{20.7}$$

where $d(t)$ denotes the discount factor for time t given by

$$d(t) = \exp\left(- \int_0^t r(u)\mathrm{d}u \right), \tag{20.8}$$

with $r(u)$ the short rate. We define the survival probability as in (4.1)

$$q(t) = \exp\left(- \int_0^t \lambda(u)\mathrm{d}u \right). \tag{20.9}$$

We now turn to the discretization of (20.7). The trapezoidal rule is used to approximate the integrals. Credit spreads and interest rates are assumed to be independent. This is a classical assumption. The derivation also depends on the martingale property of the LIBOR rate.

In the example we have assumed a flat interest rate $r(u) = r$ and a flat credit curve $\lambda(u) = \lambda$. We define the risk-free annuity

$$A = \sum_{i=2}^{N} d(t_i)\Delta t_i, \tag{20.10}$$

where t_1 denotes today and the risk-free average LIBOR is computed as

$$\bar{l} = \frac{1}{A} \sum_{i=2}^{N} L_{i-1} d(t_i)\Delta t_i, \tag{20.11}$$

which in case of a constant rate r becomes

$$\bar{l} = r. \tag{20.12}$$

We define the risky annuities

$$v = \sum_{i=2}^{N} d(t_i)q(t_i)\Delta t_i \tag{20.13}$$

and

$$\bar{v} = \frac{1}{2} \sum_{i=2}^{N} d(t_i) \left(q(t_{i-1}) + q(t_i) \right) \Delta t_i. \tag{20.14}$$

The average risky loan rate is defined as

$$\bar{f} = \frac{1}{2\bar{v}} \sum_{i=2}^{N} L_{i-1} d(t_i) \left(q(t_{i-1}) + q(t_i) \right) \Delta t_i. \tag{20.15}$$

which in case of a constant rate r becomes

$$\bar{f} = r. \tag{20.16}$$

The loss leg is given by

$$l = \frac{1}{2} \sum_{i=2}^{N} \left(d(t_{i-1}) + d(t_i) \right) \left(q(t_{i-1}) - q(t_i) \right). \tag{20.17}$$

The price equation states that the price is equal to the present value of the coupons received, the recovery rate and the final redemption at maturity

$$p = Cv + Rl + d(t_N)q(t_N). \tag{20.18}$$

Note that this depends on the assumption of a bullet amortization scheme.

The CDS spread implied by (20.7) is

$$S = \frac{1}{w} \left(C \frac{v}{\bar{v}} - F + \left(1 - \frac{Rl}{1-D} \right) \frac{D}{\bar{v}} \right) \tag{20.19}$$

where F is the funding cost, equal to the average risky loan rate

$$F = \bar{f} \tag{20.20}$$

where the investor funds at LIBOR flat and the constant w depend only on the recovery rate R and the discount D

$$w = 1 - \frac{R}{1-R}\frac{D}{1-D}. \tag{20.21}$$

If the funding cost in LIBOR flat $F = \bar{f}$ this is equivalent to the classical equation that the present value of the losses is equal to the spread multiplied by the risky annuity

$$S_l = (1-R)\frac{l}{\bar{v}}. \tag{20.22}$$

The spread B of a par asset swap is given by

$$B = C - \bar{l} + \frac{D}{A}. \tag{20.23}$$

Using (20.19) and (20.23) the implied basis can be determined.
    Where a nonzero funding margin needs to be used

$$F = \bar{f} + m, \tag{20.24}$$

where $m \neq 0$, (20.19) and (20.22) are not equivalent.

20.3   NUMERICAL RESULTS

Figure 20.1 shows results for the basis implied from the bond price. In these results we assume that the investor is funding at LIBOR flat and typical values for the recovery rate, ranging from 0 to 80%, were used. As expected, all bonds have a different implied basis, as their average

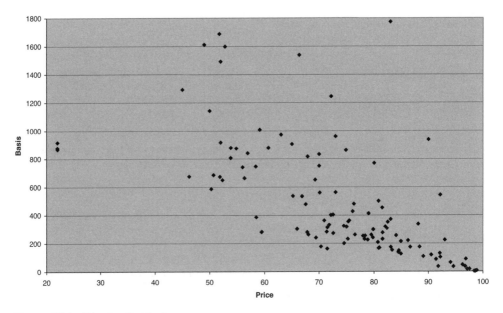

Figure 20.1   Price implied basis

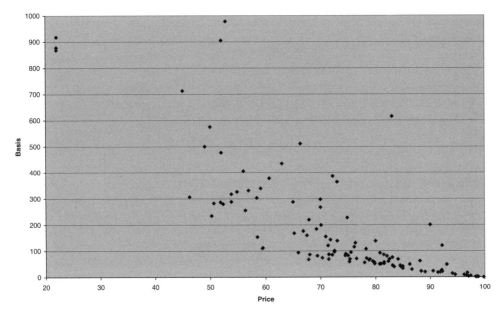

Figure 20.2 Price implied basis with an assumed recovery rate of $R = 0$

life, coupon and price are different. As some bond prices are distressed, there is a wide range of values obtained for the basis.

Figure 20.2 shows results for the basis implied from the bond price with an assumed recovery rate of $R = 0$. Comparing Figures 20.1 and 20.2 shows the impact of the recovery rate assumption.

Part V
Dynamic Credit Portfolio Management

21

Long Memory Processes and Benoit Mandelbrot

Do not go where the path may lead, go instead where there is no path and leave a trail.
Ralph Waldo Emerson

21.1 INTRODUCTION

The assumption of a Gaussian process is a cornerstone of modern mathematical finance and is present in almost every book from theory of investment to the theory of option pricing. It is common mathematical behavior of almost every professional quantitative analyst working in financial institutions to assume that underlying any observed financial instrument there is a martingale and, therefore, an equivalent martingale measure.

Hence, before looking at data or analyzing graphs to gain insight about the underlying process, the community of quantitative analysts working in banks begin any model by *postulating the absence of arbitrage* and *axiomatically assuming market completeness*. Additionally, for convenience purpose – that is, for ease of use or mathematical tractability – the chosen martingale is almost always the Gaussian process.

In this chapter we discuss some of the problems and highlight the inappropriateness of the current Gaussian framework largely used by academic and financial market practitioners alike. This chapter is based on the seminal and original work of Benoit Mandelbrot (private communication, 2009). In Section 21.2 we describe some properties of the price processes of financial instruments and we present evidence against the Brownian motion assumption. In Section 21.3 we describe the classical study of the Nile river by Hurst as an example of a long-term memory process. This particular study, encountered during a course on fractals in 1992 (see Mandelbrot, 1982 for details) served as inspiration in the market downturn of 2002, when the systemic correlation had gone up enormously, to identify the problems of the securitization instruments kept in the portfolios of the banks.

21.2 ECONOPHYSICS, FAT TAILS AND BROWNIAN MOTION

As described in more detail in Mandelbrot and Hudson (2004), the Brownian motion model that underlies the work of Black and Scholes dates back to Bachelier in 1900. Mandelbrot and Hudson also show via many examples that the model does not fit reality. Despite evidence against the Gaussian framework, it is still the approach used in practice. An example of its shortcomings is the volatility smile for options. In the last 10 years high frequency data has become available, giving rise to statistical studies that proved the unsuitability of the Brownian motion hypothesis.

In order to understand the problem, we recall that Bachelier proposed Brownian motion as a model of market fluctuations. That is, the returns of a certain instrument are independent and identically distributed normal variables. The hypothesis has the advantage that it is simple and easy to manipulate; the disadvantage is that it fails to reproduce reality, and several studies have come to this result (see e.g. Plerou et al., 1999), for individual stocks, and Gopikrishnan et al., 1999, for indices. In those studies, it is shown that the distribution of returns is non-Gaussian and follows power laws, that is Pareto. This is precisely the sort of results reported in the classical study of cotton prices by Mandelbrot (1963).

We observe that volatility outbursts are extremely correlated and follow what is known as *volatility clustering* – that is, they tend to be persistent in the periods of turbulence (see e.g. Lo, 1991).

Consequently, the higher moments of the price *change scale anomalously* with time. Another important characteristic of the pricing process is the phenomena of *self similarity* of the volatility outbursts. In a nutshell, an object is said to be self similar if it is exactly or approximately similar to a portion of itself. Self similarity is a typical property of objects known as *fractals*, and we refer, for example, to Mandelbrot (1982) for details. Related problems that begin slowly and evolve to a turbulent phase can be seen in the so-called sandpile problems studied by Bak et al. (1987). Grains of sand fall slowly, forming a pile. At some characteristic angle of the pile there is an avalanche and the sandpile is destroyed. The sandpile model is an example of a dynamic system exhibiting what is called *self organized criticality* (SOC). The concept has been observed in phenomena occurring in many fields, and is related to the study of complexity in nature, see e.g. Bak (1996). It has also been observed in what is called *cellular automata*, that is, discrete models built on a grid of cells usually on a finite number of dimensions. Each cell can be in a finite number of discrete states, and the state at time t is a function of the states in neighboring cells at time $t - 1$. The functions that determine the states may be very simple, and an interesting point in the study of automata is that with very simple rules one may generate time series which are deterministic but unpredictable. As an example, we mention the well-known John Conway's Game of Life (see e.g. Garcia et al. 1993, and the references therein for details). For our purposes, it is important to mention that SOC is commonly observed in dynamics of non-equilibrium where the driving factors typically change slowly in time. They are closely related to fractals as both show power law behavior.

There is quite a lot of evidence pointing in the direction that the price change process is quite different from the classical Brownian motion in widespread use in mathematical finance. That is, one not only observes nonlinear correlations between price and volatility, but also extreme events are much more probable than expected by the Gaussian distribution. Those deviations or *anomalies* from the Gaussian distribution imply the existence of multifractal scaling properties (see e.g. Mandelbrot (1997, 1999) or Fischer et al. 1997). They are quite important both for pricing and for hedging purposes of option contracts, and one needs to have process characteristics for different time horizons. Similar properties have been observed and treated within the context of turbulent flows where scaling and multifractal analysis have been used, see e.g. Frisch (1997).

Understanding the pricing process is very important in itself for very many practical reasons. Hedge and risk parameters are certainly more in line with reality. We refer to, for example, Calvet and Fischer (2001, 2004) for reports on successful application of multifractal models for volatility purposes. Those models are certainly not as tractable as their Gaussian competitors and there are many practical issues to be taken into account. We refer to Borland et al. (2005) and the references therein for a paper on Mandelbrot's work and the difficulties underlying those approaches.

21.3   LONG-TERM MEMORY AND THE NILE RIVER

The dynamic of the Nile river flood has been carefully studied by Hurst (1956). In this section we describe the so-called Nile river flood problem in conjunction with long-term memory processes, and we draw the parallel with the securitization business model for financial institutions. We refer to Mandelbrot and Hudson (2004) (Chapter IX) and the references therein for more details.

Back in 1906, Harold Hurst arrived in Egypt to solve the problem of the Nile floods. At that time, Egypt was ruled by Great Britain whose mills located in Manchester needed the cotton produced in Nile valleys. The production of cotton, however, was deeply affected by droughts and river floods. Observe that discharge of water in the Nile varied enormously, from 151 billion cubic meters in the flood of 1878 to 42 billion cubic meters in the drought period of 1913. Another dry period followed just years later. That is, periods of droughts would cluster among themselves and the same would happen with the periods of flood. The main problem was not to forecast the flood or the drought but to come up with the size of the dams that should be built in order to accumulate the several years of flood water to use during the periods of drought. That is, Hurst needed to solve a complex extreme value problem.

The typical solution at the time was to *assume* independent increments. Assume one intends to replace a dam that is 25 years old for which one has the historical range between the largest and the lowest flood for that period. If the widening of the range follows the typical independent increment assumption of a Gaussian process, one may expect that it goes with the square root of the time scale. That is, if one wants a dam to resist for the next 100 years, the time scale is four and the size of the new dam should be twice as large as the old one. Hurst observed that the increments were not independent and that the size of the floods were *sequence dependent*. Additionally, there was a scaling relation between the ratio highest over lowest and time and it was not 0.5 as in the independent increment assumption but 0.73!

For our purposes it is important to note that the problem faced by Hurst can easily be put in the context of correlation dynamics. Assume there are reservoirs around the Nile, for example, in the form of caves that accumulate water for a time. Year after year the reservoirs are slowly being filled until at a certain point in time there is a year with a lot of rain when all the reservoirs are filled and there is a large flood. If in the following year there is another heavy rainy season, given that the reservoirs are all still full there is another large flood. The years of rain in which the reservoirs are slowly being filled can be seen as years in which the correlation of water levels in the reservoirs is increasing. With time, however, sequential periods of dry season will empty the reservoirs bringing the correlation among the water levels in the reservoir slowly to zero. The periods of very large floods will then follow the dynamic correlation processes of reservoir water levels, where the process of filling and emptying follows a very slow drift. The analogy between this process and the impact of the securitization activity in the levels of systemic risk among financial institutions will be explained in the next chapter.

21.4   CAPITAL ASSET PRICING MODEL

The foundations of what is known as modern portfolio theory began with the work of Markowitz in the early 1950s (Markowitz, 1952). The concept of efficient frontier is fundamental to the development of the *Capital Asset Pricing Model (CAPM)* by Jack Treynor, William Sharpe, John Lintner, Jan Mossin and, more recently, Eugene Fama. Ultimately, the

CAPM model, and the Gaussian assumption underlying it, justifies investing in a portfolio of assets, taking systemic risk, instead of taking positions on single name instruments and having the idiosyncratic risk on these names.

The Gaussian assumption underlying CAPM may certainly be flawed, as discussed by Mandelbrot and Hudson (2004). Nevertheless, one is still better off investing in a portfolio of assets, taking systemic risk, than in a single name in the portfolio, taking the idiosyncratic risk associated with this particular name, all other elements, such as rating and maturity, remaining equal. As an ABS is constituted of a portfolio of assets, any portfolio manager is in principle better off investing in such an instrument than in a single name bond. The recent default of Lehman Brothers is another example of the advantages of an ABS: the recovery rate on a Lehman bond has been 8.625%, while for the worst AAA ABX.HE index – that is, the 2007 vintage – one can still recover 30% of the investment. This sort of argument, together with the issue of *innovation* and information technology, explains the recent boom in *exchange traded funds (ETF)* in the equity market. The problem, however, becomes how to build and manage an ABS and a portfolio with those instruments. In the next chapter we show the importance of the securitization business model for the economy, and in Chapter 23 we present a framework to be put in place by financial institutions to support such an important business activity.

22

Securitization and the Credit Crunch

*There are 10^{11} stars in the galaxy. That used to be a huge number. But it's only a hundred billion.
It's less than the national deficit! We used to call them astronomical numbers. Now we should call
them economical numbers.*
Richard Feynman

22.1 INTRODUCTION

As we have seen in this book, *securitization* refers to the pooling and packaging of financial
assets in the form of new securities that are sold to investors. Via securitization, financial
institutions create instruments that can be sold into the market instead of being kept on the
balance sheets. That is, it brings liquidity to a potentially illiquid instrument that would
otherwise remain in hold to maturity on the balance sheet of an institution. On the issuer
side it improves leverage ratios, the efficient use of capital, and lowers the cost of funding.
Additionally, it permits the institutions to focus on the business side instead of managing the
assets on the balance sheet. From an investor point of view, the investment on a pool of assets
inherently implies diversification. An insurance company can get exposure to an emerging
market asset class by investing on a senior portion of the capital structure of a portfolio of
securities. Via the same mechanism a pension fund can get access to a pool of credit card
receivables or auto loans.

This was the securitization business model until June 2007 when the credit crunch brought
up additional awareness for the consequences underlying the business model. On the one
hand, the diversification benefits allowed an increase in leverage especially in *off balance
sheet* transactions of the financial institutions. On the other hand, however, by substituting a
single name instrument – such as a single name bond – by a securitization note – such as a
CDO note – the investor inherently substitutes idiosyncratic with systemic risk.

As we have seen, the credit crunch was ignited by the subprime mortgage-backed securities
in the portfolios of financial institutions. Since then, amplified by extreme leverage and the late
response of policy makers to the roots of the problem and its implications, what was supposed
to be a problem related to subprime mortgages in the US *slowly* spread to involve the real world
economy. In this chapter we discuss the implication behind the securitization business model.

The chapter is structured as follows. In Section 22.2 we give a pictorial view of the *correlation dynamics* underlying the securitization process. In Section 22.3 we show economic
evidence on the importance of the securitization business model guiding the readers to the
proposal presented in the next chapter.

22.2 CORRELATION AND MORTGAGE-BACKED SECURITIES

In Chapter 13, we showed how variations in the dependency on the systemic factor affect
the correlation among the different tranches of the capital structure. Although investments in
ABSs eliminate the issues of idiosyncratic risk it puts on the table a more subtle issue of how to

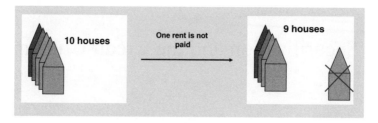

Impact on economic activity:
- **Construction companies**
- **Real estate rental and vendors**
- **Housing accessories**
- **banks and other financial companies**

One delay in rental payments is immediately noticed by investors

Figure 22.1   The impact of 10 houses on the economy

treat the systemic risk embedded in the structures. What we show below via an example is how the dynamics of the change in correlation take place, building an argument for the necessity of following that dynamic. As experienced during the credit crunch, the diversification benefits of the instrument come at the price of potential increases in the level of *systemic* risk to the portfolio, implying a higher cost of regulatory capital than the one that had been taken by Basel II.

In an article from June 2005, Laing (2005) reported that in the opinion of Robert Schiller there was a housing bubble in the US and that prices could fall as much as 50%. Laing writes the following:

> ... housing busts, unlike bear markets on Wall Street, often start almost imperceptibly and unfold slowly. They're difficult to detect in their early phases, in part because accurate price data on comparable-home sales is hard to come by.

We give an example in order to clarify the credit crunch and its relation with the economy, the issues of regulation, and the securitization business model of financial institutions.

Assume one builds houses to rent out as shown in Figure 22.1. The impact on the economic activity, that is construction companies, realtors, housing accessories, banks and other financial companies, is the one of *ten houses*. For the sake of simplicity, let us suppose the gross return on the investment is about 10%. One delay in payments is immediately seen by the investor.

Assume as an alternative, as shown in Figure 22.2, that the investor decides to *securitize* the cash flow of the houses while keeping a margin. The investor buys 100 houses and issues ABS notes, getting the cash to buy more houses and again issuing ABS notes, until 10 rounds of ABS notes have been issued. The total number of houses involved becomes 1000. The positive impact on the economy: construction companies build more houses; there are more houses to sell; more accessories are sold; there is a significant increase in banking and financial activity; and, as a consequence of the economy of scale generated by the securitization process, houses become more affordable. If the margin retained by the investor is 1%, she will make 1% on 1000 houses and will have gotten rid of all the problems of administering the maintenance of the houses, e.g. making sure that insurances are paid and that repairments in the house

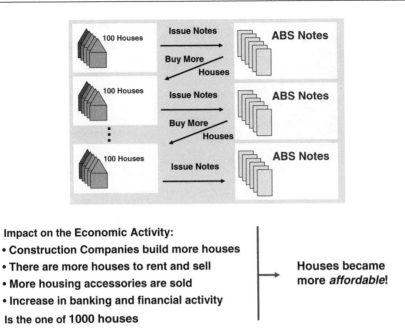

Figure 22.2   The impact of 1000 houses on the economy

are made at an appropriate time. The same securitization algorithm can easily be applied to other asset classes – autos, aircraft leases, student loans, credit card receivables – making the economy much more efficient and the costs of goods and services cheaper. The investors who bought the ABSs will have the benefit of diversification, exposing themselves to systemic effects instead of to idiosyncratic risk.

The catch comes when defaults begin to happen. If one tenant is not paying the rent, as shown in Figure 22.3, it is only one delinquency in a portfolio of 100 houses, and this is less noticeable than one in 10. The cause of the delinquency may be a divorce or a sickness or any idiosyncratic issue related to one particular household. However, the delinquency may come from a more systemic source that is common to a large portion of the population. The important point to keep in mind is that delinquencies only begin to be noticeable when there is already *widespread* troubles with the whole sector, as shown in Figure 22.4. From one default on one ABS to several defaults in several ABS notes the *correlation* between the different tranches increases significantly and the problem becomes systemic, potentially affecting the whole economic activity.

The dynamic of the process can be seen in Figure 22.5. In the initial phase, delinquencies are idiosyncratic and imperceptible, and the correlation between the instruments is very low. Then it evolves *slowly* to a second phase in which the delinquencies increase systemically and the problem becomes detectable. At this point the correlation has increased significantly. Finally, it passes very quickly to a phase of total awareness of a widespread problem, and the correlation has exploded to barely one and, depending on the size of the market and the stage in the economic cycle, potentially affecting the whole economic activity.

As we have seen in the credit crunch that began in June 2007, the levels of systemic risk can become high enough to affect the survivability of the financial system as we know it. With

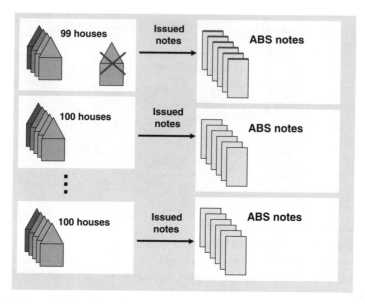

- **The impact of one loss is practically not noticeable**
- **Very low *correlation* among ABSs**

Figure 22.3   The impact of 1 delinquency in 100

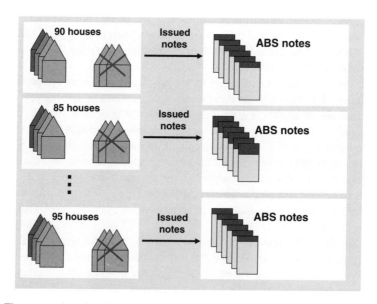

- **There are already widespread problems in the sector**
- ***Correlation* increased significantly**

Figure 22.4   The impact of several delinquencies in a portfolio of MBSs

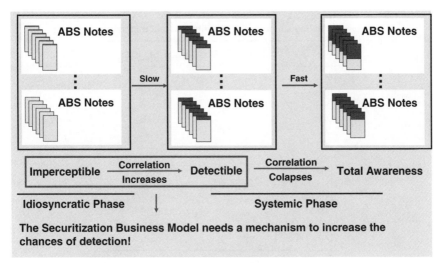

Figure 22.5   The dynamic of correlation

respect to the securitization activity there are then two possibilities left: either there is an end to the activity, or mechanisms should be created to avoid systemic risk reaching catastrophic levels. The dynamic mentioned here is very similar with the long memory problems described in Chapter 21.

The sort of long memory process that slowly evolves into a situation of turbulence has two possible solutions. First, the solution is similar to the dam problem faced by Hurst – that is, one needs to take a much larger cost of capital than is currently observed. This is similar to putting the instrument in a buy and hold portion of the portfolio, and the correlation used for cost of capital would take into account the worst possible case. Such a calculation has been made in Chapter 13. The cost of capital associated to this solution may kill the business activity. The second solution designed to foster the securitization business model at the lowest possible cost of capital means a dynamic framework in which the instruments are put on mark to market while managing the risks via the standardized credit indices.

In the next section we present evidence of the benefits of the securitization activity to the economy, and look at the ingredients of a framework that needs be put in place to move forward with the securitization activity. We would like to stress that an integral part of the solution passes by CDSs and standardized credit indices. The framework is discussed in more detail in the next chapter.

22.3   SECURITIZATION AND ECONOMIC GROWTH

As described in Chapter 8, synthetic instruments offer several advantages over cash instruments. Deals with synthetic collateral will go through faster than when cash instruments are involved. The growth can be seen in Table 22.1 and the current distribution is shown in Table 22.2.

Table 22.1 Outstanding notionals for CDSs, including single names, multinames and tranches

Year	Size (USD trillion)
1997	0.2
1998	0.4
1999	0.6
2000	0.9
2001	1.2
2002	2.2
2003	3.8
2004	8.4
2005	17.1
2006	34.4
2007	62.2
2008 (ISDA)	54.6
2008 (DTCC)	33.6

The securitization activity brings several benefits for the economy. It transforms illiquid assets into market tradable ones, potentially releasing capital trapped in low margin illiquid assets to be used elsewhere. In this way, it can be seen as an alternative source of funding. Via the tranching technique, securitization offers investors exposure to different portions of the capital structure. A conservative investor can have access to asset classes that would be unaccessible otherwise. Moreover, introducing credit enhancement techniques makes the structures even more appealing to a broader pool of investors, which are attracted by the risk-return trade-off, thereby potentially decreasing the costs of funding of the financial institution. For example, consider an insurance company that gets access to an emerging market debt instrument by investing on an AAA tranche of an emerging market CDO. This implies that the higher in the capital structure one invests, the lower is the exposure to idiosyncratic risk and the higher is the exposure to systemic risk. Hence, in a systemic credit event, the probability that losses will affect the higher-rated tranches increases. Tranching, however, introduces the effect of *negative convexity* – that is, the effect that a widening of credit spreads has a stronger impact on prices than a narrowing and that prices decline at an increasing rate the more the spreads widen.

It happens, however, that securitization products and investment strategies incorporate additional leverage. In Chapter 15 we covered the CPDO strategy and the use of leverage in the synthetic credit derivatives market. Another example of a structured credit product, incorporating additional leverage, is the *leveraged super senior* (LSS). Under this strategy a certain amount is invested in the very upper level of the capital structure, with a leverage factor that can vary from 2 to 10. The strategy is typically rated AAA and offers a significantly

Table 22.2 Distribution of outstanding CDS notionals

CDS type	Size (% of total)
Tranche	10.1
Index	44.0
Single name	45.8

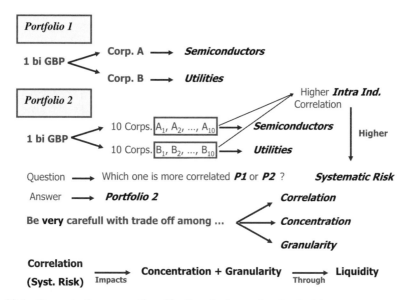

Figure 22.6   Concentration versus diversification: the issue of systemic risk

higher return, depending on the leverage factor, in comparison with single name exposures of the same rating.

More importantly, the securitization activity transforms the risk characteristics of the financial institutions' credit portfolio. As before, it reduces the exposure to idiosyncratic risk and increases the exposure to systemic risk. An example illustrating the non-trivial interplay between correlation and systemic risk that characterizes securitization is shown in Figure 22.6. Consider two alternative investment strategies involving the same amount, say one billion USD, equally divided over two sectors: financials and semiconductors. In Portfolio A, one has an exposure to two companies each belonging to one sector, and each company accounts for half of the total investment. In Portfolio B, one has an exposure to 20 companies, 10 from each sector, and each company accounts for five percent of the total amount invested. Observe that although Portfolio A is more exposed to idiosyncratic risk, Portfolio B is certainly more exposed to systemic risk, as the level of exposure to the market as a whole increases. For a detailed study on the interplay concentration versus liquidity we refer to Basel (BIS, 2008).

In general there is a high correlation between economic growth and spreads. Via securitization, leverage is used to increase the offer, potentially reducing spreads and so increasing economic growth. An intuitive example of this dynamic has been shown in Section 22.2. The increase of the securitization activity in the US from 1985 to 2007 can be seen in Table 22.3. The proportion of securitization instruments has gone from 5% in 1985, to 16% in 1990 and finally 25% in 2007, coming from USD 667 billion in 1985, to USD 1.9 trillion in 1990 and finally reaching a market of USD 12 trillion in 2007. Additionally, we show in Table 22.1 the growth of the synthetic credit derivatives instruments from 1997 to 2008. All this growth came with a quite large increase on leverage in the banking activity. The usual leverage ratios for banks has been around 10. Table 22.5 shows estimates for the leverage ratios of six large American banks (see Eavis (2009) for details). The increase in the securitization activity closely related to the

Table 22.3   US market securities

Year	Equities	Corporate	ABS	Treasury Sec.	Agency Sec.	Mortgage Sec.	Money Markets	Muni Bonds
1985	2 270.4	776.5	0.9	1 437.7	293.9	372.1	847.0	859.5
1986	2 682.2	959.3	7.2	1 619.0	307.4	534.4	877.0	920.4
1987	2 710.3	1 074.9	12.9	1 724.7	341.4	672.1	979.8	1 010.4
1988	3 075.6	1 195.7	29.3	1 821.3	381.5	772.4	1 108.5	1 082.3
1989	3 813.0	1 292.5	51.3	1 945.4	411.8	971.6	1 192.3	1 135.2
1990	3 531.3	1 350.4	89.9	2 195.8	434.7	1 333.4	1 156.8	1 184.4
1991	4 847.8	1 454.7	129.9	2 471.6	442.8	1 636.9	1 054.3	1 272.2
1992	5 422.0	1 557.0	163.7	2 754.1	484.0	1 937.0	994.2	1 295.5
1993	6 296.9	1 674.7	199.9	2 989.5	570.7	2 144.7	971.8	1 361.8
1994	6 317.5	1 755.6	257.3	3 126.0	738.9	2 251.7	1 034.7	1 325.9
1995	8 481.3	1 937.5	316.3	3 307.2	844.6	2 352.1	1 177.3	1 268.3
1996	10 279.6	2 126.5	404.4	3 459.7	925.8	2 486.1	1 393.9	1 261.8
1997	13 292.8	2 359.0	535.8	3 456.8	1 022.6	2 680.2	1 692.8	1 318.7
1998	15 547.3	2 708.5	731.5	3 355.5	1 300.6	2 955.2	1 977.8	1 402.9
1999	19 522.8	3 046.5	900.8	3 281.0	1 620.0	3 334.2	2 338.8	1 457.2
2000	17 627.0	3 358.4	1 071.8	2 966.9	1 854.6	3 565.8	2 662.6	1 480.9
2001	15 310.6	3 836.4	1 281.1	2 967.5	2 149.6	4 127.6	2 587.2	1 603.7
2002	11 900.5	4 099.5	1 543.3	3 204.9	2 292.8	4 686.4	2 545.7	1 763.1
2003	15 618.5	4 458.4	1 693.7	3 574.9	2 636.7	5 238.6	2 519.9	1 900.5
2004	17 389.3	4 785.1	1 827.8	3 943.6	2 745.1	5 455.8	2 904.2	2 031.3
2005	18 512.0	4 960.0	1 955.2	4 165.8	2 613.8	5 915.6	3 433.7	2 225.9
2006	20 909.3	5 365.0	2 130.4	4 322.9	2 660.1	6 492.4	4 008.8	2 403.2
2007	21 463.5	5 825.4	2 472.4	4 516.8	2 946.3	7 210.3	4 140.2	2 617.8

increase on the credit derivatives market implies an increase in the leverage ratio of financial institutions. The impact of all this activity on the economy can be seen in Table 22.4, as can evidence of the impact of the increase in the securitization activity by the dramatic decrease in spreads for Aaa and Baa corporates for the period 2000 to 2007. At the same time, unemployment reduced from 5.8 in 2002 at the last end of the internet bubble explosion to 4.6 in 2007. The impact of securitization is even more striking on consumption levels that can be measured by the levels of savings that went from 9.0% in 1985 to 7% in 1990, 2.3% in 2000 and finally 0.4% in 2007. The increase in securitization and leverage, however, implied an inherent increase in the level of systemic risk for the economy. From Tables 22.1 and 22.3 we see that the total market for securitization and synthetic credit derivatives rose from USD 4.4 trillion in 1997 to a staggering USD 67 trillion in 2007, for which the contribution of synthetic instrument is USD 54.6 trillion. Moreover, we note from Table 22.2 that the proportion of multiname synthetic instruments is about 54%.

A simple evidence of the impact of securitization in an industry can be seen in Table 22.6 where we show the year over year contraction in the new passenger vehicle registrations by manufacturer. The problem is also visible on this webpage[1], which shows a photo of the test facility of Nissan Motor Manufacturing Ltd., the largest car plant in the UK and the most productive in Europe. The factory's parking lot is overflowing and the test track facility is used

---

[1] http://www.zerotohundred.com/2009/auto-news/problems-at-nissan-test-track-used-as-parking-lot-for-unsold-cars

Table 22.4   US economic data

Year	Corp Aaa	Corp Baa	Munis HG	Unempl. rate	Personal savings	Real GDP change
1985	11.37	12.72	9.18	7.2	9.0	4.1
1986	9.02	10.39	7.38	7.0	8.2	3.5
1987	9.38	10.58	7.73	6.2	7.0	3.4
1988	9.71	10.83	7.76	5.5	7.3	4.1
1989	9.26	10.18	7.24	5.3	7.1	3.5
1990	9.32	10.36	7.25	5.6	7.0	1.9
1991	8.77	9.80	6.89	6.8	7.3	-0.2
1992	8.14	8.98	6.41	7.5	7.7	3.3
1993	7.22	7.93	5.63	6.9	5.8	2.7
1994	7.97	8.63	6.19	6.1	4.8	4.0
1995	7.59	8.20	5.95	5.6	4.6	2.5
1996	7.37	8.05	5.75	5.4	4.0	3.7
1997	7.26	7.86	5.55	4.9	3.6	4.5
1998	6.53	7.22	5.12	4.5	4.3	4.2
1999	7.04	7.87	5.43	4.2	2.4	4.5
2000	7.62	8.36	5.77	4.0	2.3	3.7
2001	7.08	7.95	5.19	4.7	1.8	0.8
2002	6.49	7.80	5.05	5.8	2.4	1.6
2003	5.67	6.77	4.73	6.0	2.1	2.7
2004	5.63	6.39	4.63	5.5	2.0	4.2
2005	5.23	6.06	4.29	5.1	0.5	2.3
2006	5.59	6.48	4.42	4.6	0.4	2.9
2007	5.56	6.48	4.42	4.6	0.4	2.2

to park the new cars. Moreover, this is not the only remarkable car park. The port of Zeebrugge in Belgium has three square kilometers of car terminals. By the end of February 2009 these three square kilometers had been filled up with 175 000 cars, making it one of the largest car parks in the world.

All of what is said in the last paragraph means that stopping the securitization activity will reduce leverage and economic growth. This also means reducing the levels of systemic risk exposure and, as such, correlation among portfolios of financial institutions. This is done at the cost of decreasing consumption and consequently an increase in unemployment. This will bring higher costs for the state at a time when the population in the developed world is aging, bringing problems of budget financing for pension funds and municipalities as the tax pool of

Table 22.5   Estimated leverage ratio of American financial institutions

Financial institution	Leverage ratio
Citigroup	46.7
Bank of America	31.7
J.P. Morgan Chase	25.8
Goldman Sachs	20.6
Wells Fargo	15.5

Table 22.6 New passenger vehicle registrations by manufacturer

AUTO manufacturer	YoY
VW Group	−20.1%
Ford Group	−21.8%
Jaguar Land Rover	−49.2%
Renault	−33.9%
GM Group	−35.4%
Fiat Group	−26.0%
Toyota & Lexus	−31.5%
Daimler Group	−30.5%
BMW Group	−32.4%
Nissan	−25.5%
Hyundai	−16.3%
Mazda	−16.7%
Honda	−27.0%
KIA	−28.7%
Suzuki	−28.5%
Mitsubishi	−41.8%
Chrysler	−53.2%

the economically active population goes down. At some point of the process money will have to be printed, increasing inflationary pressures with eventual increases in currency volatilities.

The solution to the problem, then, is to maintain the securitization activity but build a portfolio framework in which the systemic risk for those exposures can be appropriately managed. This means creating a structure to manage the exposure of the portfolio to the dynamics of systemic correlation. As such, the correlation for each ABS asset class should become an observable market parameter. It implies the creation of tranche instruments for the respective asset class that are liquid and exchange traded. It also implies transparency for pricing models that are needed to give hedge parameters. Keeping an eye on correlation means having the instruments put on mark to market, otherwise the cost of capital would become prohibitively high. Additionally, capital costs have to be portfolio-dependent, implying the necessity of a dynamic framework for capital costs purposes. The framework in question has to take all those points into account and such a framework is presented in the next chapter.

23

Dynamic Credit Portfolio Management

Ignorance more frequently begets confidence than does knowledge: it is those who know little, and not those who know much, who so positively assert that this or that problem will never be solved by science.

Charles Darwin

23.1 INTRODUCTION

At the heart of the crisis that started in the June 2007 are the loan securitization markets – that is, the securitization markets for commercial and residential mortgage loans, credit card receivables, leveraged loans, and so on. Broadly, the securitization of loan assets has become a key part of the business model of many large financial institutions. Ultimately, it has enabled institutions to transform very illiquid assets into marketable instruments that can be sold into the market. This has led to an interplay between the financial institutions that, on the one hand, shed loans via securitization and, on the other hand, took securitization products on their books.

It should be clear by now that pooling credit assets, and investment in the securitization products – specifically high-grade CDO tranches – represent relatively strong exposure to systemic risk. The correlation among the collateral, the negative convexity, introduced by tranching, and the huge leverage within these products or investment strategies reinforces the strength of the exposure to the systemic risk. Additionally, as shown in Chapter 13, within a portfolio context the dependencies between the securitizaton notes may become, much stronger than between single name bonds and loans. Hence, these risk characteristics imply a relatively stronger exposure of the credit portfolio to the systemic events. This is illustrated well in the crisis by the speed and the extent that an initial systemic event, the falling US house prices and the subsequent increase in mortgage delinquencies, translated in write-offs and losses throughout the entire financial system.

In Chapter 13 we have shown that the correlation between tranches of the capital structure may vary significantly with the variation in systemic risk. In Chapter 22 we made a case for the importance of securitization for the economic activity – that is, we have shown the catastrophic consequences of the reduction of securitization. We have also shown the need to follow up on the dynamics of systemic correlation to detect the level of systemic risk underlying the structures. From the parallel with the examples described in Chapter 21 we know that the correlation dynamic is a long term memory process and as such does not follow the Gaussian assumptions. In the Nile River studies we saw that the solution presented by Hurst was to adopt a more appropriate probability distribution that gives a better estimation of the frequency of the so-called extreme events and therefore of the size of the dam. This suggests that in the case of securitization, inspired by the results of Chapter 13, the solution for the systemic risk accompanying the securitization activity is to increase the regulatory capital cost for those instruments in the portfolios of the banks. This would imply a high level of correlation given that one may want to adopt a prudent approach – that is, using the highest correlation assuming a long term buy and hold strategy, potentially killing the activity or reducing it dramatically.

An alternative solution, designed specifically to foster the securitization business model at the lowest possible cost of capital, while keeping transparency, is to put the securities in mark to market while managing the risks via the standardized credit indices. This framework is described in detail in this chapter.

The chapter is organized as follows. In Sections 23.2 and 23.3 we discuss respectively how the systemic risk factor is introduced under the regulatory Basel II Internal Rating Based (IRB) framework and the general portfolio credit risk models. In Section 23.4 we address the securitization activity and particularly focus on how correlation between the collateral was taken into account. We show that indeed the use of the rating agency models by structurers had an implicit assumption of liquidity in the securitization markets. In Section 23.5 we very briefly return to the pricing algorithm described in Chapter 9 for standardized credit indices, stressing the differences with respect to the rating and regulatory capital algorithms. We specifically show the importance of the standardized CDS indices for the pricing and trading of CDOs. Section 23.6 brings the different elements of previous sections together, as we discuss short-term Dynamic Credit Portfolio Management. Again we show that liquid standardized credit indices are necessary for the short-term hedging of the *mark to market* value of the credit portfolio. Additionally, we discuss that, in general, transparent and liquid standardized credit indices for the loan securitization markets, in contrast to the corporate bond securitization markets, are absent. We see this absence as an important feature contributing to the dislocations in the loan securitization market. Moreover, increased transparency and liquidity of standardized credit indices is essential in order for the loan securitization market to develop further.

The more financial institutions depend on the markets for their business, the more do the evolving financial and economic conditions and the changing risk characteristics of investment products – due to *financial innovation* and development – plead for dynamic risk management frameworks. Two crucial aspects of a dynamic risk management framework are portfolio dependency and frequent updating of the assumptions underlying the models. Therefore, building on the commonly applied static Ratings Based Approach, we describe in Section 23.7 the main concepts of a dynamic credit management framework. Central to the framework are the concepts of standardized credit indices, economic capital, stress tests and scenario analysis.

23.2   REGULATORY CAPITAL AND BASEL FORMULAS

The development of the BIS document *International Convergence of Capital Measurement and Capital Standards* – hereafter the Basel II framework – and its current implementation in the different jurisdictions, has been guided by two important developments: first, the increased use of sophisticated models by large financial institutions to manage their credit portfolios and, second, the acknowledgment by the supervisory community of the failures (see Jones (1998), of the regulatory rules established by the 1988 Basel Accord, commonly known as Basel I). After its assessment of the financial institutions' internal models, the Basel Committee concluded that these models were, due to the insufficient degree of comparability across models and the calibration restrictions stemming from data scarcity, not ready to be used for regulatory purposes.

For this reason, Basel II used the so-called *ratings based approach* (RBA). Under this approach, the credits of the bank's portfolio are grouped in homogeneous pools or buckets of credits with the same characteristics. For the *internal ratings-based* (IRB) approach these characteristics are: the borrower's rating; the loan type (that is, sovereign, corporate, project financing or ABS), the seniority (senior secured or subordinate); and the maturity. Each unit exposure in a common bucket receives a predetermined fixed capital charge. Hence, this approach makes that the capital charges are *portfolio-invariant*, that is, the capital charge only depends on the characteristics of the exposure, its rating, and *not* on the characteristics of the portfolio, of which it is part.

Gordy (2003) shows that the portfolio-invariance condition holds for risk-factor models if the portfolio is asymptotically fine-grained (this is a *first* assumption), and there is only one single systemic risk factor (this is a *second* assumption). The asymptotic single risk factor (ASRF) model underlying the IRB formulas is based on the Merton model (see Chapter 2), and the work of Vasicek (2002). Hence the *whole Basel II regulatory capital framework has been based on a single factor Gaussian model*. The probability of loss of an exposure conditional on a single systemic risk factor (X) is given by

$$P(X) = \Phi(y_A) \qquad (23.1)$$

with

$$y_A = \rho X + \sqrt{1 - \rho^2} \xi_A \qquad (23.2)$$

where PD is the one-year probability of default. The parameter ρ introduces the dependence of the asset value of a borrower on the systemic risk factor (X), the general state of the economy. Additionally, it *also determines the correlation between the two returns y_A and y_B* which drive the borrower default for exposures A and B which is equal to ρ^2. These asset correlations importantly determine the shape of the IRB risk weight formulas. The correlations vary between the different asset classes, since these different sorts of borrowers significantly differ in their dependence on the general economy. For instance, large corporates tend to depend more on the general economic state and thus to have a higher correlation than the retail portfolio, of which the borrowers are only weakly interlinked. The correlations for the different asset classes are predetermined via asset correlation in the IRB formulas, see BIS (2005) for details. As the dependencies between the obligors are *fixed* in the IRB approach, the focus of the market participants is put on the PD variable and, additionally, the loss given default (LGD) and exposure at default (EAD) variables for the advanced IRB.

From the two assumptions – asymptotically fine-grained portfolio and one single systemic risk factor – the additivity condition is derived, meaning that the risk assessments can be conducted at the individual exposure level and the results can be added up to give the risk assessment of the portfolio. However, if the two assumptions do not hold then the bottom-up approach is likely to give an inaccurate assessment of the credit portfolio risk. Though, for the reasons of its relative simplicity, the supposed inadequate stage of development of the credit portfolio models for regulatory purposes at the time, and the fact that the validation of the inputs is more convenient and easier than the validation of the entire models, the bottom-up approach was opted as basis for the first pillar IRB capital charges (BIS, 2006).

In the real world, credit portfolios are not asymptotically fine-grained; they are finite and, moreover, credit defaults and their dependencies depend on more than one single risk factor, such as the global business cycle, for example. The interplay between technology and innovation means that the correlation between two asset classes may certainly evolve in time, as we have seen in Chapter 13. Market evidence shows that if a whole set of investors begins to push for the same strategy the correlation between the asset classes involved will eventually increase in time. Hence, the marginal contribution of a single exposure to the total risk of the portfolio depends on the composition of the portfolio toward single names or other *local* risk factors. Therefore, the sum of the IRB capital charges might understate the risk of the portfolio depending on its composition, relative to the well-diversified basis portfolio used for the calibration of the IRB formulas.

The implications, in terms of incorrect assessments of the risks, from the violation of the first assumption and methods to capture the single-name concentration have been reported in Gordy and Lütkebohmert (2007) and Heitfield et al. (2005). From the second assumption, it thus follows that the ASRF model does not capture the sector concentration risk, as it does not allow for the rich dependency structure between the credit defaults of obligors. Since the sector concentration risk concerns dependencies, the issue is not straightforwardly measurable and remains technically challenging, as will become clearer in the following sections. Both issues of single name concentration risk and sector concentration risk are supposed to be addressed in the second pillar of the Basel II framework.

As a resumé of the current Basel II framework, we mention the following points, and we refer to the seminal work of Gordy (2003) for details. Capital charges are supposed to be *portfolio independent* – that is, they depend on the characteristics of the securities in itself and not on the portfolio in which they are held. The main reason for this is said to be stability. That is, *portfolio dependent* capital charges would cause the costs of capital to change on a daily basis and a position booked as a profit on one day could be unprofitable the next day just because the portfolio changed. The four next assumptions are:

1. *fine grained* portfolio composition;
2. regulatory capital is defined within a value-at-risk (VaR) paradigm;
3. there is one systemic factor driving the whole economic activity; and
4. both the systemic and the idiosyncratic risk factors follow a Gaussian standard normal distribution.

It can be proven that, with the assumptions above, the cost of capital is portfolio invariant and the total capital cost of a portfolio is the sum of the costs of the individual components in the portfolio (see Gordy, 2003). In the next sections we explain why this framework is inadequate for the securitization business model and propose a dynamic credit portfolio management framework based on stress tests, scenario analysis and mark to market based on the standardized credit indices as a solution for the securitization business model for financial institutions.

In order to adapt to the problems observed during the credit crunch, it has recently been proposed to update regulatory capital charges that would be dependent on the levels of iTraxx and CDX (see Gordy, 2009). However, the proposal seems to be in a preliminary phase.

23.3   PORTFOLIO CREDIT RISK AND ECONOMIC CAPITAL

Economic capital (ECAP) is the amount of capital set aside by a financial institution in order to prevent its net asset value falling below the level that could affect its business or hinder the pursuit of its strategic objectives. While regulatory capital (RC), as explained in Section 23.2, is the capital *required* by the regulators, the ECAP is a firm's *internal* estimate. As we focus on credit risk in this book, we will discuss ECAP in the context of credit risk management only.

For the determination of ECAP and its allocation, the tail of the loss distribution is crucial. A *key* parameter that affects this tail is the *correlation*. This section is divided in two subsections.

The first is dedicated to the computation of economic capital and its allocation. The second gives a brief discussion of the methodologies employed to introduce the correlation parameter into the credit risk systems. The main objective is to show that there has been no standard practice on the correlation assumptions entering ECAP calculations. As a good deal of the material presented in this section is already standard in the literature, we will focus on the issues that are less well known.

23.3.1 Economic capital allocation

The initial step when estimating the economic capital of a credit portfolio is the generation of its loss distribution. In this section we describe the general methodology underlying the most widespread approaches, and we refer to Gupton et al. (1997) and Moody's (2002) for more details. The factor approach, as described in Chapter 3, is basic for the generation of the loss distribution and assumes that the return of each asset i in the portfolio is given by

$$Y_i = \alpha X_i^m + \sqrt{(1 - \alpha^2)}\xi_i \tag{23.3}$$

where ξ_i is the standard normal distributed idiosyncratic factor, and X_i^m is the market factor often represented by an industrial and a country factor and given by

$$X_i^m = \omega_{ind} I_i + \omega_{country} C_i \tag{23.4}$$

where ω_{ind} and $\omega_{country}$ are the industry and country weights. To introduce the dependencies, the widely-used approach is the Gaussian copula as described in Chapter 3. For historical reasons, VaR has been taken as the standard market measure for ECAP calculation. Using the VaR measure the ECAP of a bank is defined as (see Figure 23.1):

$$ECAP(L, q) = VaR(L, q) - E[L] \tag{23.5}$$

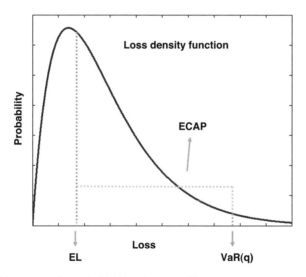

Figure 23.1   Linking economic capital, VaR and expected loss

that is, ECAP is defined as the amount of capital the bank is supposed to set aside to serve as a buffer for any *unexpected loss* defined as an event of probability $(1 - q)$. As an example, assume that the financial institution targets an AA rating, the quantile q in this case is 99.97%.

Once the loss distribution has been calculated, certain risk measures need to be determined to allocate the ECAP among the business lines. The selection of an appropriate risk measure is an important issue in itself. The recent increase in competition and its pressure on business margins has strengthened the need for the efficient use of ECAP and its allocation among the different entities and business lines of a financial conglomerate. Although VaR has been widely used in the evaluation of the total ECAP, it is well known that it is *not a subadditive risk measure*. In Appendix A we give a brief description of some approaches used to allocate capital and mention some of the difficulties with those techniques. We refer to Artzner et al. (1999) and Tasche (2004) for the issues of coherent risk measures and the allocation of economic capital.

23.3.2   Different correlation assumptions

As we are dealing with quantiles, *the tail of the loss distribution is crucial.* Dependencies between the credit defaults strongly determine the tail. Hence, the modeling assumptions made to capture these dependencies significantly determine the accuracy of the risk estimates, see Figure 23.2.

In general, risk models make use of *correlation* to introduce these dependencies. We refer to Embrechts et al. (1999) for a reference addressing the common pitfalls related to the correlation concept as a measure of dependency. In this section we briefly discuss the different approaches used to derive the default correlation parameter and the lack of consensus among market practitioners on the methodologies to incorporate the default correlation estimates in the risk models.

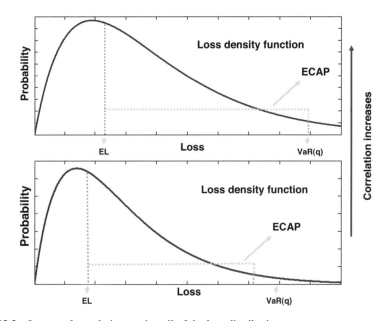

Figure 23.2   Impact of correlation on the tail of the loss distribution

Table 23.1   Asset correlations derived from default data

Source study	Data source	Results
Duellmann et al. (2006)	KMV	10.1%
KMV (2001)	Undisclosed	9.46%–19.98%
Fitch (2005)	Equity	intra 24.09%, inter 20.92%
Lopez (2002)	KMV Software	11.25%

Correlation is a second order moment and, up to now, not directly observable. The number of defaults (of obligors) is relatively limited, and there are generally insufficient observations to adequately calculate the default correlations from the actual defaults. As an alternative to the scarcity of default data, market participants have established different techniques. A first general technique is to derive the default correlation from the asset correlations, calculated from the asset data, e.g. equity returns and credit spreads. The technique allows one to go from asset correlation to default correlation and vice versa, allowing the comparison of the asset correlation implied from the limited default data. The theory that permits one to link the data-scarce default process to the data-rich asset return process has been described in Chapter 2 and is based on the Gaussian assumption. Tables 23.1 and 23.2 show the results of different studies that derive asset correlations from default and asset returns respectively. It is clear that not only the range of correlation estimates of the individual studies is quite large but also the estimates differ importantly between the studies. We refer to Chernih et al. (2006) for a more detailed discussion on the different studies.

In several studies the default correlation is derived from the correlation between the equity returns. We note, though, that as reported in de Servigny and Renault (2003) the link between the two is quite poor. As an example of the careful interpretation that the derived correlation estimates require, Table 23.3 depicts the default correlation between Belgium, France, Germany and Greece calculated using equity index returns. Generally, one would expect that the correlations between Belgium, France and Germany would be higher than the correlation between France, Germany and Greece. As we see in the table, that is *not* the case. An explanation for these counterintuitive results is that the Belgian equity index (BEL 20) has a relatively high weight of financials, which is not the case for Germany and France.

Table 23.2   Asset correlations derived from asset data

Source study	Data source	Results
Gordy (2002)	S&P	1.5%–12.5%
Cespedes (2000)	Moody's	10%
Hamerle et al. (2003)	–	max 2.3%
Hamerle et al. (2003)	S&P 1982–1999	0.4%–6.04%
Frey et al.	UBS	2.6%, 3.8%, 9.21%
Frey & McNeil (2003)	S&P 1981–2000	3.4%–6.4%
Dietsch & Petey (2004)	Coface 1994–2001 AK 1997–2001	0.12%–10.72%
Jobst & de Servigny (2004)	S&P 1981–2003	intra 14.6%, inter 4.7%
Duellmann & Scheule (2003)	DB 1987–2000	0.5%–6.4%
Jakubik (2006)	BF 1988–2003	5.7%

Table 23.3   Typical country correlations extracted from index equity returns

	Belgium	France	Germany	Greece
Belgium	1	32%	29%	5%
France	32%	1	92%	38%
Germany	29%	92%	1	35%
Greece	5%	38%	35%	1

An alternative methodology employed by market participants is to infer default correlations from rating migrations. This methodology has been used by a rating agency for their corporate CDO tool.

In the next section we discuss more in detail the methodologies employed by the rating agencies to evaluate the correlation parameters for the structured products. We have shown in Chapter 13 how variations on the systemic correlation affecting the collateral returns affect the different tranches of securitization products. Additionally, we have also shown that the impact is indeed maturity dependent. This has a significant implication for the cost of ECAP of securitization products in the portfolios of financial institutions. However, studies that specifically tackle the correlation issues for structured products are very limited. The current credit crunch is a demonstration that this issue has not received the necessary coverage by market participants.

Most studies, with a few exceptions, do not address the issue of time horizon, as can be seen in Chernih et al. (2006). Using 10 to 20 years' data to calculate correlations would give a more robust estimate than results using 3 to 5 years' data. The use of long dated datasets, however, has the potential to include correlation patterns that have changed in recent years. For instance, the recent enormous development in information technology may have changed the nature of the markets, making past data less relevant.

23.4   SECURITIZATION AND CDO MODELS

The objective of this section is to show the importance of the correlation and the liquidity assumptions underlying the use of the rating agency tools by structuring desks.

Figure 23.3 depicts the concept of securitization for the management of RCAP/ECAP before the credit crunch. As shown in Table 7.1, the business rationale stems from the observation that the cost of capital of a single bond (idiosyncratic risk) of a certain rating, *ceteris paribus*, is equal or higher than the cost of capital of a securitization note of the same rating (systemic risk) and maturity.

As we have seen recently, when using the rating agency algorithms to get a spread the structurers were implicitly making an assumption of liquidity of the structured market. This can be understood as follows. The rating agency algorithm is based on the Gaussian copula model described in Chapter 3 in which the returns are given as in (23.3) and (23.4). Once the loss distribution has been generated, the rating of the tranche depends on the level of subordination under it – that is, how much loss may happen before the tranche begins to be affected. In order to determine a rating for a tranche one takes the expected loss (EL) of the tranche into account, thereby employing a mapping between EL of a tranche and the rating attributed to it. Others base their approach on the so-called *first dollar loss* methodology,

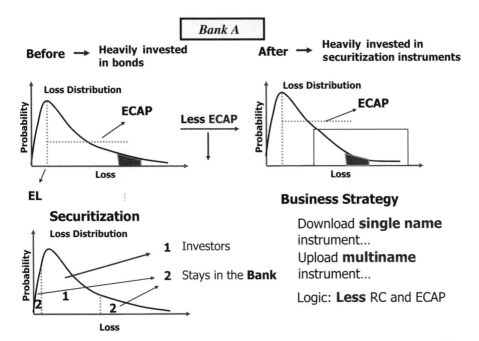

Figure 23.3 The process used in the industry to reduce regulatory/economic capital via securitization while investing on those instruments

supposed to be more in line with a VaR methodology. We refer to Neugebauer (2004) for more details. The rating concept is shown in Figure 23.4.

Once the rating of the tranche is determined, the structurers went to the market in search of *similar deals* with the same rating. The spread of the tranche being structured is assumed to be close to the similar deal found in the market. The rating-based *algorithm* used by the

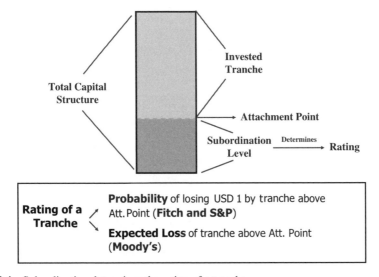

Figure 23.4 Subordination determines the rating of a tranche

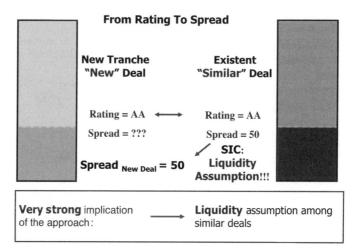

Figure 23.5 Spreads from rating implies liquidity assumption

structuring desks to *determine* the spreads of the new tranche is depicted in Figure 23.5. It happens, however, that, as shown in several chapters in this book, the standardized credit indices are the instruments created to bring liquidity to the credit market and to be used in the pricing discovery process of the bespoke deals. A possible alternative for the market would be to first discover via the indices the relation between spreads and rating and only then infer the spreads of the bespoke tranches. This point is shown schematically in Figure 23.6

The correlation matrix used in the generation of the loss distribution depends on the type of asset class of the collateral of the securitization note. There are differences in the correlation matrices used. The differences become particularly striking when the collateral was ABS notes in the CDOs of ABS. We refer to Fu et al. (2004) and Toutain et al. (2005) for a description

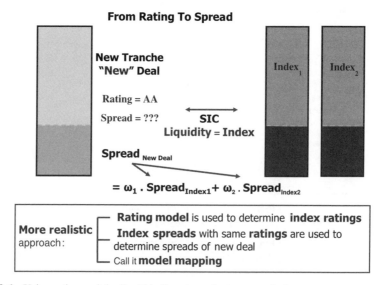

Figure 23.6 Using rating and the liquid indices to evaluate a new deal

Table 23.4   Statistics on intra and inter industry asset value-like correlation

	DRTM		G-Corr	
	Intra%	Inter%	Intra%	Inter%
Average	12	3	15	13
Min	4	1	11	10
Max	25	4	26	16
StDev	6	1	3	1

of correlation methodologies for both corporates and structured finance CDOs respectively. Observe, however, that the studies mention the issues of scarce data and the difficulty of deriving an adequate methodology to cope with it for both asset classes. Table 23.4 shows some statistics on intra and inter industry asset value-like correlation for the corporate asset class. One approach, called Global Correlation (G-Corr), is intuitively similar to the idea of asset correlation although it uses a regression model among the factors, that is industries and countries. The second approach, known as Directional Rating Transition Matrix (DRTM), evaluates default correlation from rating transitions. We refer to Fu et al. (2004) for details.

When the collateral is composed of structured products, as in a CDO of ABSs, the difference in methodologies and in correlation matrices are more significant. One approach is to use an *add-on* approach that depends on the structured finance sector (subdivided in global, meta, broad and narrow), regional, or vintage. The other approach is the so-called *drill down* approach. The idea behind this latter approach is to take the underlying references within the ABS CDO transaction into account (see Figure 23.7). The purpose was to better capture the level of correlation among the ABSs in the collateral portfolio. Moreover, it is worth mentioning that Gilkes and Drexler (2003) and Neugebauer (2004) have reported that the correlation between the ABS collateral in a CDO of ABS transaction is much higher than the correlation among simple corporate bonds.

Note that default probabilites and correlations, derived from studies on historical data, have been used to determine the loss distribution of securitization instruments. This means that

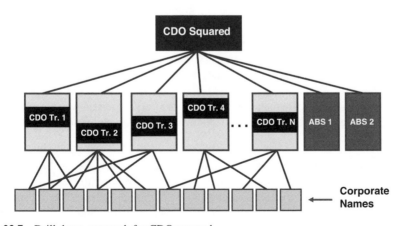

Figure 23.7   Drill down approach for CDO squared

Table 23.5   AAA attachment points for TABX.HE BBB and BBB- using a rating agency methodology before (old) and after (new) the credit crunch for different values of the recovery rate

RR (%)	TABX.BBB		TABX.BBB-	
	R.A. old (%)	R.A. new (%)	R.A. old (%)	R.A. new (%)
0	30.0	67.5	35.0	75.0
25	22.5	50.6	26.3	56.3
40	18.0	40.5	21.0	45.0

there is the *implicit assumption of a long term buy and hold strategy* when determining the rating of the tranche.

Once the loss distribution and the rating of a tranche have been determined, the spread of the tranche is derived by comparing the structure with a similar deal in the market. Therefore, inherent to this approach is the *implicit assumption of market liquidity*.

This was the securitization framework until before the credit crunch. More recently, the agencies have updated their methodologies making it considerably harder to attain the AAA rating for CDOs of ABSs. In Table 23.5 we compare the attachment points for obtaining the AAA rating with the collateral of TABX.HE BBB and BBB- indices for the 07-2 07-1 series, using the old and the new methodologies of a rating agency under different recovery rate assumptions.

23.5   CDO PRICING

Standardized synthetic CDO indices are for credit markets what equity indices are for equity markets. They were created to bring liquidity to the credit market as they facilitate direct investments into a standardized credit portfolio, taking short positions and offering a key mechanism for the pricing discovery process of bespoke portfolios of the underlying asset class. An indication of their importance is shown in Table 22.1. The volume of index-related instruments has grown to at least USD 33 trillion in 2008.

As shown in Chapter 8 for the iTraxx/CDX tranches and in Chapter 18 for the TABX tranches, the pricing of standardized credit indices and their tranches is rather complex when compared to equity indices.

The pricing set up is identical to the one of Basel II risk weights. The main reason for this choice is simplicity: a 1-factor model needs much less computing time for pricing, calibration and generation of hedge and risk parameters than a 2-factor model. Additionally, it has advantages for the pricing of bespoke tranches using correlation mapping techniques, as seen in Chapter 12.

For pricing the indices the input parameters differ in a very important way when compared to the models described for rating, risk and RCAP evaluation. For corporate indices the required parameters are as follows:

1. *Recovery rates (RR)*. Until before the credit crunch the recovery rate has been traditionally set at 40%. As described in Chapter 9, the recent failure to recover distressed prices for very senior tranches of CDX has made the market aware of this dependence and initiated a search for alternative inputs for the recovery rates, stressing it at 20%, while also testing stochastic recovery rates. The RR, however, is just a number agreed by market participants for pricing

purposes. It does not need to have any coherence with internal calculated recoveries for Basel II or any other purpose.

2. *Probabilities of default (PD)*. The probabilities of default are risk-neutral probabilities, implied from CDS quotes. There is no relation with the historical probabilities generally used for the rating approaches and nor with the internal PDs evaluated for regulatory capital purposes.

3. *Correlation*. The correlation parameter is the one that *matches the observed tranche quotes*. Again, there is no link between historical correlations used for rating or risk management systems and the ones used for pricing purposes. There is no link with the *static* correlation implicit in the Basel risk weights. Additionally, we recall that each tranche has a correlation input that ultimately represents how the market perceives the levels of systemic risk affecting the different tranches.

In Chapter 9 we addressed the important concepts of implied or compound correlation and why the market came up with the concept of base correlation. We have also shown the differences between using the Gaussian and the Lévy-based approaches. We have shown that the pricing of bespoke CDOs depends on the correlations implied from the spreads of the liquid standardized indices. In other words, one uses the concept of risk-neutral pricing for correlations, in the same way that volatility of equity is derived from traded options. We have shown in Chapter 11 the importance of the base expected loss concept as an arbitrage-free approach for interpolation purposes. Note that a lot of reliance is placed upon interpolation methodologies: the price of a bespoke tranche may vary significantly depending on the interpolation methodology used. This has been discussed in Chapter 12.

23.6 CREDIT PORTFOLIO MANAGEMENT AND CORRELATION MAPPING

The standardized synthetic credit derivative indices are the appropriate market instruments to manage the systemic risk of the credit portfolio. This explains their strong growth. We focus on the relation between the credit turmoil that started in the summer of 2007 and the need for enhanced transparency in the loan securitization market and the standardized indices. This is required for the securitization business model to develop further.

The securitization activity over the recent years has become strategic for the financial institutions as it permits the efficient use of regulatory and economic capital. Transferring assets through securitization not only frees a firm's capital but also provides a tool to shed concentrated exposures.

Before the credit crunch, a securitization note required a cost of capital equal or lower than that of a single name bond or loan with the same rating and maturity. Moreover, it is well known that for the same rating and maturity the securitization note has a higher spread than the individual bond or loan. Two common arguments were traditionally provided by market practitioners for this higher spread. First, the complexity of the securitization deals implies higher processing costs both in terms of systems and in human capital. The second argument is the so-called *rating change momentum*. Although ratings of securitization notes are reported to be more stable, when conditioning on rating changes, the variations in ratings are much faster than the variations for single name instruments (see Batchvarov et al., 2003). This was observed during the CDO debacle of 2002 and during the more recent credit crisis when high grade tranches have been downgraded very fast from investment grade to junk and even default.

In general, these features increase the extent and speed of a systemic event materialising in price declines and losses for these securitization notes. This sort of phenomena is typical of the self-organized criticality and long-term memory processes discussed in Chapter 21 of which the sand pile problem is just an example (see Bak et al., 1987 and Mandelbrot, 2002). In a portfolio context, we have seen that the dependencies between the securitization notes, compared to dependencies between single name bonds or loans, are in general relatively stronger. Notes of single name CDOs when inserted in a portfolio are closely related to the portfolio of a CDO of ABS. Hence, these risk features strongly influence the risk characteristics of a credit portfolio, thereby leading to significant exposures and high sensitivity to systemic events. The combination of inadequately attributing the *changes in risk characteristics to illiquidity* and absence of *appropriate standardized indices* are very important elements that have led to the severe dislocations in the loan securitization market that is at the heart of the credit crisis.

Before the credit crunch there was a general trend toward fair value accounting. A growing share of banks' credit assets were measured at fair value for financial reporting purposes: trading, available-for-sale and fair-value option assets, and had thus been repriced on a regular basis. The trend reflected a greater liquidity and tradability for an increasing number of credit products and risk parameters, and offered the potential for a more *active* management of credit risk exposures.

However, despite the strong development of securitization, bespoke securitization deals are rather illiquid. For the mark to market management of securitization transactions, one needs *liquid* credit reference instruments. We focus on the standardized indices not only for the management of portfolios composed of securitization notes, but also to serve for the management of the systemic risk of the credit portfolios or subportfolios of the financial institution. As an example, we refer to Martin and Tasche (2007) for a technique to evaluate the proportion of systemic risk and as such *hedgeable* via an appropriate credit index within a credit portfolio. We refer to Section 23.7 for a more detailed discussion.

The recent creation of the standardized credit indices represents a huge technological innovation for credit portfolio management. Their main purpose has been to bring liquidity, via *standardization*, to the underlying credit market. These instruments increase the liquidity in three ways. First, on a deal by deal basis, the standardized indices help in the so-called *price discovery process* of the illiquid bespoke securitization deals. Second, on a portfolio basis, they help to hedge a full portfolio of credits. Finally, by referencing issuers, they may serve as a factor to increase the liquidity of otherwise very illiquid issuers.

As described in Chapter 9, a key parameter for the pricing of the bespoke transactions is the risk-neutral correlation. It is precisely for implying this parameter that standardized and liquid credit indices are essential. Additionally, the fact that the standard model is a 1-factor makes pricing a more straightforward process. As shown in Chapter 12, pricing bespoke tranches means finding appropriate correlation values that are derived from the correlation curves of the standardized liquid credit indices. Despite the simplicity behind 1-factor models, several techniques are still used in the market to interpolate the standardized correlation curve and they may lead, on a deal by deal basis, to considerable price differences. The pricing techniques currently available are indeed much more an art than a science. We have given examples of mapping loss distributions of bespoke CDOs. The mapping techniques can easily be generalized to map different portions of the loss distribution of the financial institution's credit portfolio into the loss distributions of appropriate standardized indices.

A very important point is that the framework used for pricing the corporate standardized credit indices is well established and known by market practitioners. For the ABSCDO market, however, the same cannot be said. The collateral of the ABX.HE index and its TABX.HE tranches are ABCDSs and as, described in Chapter 16, the protocol has just recently been updated. The instruments are still illiquid and, as a result, quotes for ABCDSs on subprime MBSs are not readily available. Moreover, as discussed in Chapter 19, there is currently *no standardized market approach* to price either the indices or their tranches. Given the size of the mortgage market and the credit crisis, we review some points on securitization, risk management and regulatory capital for securitization notes of MBS. We stress that the links among pricing transparency and dynamic credit portfolio management are key to the survival of the securitization framework for financial institutions.

We start with the rating agency rules for the structured products of ABS. We have seen that the rating agencies use as input parameters in their models, historically estimated probabilities of default, recovery rates and correlations. The rating agencies have differed strongly with respect to the correlation estimates introduced in their models. Hence, although the rating agencies were well aware of data issues, it is clear that their rules had not adequately captured the risk characteristics of the securitization notes.

The Basel II capital charges, on the other hand, have been constructed to be portfolio invariant and to be additive (see Section 23.2). To fulfill these conditions, the assumptions of asymptotically fine-grained portfolio and of one single systemic *Gaussian* distributed risk factor were made. As the correlation estimates are calculated on portfolios that did not include recently developed securitization products, such as ABS CDOs, we can conclude that the systemic nature of these securitization instruments may have been underestimated. Additionally, we have seen in Chapter 13 how a variation in systemic correlation affects the correlations between different tranches in the capital structure. This suggests that the correlations may certainly be affected by the business cycle.

In Section 23.3 we mentioned that the credit portfolio risk methods of the financial institutions may have failed to take the correlation parameter of the securitization investments, and thus the systemic risk of the investments, sufficiently into account. The interplay of the financial institutions during recent years led to freeing idiosyncratic exposures via securitization and investing in securitization products. This business model is shown in Figure 23.3. This model has been driven by the benefits of capital relief, fee income, obtaining additional funding sources and relatively high spreads on securitization investments. As the correlation parameter generally entered in the risk methods for the securitization investments was the same as the one for the single name bonds or loans, the necessary increase in the economic capital due to the higher real correlation from the stronger exposure to the systemic risk was not recognized – hence giving a false impression of increased diversification. In other words, in general, *the risk methods of the financial institutions have failed to adequately account for the risk dynamics of the securitization investments*. More specifically, the dynamics of the correlation process, key driver of the securitization business model, have not been taken into account.

The difficulties underlying the pricing of the ABX.HE index and its tranches in terms of a generalized lack of standardized practices strongly limits the transparency in this market. There are several issues behind it. First, the information available to market participants on the CDS of ABS quotes is severely limited. Hence, in contrast to the corporate sphere in which a view on risk-neutral default probabilities is readily available from the CDS market, it is much less straightforward for the ABS case.

Second, as demonstrated in Chapter 19, an important input parameter for the pricing of ABCDSs is the *prepayment* assumption (CPR). The assumption has a considerable impact on the duration of the instrument and therefore on the implied default probabilities. We have shown that it is not possible to recover observed market prices for the TABX.HE BBB-tranches by adapting the 1-factor corporate model if the prepayment assumptions given by the remittance reports of the underlying ABS instruments are used. Moreover, under the 1-factor model the market's view on prepayments was significantly lower than the ones contained in the remittance reports. We know the importance of the indices for bringing liquidity to the underlying asset class. We also know that the 1-factor model offers straightforward and ready-to-use approaches for correlation mapping. Those techniques are key for valuing hedge parameters essential for portfolio management purposes. One obvious solution to this problem is the adoption by market participants of a *risk-neutral* CPR for index pricing purposes, just as has been done for the recovery rate.

Table 23.5 shows that, using rating agency models prior to the credit crunch, the required subordination for an AAA rating was between 21% and 35% for TABX.HE BBB- depending on the recovery rate assumption. On the other hand, the tranche [40%–100%] has been trading *below 90%* since March 2007 already, as shown in Figure 19.4. Either the market was correct – the [40%–100%] was not worth its AAA rating and there was a problem with the rating methodology – or the market was wrong. Today we know the answer. One conclusion that can be drawn is that very important information related to the deterioration of the subprime MBS market was available in the standardized credit indices and this was not perceived or understood by several market participants.

A general remark that applies to rating agency rules, credit portfolio risk methods and the Basel II securitization framework is that data on ABS was absent when deriving the parameter estimates. This is not the same as saying that there was no evidence in the market to show that the increase in the systemic risk was not there. Anybody who priced senior CDO tranches in September 2002, during the burst of the internet bubble, has experienced the impact of the increase in systemic risk on the levels of capital costs of those tranches. The convexity feature is another indication of potential problems with the asset class. Remarks as the one by Robert Schiller (see Laing, 2005), remarks by the rating agencies on the lack of data, and the presentation by Garcia (2006), are all indications that market practitioners were well aware of the problems and some had taken action!

In the next section we propose a framework that integrates all these points in a dynamic credit portfolio framework designed to support the securitization business model of a financial institution.

23.7   STRATEGIC CREDIT ECAP MANAGEMENT

The credit crisis shows that the securitization business model and the recent general innovation in the credit space, such as the development of ABS CDOs, have important consequences for the management of the credit economic capital of a financial institution. To this end, we describe the main concepts of a credit ECAP framework that builds on the current static ratings-based approach in order to enhance the flexibility of the framework. The proposed framework addresses the changing risk characteristics in the banking industry and incorporates a structure for the active management of the credit portfolio. In general, the capital consumption, as determined in the risk systems of the firms and the Basel II framework, has been calibrated on certain portfolios from the past and, therefore, may not represent the current composition of an institution's portfolio. The credit crunch unveiled an underestimation of the correlation on structured products. The changing risk characteristics may not have been detected as sufficient data was not yet available to quantify these changes. The proposed framework is dynamic as it is based on two main aspects: portfolio dependency and time varying assumptions.

The objective of the firm is to optimize the risk-return trade-off and to preserve capital return ratios at predefined levels under different market conditions. In Section 23.3, we determined the *economic capital* (ECAP) as the amount of capital to be set aside by a financial institution in order to prevent its net asset value falling below the level that could impact its normal business activity (short- to mid-term time-horizon), or would hinder the pursuit of its strategic objectives (long-term time-horizon). Hence, the framework to monitor the economic capital consumption should incorporate the evolution of capital on a mid term (one year) and on a multi-year horizon. The remaining discussion is twofold: the framework for dynamic credit ECAP calculations, and the active ECAP management.

23.7.1 Dynamic credit economic capital calculations

The proposed framework is designed to be *dynamic* in contrast to the static ratings-based approach currently employed. This is attained by:

- first, making credit risk – and consequently capital consumption – portfolio dependent;
- second, introducing time varying assumptions, by including the impact of scenario analysis and stress tests on the input parameters;
- finally, by updating the cost of capital to be used within the ratings based system on a regular basis.

Portfolio dependency is required to make the cost of capital dependent on the composition of the portfolio and to capture its changing nature. This can be illustrated by the following two examples. First, consider two banks, M and N with USD 1 billion and 10 million of Brazilian bonds respectively in their portfolios. Assume they intend to add USD 100 million of the same bonds to their portfolios. By making the cost of capital portfolio-dependent, one intends to better access the complex and intricate issues of concentration and diversification of the portfolios of each bank. Second, consider a bank that had large positions on ABSs five years ago. Assume the bank rolls the positions in time in a way to keep the whole composition of the portfolio constant. Financial innovation changed the nature of the market, increasing the level of correlation on that asset class, so the cost of capital of the portfolio should have increased from five years to now.

Before turning to the scenario analysis, the first important step is to make a sensitivity analysis of the portfolio loss distribution with respect to each model parameter. The difficulty of the approach resides in determining the degree of change that one needs to make in the input parameters: risk-free interest rates, default probabilities, transition probabilities, correlation, recovery rates and spreads with respect to risk-free rates. For instance, for the risk-free interest rates one typically applies parallel shifts of 50 to 100 bps, and changes the inclination the curve, e.g. steepening the curve by 25 bps. Spreads can be moved up and down by a factor of 10%. Changes in default probabilities or in the transition probabilities depend on the rating. The variations in correlations depend on the actual correlation stressed, e.g. equity or spread correlations. Observe that during the sensitivity analysis phase, one is not interested in the actual cause of the variations in the parameters. The variables are normally changed one at a time as if they were independent of each other. The advantage of the approach is its simplicity in terms of data and implementation. A big disadvantage of the analysis is the fact that simultaneous movements of the variables are not captured. In reality, the parameters change simultaneously, potentially causing highly nonlinear effects in the economic capital measures.

Scenario analysis is key to introducing the time-varying assumptions and to incorporating the forward-looking perspective in the decision-making process. Two broad types of scenario analysis can be distinguished: historical scenario analysis or hypothetical scenario analysis. There are at least two advantages of the first type. First, data is more readily available. Second, historical scenario analysis immediately receives the required credibility as the scenario actually happened in the past. However, it also has at least two disadvantages. First, the credit portfolio may have been built to survive those historically experienced shocks. Second, the scenarios do not take into account the economic realities and the development in the credit assets. For instance, standardized credit derivatives indices have been created in recent years and did not exist prior to 2002. Anecdotal evidence has it that during the credit crunch some market players were using the crossover index for hedging purposes independent of the nature of the portfolio. Hence, the existence of new instruments changes the dynamics of the market and may make a good deal of the historical-based scenarios irrelevant.

Hypothetical scenario analysis may partly resolve the disadvantages of the historical scenarios and offer the possibility to introduce the forward-looking perspective. They should be based on a thorough analysis and understanding of the economic and financial environment, with forecasts depending on the potential evolution of the environment and identification of how different risk factors could potentially play. The disadvantage of the approach is the difficulty in giving credibility to the scenarios. The more unique and important a scenario may be, the harder it potentially is to make it convincing.

To capture a wide array of potential economic evolutions while keeping it simple, we propose a framework that includes three regimes: bullish, neutral and bearish. That is, we assume that economic activity can be divided into separate regimes: bullish and bearish meaning expansion and contraction respectively. We refer to Hamilton (1989) and the references therein. For each regime, different scenarios are considered. For each scenario, one has to determine how it could affect the input parameters. The bullish scenarios represent expanding credit cycles typically involving tight spreads and consequently low defaults. Recent historically bullish scenarios are the internet bubble of the mid 1990s, or the last five years in which credit spreads have become extremely tight. Examples of bearish scenarios could be: the savings and loan crisis (1980 and 1990), the Mexican peso crisis (1994), the Asian currency crisis (1997), the Russian crisis, the LTCM debacle (1998) and, more recently, the credit crisis. The recent ups and downs in the post-credit crunch can be stressed using scenarios of the 1970s in which we had the oil shock with enormous increase in inflation.

The challenge, then, is to determine the impact of the different scenarios on the input parameters. The relationship between transition probabilities and the business cycle has been studied in Nickell et al. (2000) who found that transition probabilities change during periods of low, medium and high growth of GDP. Bangia et al. (2002) proposed adapting the transition probability matrix for two regimes: expansion and contraction. They found that the ECAP should be around 30% higher during recession periods. The two studies assume constant recovery rates.

We refer to Altman et al. (2006) for a study showing the close link between recovery and default rates, and to Altman et al. (2001) for a first study showing how the 99% VaR varies if that relation is taken into account. More recently, Chava et al. (2006) and Bruche and Gonzalez-Aguado (2008) proposed models that combine default probability and recovery rates to model expected loss. Bruche and Gonzalez-Aguado found that the time variation of recovery rate distributions amplifies risk although the effect is smaller than the impact of the time variation of default probabilities to the systemic risk. As we have described in Sections 23.3 and 23.4 the default correlation is one of the hardest input variables to determine although it has a crucial impact on the determination of the ECAP. It is reported in Lucas (1995), Bahar and Nagpal

Table 23.6 Impact on the credit VaR at different quantiles when going from a growth to a recession scenario

	95%	99%	99.7%	99.9%
Correlation contribution	30%	39%	40%	56%

(2001) and de Servigny and Renault (2002) that default correlations tend to increase over the time horizon. Over a one-year horizon the defaults would be rather firm-specific, while over a three-to-five year horizon defaults could be caused by an industry-wide crisis. The sensitivity of the tranche correlation with respect to systemic correlation has been discussed in Chapter 13. In Table 23.6 we show the impact of the increase in correlation on the credit VaR at different quantiles when the economic cycle goes from growth to recession. Observe that during a recession the correlation increases, and as such the VaR of a position at a certain quantile increases. Moreover, the higher the quantile, the higher the impact of an increase in correlation. The implication is that if one entered on a position during an expansion and hedged that position, once evolving to and through a recession as the VaR increases more with correlation, the hedges that had been calculated during the expansion will not be enough. So changes in correlation from an expansion to a recession means that one will be insufficiently hedged when the economic cycle tightens.

We now turn to the different steps to compute the ECAP of the credit portfolio. For each scenario of each regime one generates the loss distribution and consequent ECAP on both portfolio and position level. As depicted in Figure 23.8 the scenarios will have been elaborated taking into account aggregated views on the credit assets of the portfolio – that is, future defaults, spreads, recovery rates and correlations – and the economic conditions – that is interest rates and correlations. With a weight attributed to each scenario we obtain an ECAP estimate for each regime. Similarly, each regime receives a weight and the total ECAP is given by the weighted average of each regime's ECAP. The weights associated to each regime and its scenarios are certainly subjective as each bank has its own assessment of the impact of economic conditions on its portfolio. But this happens anyway when an investor takes an investment decision, and the difference now is that the decision-making framework is explicit

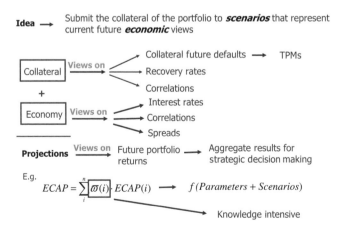

Figure 23.8 Scenario analysis

Table 23.7   Fake positions are used to build an interpolation table for the evaluation of the portfolio-dependent risk weighted assets

Position	Amount	Rating	Maturity	Sector
Real	N_1	A	M_1	S_1
Real	N_2	A_2	M_2	S_2
:	:	:	:	:
Fake	10 mi	AAA	1 year	Financials
Fake	10 mi	AAA	5 year	Financials
Fake	10 mi	AAA	10 year	Financials

and can be measured. In order to cope with the inherent dynamic nature of the economic activity the framework has two ingredients. First, during the scenario analysis phase the input parameters have also been stressed to account for the impact of structural changes in the economy. Second, the entire analysis is to be updated on a regular basis, say quarterly.

As an example, in order to calculate the risk weighted asset (RWA) of a new position one adds some fake positions to the portfolio (see Table 23.7). The whole set of simulations is performed to generate a table of RWAs for AAA financials positions of 10 million for one, five and ten years. The same is done for positions of one million and one billion. The same approach is taken for a set of ratings, say AA, A, BBBs, sectors and maturities. Once the RWA table has been generated, the RWA of the new position is obtained by interpolating from the table. The RWA table is updated regularly, every three months, and depends on the type of the portfolio and risk necessities of the financial institution.

In practice, the framework is used to generate the capital costs for a rating-based economic capital approach. This approach has several advantages. First, the ECAP represents the economic reality as seen by the bank. Second, it is portfolio-dependent, potentially taking into account the issues of diversification and concentration. Third, the values are updated on a regular basis. Fourth, there is already a well understood framework for rating-based systems inside a financial institution and the only additional hurdle would be to feed the tables with numbers updated on a regular basis. Fifth, unlike the current Basel framework, the impact of the different parameters on the generated weights is transparent. Sixth, the whole framework is integrated in the strategic management of the financial institution – that is, the parameters used to generate the simulations represent the internal views of the economic reality and, as such, how it could impact the investment strategies of the institution.

In the next section we will integrate the approach proposed here in the context of dynamic strategic credit portfolio management.

23.7.2   The dynamic ECAP management

The second part of the framework consists of the active management of the credit risk exposures with the purpose of attaining the predetermined strategic goals of the financial institution. Key to this active management is the alignment of the short- and mid-term activities to the long-term strategies of the institution. The central scenario analysis for the credit ECAP management provides a firm-wide view of the potential different economic evolutions/conditions on the short-, mid- and long-term.

The views on the potential developments are based on insights from the trading teams, the portfolio management teams and the strategic management team. The strategic management

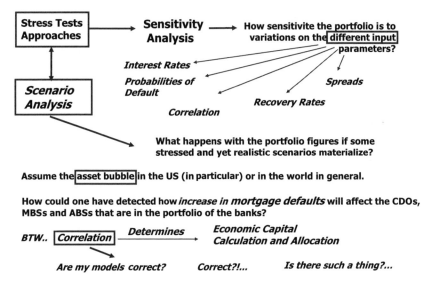

Figure 23.9   Stress tests: important parameters (Garcia, 2006)

team will regularly monitor the feasibility of the predefined long-term goals and make occasional adjustments to the firm's strategy. The first two teams have responsibility for the active management, which implies the monitoring of the risk exposures and making the corrective actions to directing the firm toward its strategic goals. The trading teams are responsible for taking (short-term) hedging positions. The portfolio management teams are responsible for the securitization of the credit portfolios to offload the concentrated exposures. They are responsible for determining the optimal use of ECAP. Note the important intersection between both activities. Once a portion of the portfolio has been selected for securitization, the process is typically time consuming and may take several months, up to one year to be completed. During these months, market conditions may deteriorate considerably, thereby, significantly decreasing the investors' interests in the securitization notes and exposing the firm to potential concentrated risk exposures and losses. It is the function of short-term active management to take positions in liquid credit indices to hedge the adverse market movements.

Underlying this management framework is a basic *feedback loop* that is constantly monitoring the short- and mid-term business evolutions with respect to the strategic objectives and, eventually, making the necessary (short- or mid-term) adjustments. A possible set-up would be a traffic light system, with a *green* light, signalling strong achievement, and a *red* light, signalling deviation from the short- and mid-term activity from their optimal business or portfolio composition, required to achieve the strategic goals. Once an activity receives a yellow or red light, action has to be taken to steer the business back to the long-term strategic goals. This system generates early warning signals supposed to detect difficulties upfront and prevent business deteriorations, and thus significant losses, materialising. Observe that a dashboard containing a summary of the results of the total ECAP and its subdivisions along business lines, important asset classes or sectors, or even individual positions should be generated for monitoring purpose and, depending on market circumstances, on a weekly basis. Figure 23.10 provides a stylized overview of the framework.

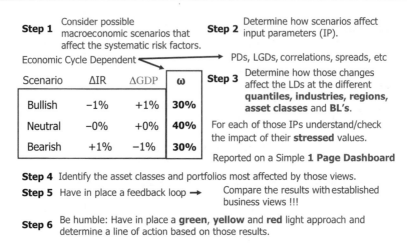

Figure 23.10   Stress tests and scenario analysis (Garcia, 2006)

The strategic goals for the institution are set by the long-term (LT) team when the loss distributions are generated using *through the cycle (TTC)* parameters. The short-term (ST) team looks at the short term for which the loss distributions are generated with *point in time (PIT)* parameters. Both groups set the scenarios and stress tests for their time horizons. The mid-term (MT) team compares the short-term results with the long-term goals and performs an analysis taking into account both TTC and PIT parameters. They are responsible for detecting mismatches between the two views and generating the green, yellow and red lights to indicate that action needs to be taken. That team fully understands the goals of the institution and can communicate with both the ST and LT teams. They also understand the capital aggregation and allocation processes on a firm-wide basis. Consider, for example, that a red light has been generated for a certain set of positions. The assets are going to be securitized or hedged via the indices. During the recent credit crunch the Basel Committe on Bank Supervision proposed an update for the cost of capital of securitization instruments. Observe that in this framework securitization instruments are supposed to be put on mark to market where the cost of capital is minimal.

To summarize, the solution for the securitization business model comes from understanding the nature of the processes underlying the securitization instruments. Any instrument substituting idiosyncratic for systemic risk implies a dependency on systemic correlation. As discussed in Chapter 21, correlation is identified as a long-term dynamic memory process. This means that the widespread Gaussian assumption is inappropriate, even though it is embedded in basically all risk systems, rating agency systems, pricing tools, regulatory framework, university courses and, more important, in the head of every market practitioner! As explained by Hurst when solving the problem of the dam, a first solution is to consider that the instruments are going to be held to maturity using a significant high correlation.

A second solution is to create a dynamic framework in which the dynamics of correlation are followed up and hedges are put in place resulting in an automatically reduced securitization activity via the market forces expressed in the indices – that is, because market participants failed to understand the dynamics of the systemic correlation process, as could have been seen in the prices of the senior TABX.HE.BBB- tranches. The proposed framework includes a monitoring process based on stress tests and scenario analysis using a short-, mid- and long-term time horizon. The short-term is related to immediate market conditions. The mid-term team functions within a *feedback loop* taking corrective measures. The focus of the long-term team is on the strategic goals. Within this approach, it is still possible to apply the Gaussian framework while giving the whole industry time to understand the properties and mathematics of the non-Gaussian world as expressed in the many and notable works of Mandelbrot.

There are several advantages behind the approach and systems proposed here. First, we keep the simplicity of the rating-based framework while adapting it on a regular basis, taking into account the fact that the capital consumption is portfolio-dependent. Second, the framework implies the creation of management teams within the financial institution that analyze the potential risks affecting the institution. The existence of a framework based on stress tests and scenario analysis will considerably increase the level of market and economic awareness throughout the financial institutions. Third, issues such as adverse impact of financial innovations have a far higher chance of being detected and captured at an early stage. Fourth, it puts economic capital at the center of the decision-making process, potentially implying a more efficient organization. Fifth, the entire framework implies the creation of a firm-wide dynamic credit portfolio management structure, including a trading desk well aware of market developments through the indices.

This implies the use of credit derivatives indices for hedging and for determining the fair value of the credit portfolio. The indices are supposed to be liquid with transparent widely-used market approaches for pricing and hedge purposes. The input parameters used in the models need to be agreed for pricing purposes. The issues of volume and transparency mean that the indices should be exchange traded. For the corporate credit indices we see that this is already a reality. At the time of writing we have seen the emergence of exchange traded credit derivatives for counterparty risk management purposes (see Grant, 2009). The next step is to bring the standardized credit indices to the exchanges. For ABX.HE and TABX.HE the market still needs to agree on many aspects, such as standardized pricing and risk-neutral parameters.

24

Conclusion

Sometimes I lie awake at night, and I ask, "Where have I gone wrong?" Then a voice says to me,
"This is going to take more than one night."
Charles M. Schulz, Charlie Brown in "Peanuts"

The main topic in this book is the securitization business model for financial institutions. From the originator point of view it permits the financial institution to distribute idiosyncratic risks to the market and remain focused on the origination process. From the investor point of view one is less exposed to idiosyncratic risks, increasing diversification and potentially the level of systemic risk. It increases the level of economic activity by increasing the levels of consumption while reducing the prices of goods and services, making them accessible to the whole population. However, the benefits come via increasing leverage. To avoid increases in the levels of systemic risk having a catastrophic impact on economic activity, as has happened since June 2007, the leverage ratios of a financial institution need to be carefully monitored and appropriately managed in accordance with the point in time of the economic cycle and the nature and long-term strategic goals of the different activities within the financial institution.

The inappropriate framework for handling securitization instruments in the portfolios of financial institutions is responsible for the huge losses observed since June 2007. We have shown that the deterioration in the MBS market was certainly observable in several standardized credit indices. The deterioration of the TABX.HE BBB- super senior tranche, which at the time was an AAA tranche, was visible since early 2007. The severe deterioration since February 2007 was visible in the ABX.HE indices. Given that commercial real estate is very dependent on the economic cycle, the same behavior is also observed in the CMBX.NA indices. It is interesting to note that the AAA-related instruments only showed the deterioration in the summer of 2007 when the problem had become systemic.

The correlation between tranches of securitization instruments depends on the level of systemic risk. The variation can be observed in the senior tranches of standardized credit indices. Just as in the Black-Scholes formula where the implied volatility is the key parameter for option pricing, in the correlation market the systemic correlation is the key parameter for tranche spreads in the capital structure. Note that the Gaussian hypothesis is a widespread assumption underlying almost every system for credit risk, regulatory capital, rating and pricing purposes. The dynamics of systemic correlation, however, follow a long-term memory process. The loss distributions are more fat tailed than the loss distribution generated by the Gaussian distribution.

The set-up outlined here has some important consequences:

1. The cost of capital changes in time. That is, a rating-based approach for capital costs *cannot be time independent*, as is the current approach.
2. If securitization instruments are put on *buy and hold* then the correlation used to evaluate the cost of capital has to be the through-the-cycle value. The cost of capital becomes very high, potentially impacting the activity. For this reason, in order to reduce the cost of capital

the instruments should be put on a *mark to market* framework where the prices are based on the appropriate standardized credit indices.

3. The instruments in mark to market bring *transparency*. The higher the transparency levels for the asset class, the higher its potential liquidity, the higher the volume, the higher the benefits for the economy.

4. The standardized credit indices should be *exchange traded* and the pricing algorithms and risk-neutral input parameters should be agreed upon by market practitioners.

5. As different asset classes react differently and portfolio concentration matters, a rating-based approach for capital costs should be *portfolio-dependent*.

6. In order to catch systemic changes early in the credit cycle, one needs to implement an Economic Capital Planning framework that mixes short-, mid- and long-term horizons integrated in a *traffic light* system:

   • The long-term horizon is used to set the strategic goals for the financial institution and assumes the use of through-the-cycle (TTC) parameters.

   • The team focusing on the short-term horizon follows up on the activity in line with the point in time (PIT) of the economic cycle.

   • The team focusing on the mid-term horizon serves as a *feedback loop* in the control system, making the link between the two. It monitors the short-term results and compares them to the long-term goals. The team doing this needs to understand the goals of the institution and should be aware of the short-term context, fully understanding the capital aggregation processes within the financial conglomerate. If short-term developments deviate dangerously from the assumption underlying the long-term goals a red light is flagged. Assets to be disposed of are either securitized or hedged using a CDS. The choice between the two options depends on the time frame and market conditions.

7. Economic capital needs to be monitored using economic parameters within a *stress test and scenario analysis framework*. A rating-based approach for capital costs can still be used, but the capital weights for the different ratings and maturities need to be updated regularly, depending on portfolio composition and market conditions.

One of the main forces behind the creation of ABX.HE standardized credit indices have been hedge funds. They have requested an instrument to take short positions on the subprime MBS market. Due to Basel regulatory capital requirements, risk capital intensive activities have been moved out of banks into hedge funds in recent years.

Many have blamed Alan Greenspan, Chairman of the Federal Reserve of the United States from 1987 to 2006, for his defense of the use of innovation for economic development and for the asset price bubble that generated the credit crunch (see e.g. Krugman, 2008). For years he was seen as a pillar of self regulation and the use of innovation for economic development. In February 2004 Greenspan warned against the high leverage of government-sponsored enterprises:

> Federal Reserve Chairman Alan Greenspan last week threw his considerable clout behind the effort to curb the growth of Fannie Mae and Freddie Mac. In candid testimony before lawmakers, he said the agencies posed potential systemic risks to the US financial system and urged that a limit be placed on the size of their balance sheets.

> Greenspan has stated his concerns about the explosive growth of government sponsored enterprises (GSEs) in the past, but the fervour with which he testified on the issue in front of the Senate Banking Committee surprised many market participants. One interest rate strategist said he believed that

because corporate America had cleaned up its balance sheet, Greenspan was turning his focus to the GSEs, which together owned or guaranteed four trillion USD worth of mortgages.

"Philosophically, he just doesn't believe the GSEs should be as big a leveraged player in the mortgage market as they are," said one strategist. "The concentration of risk is what disturbes Greenspan."

The agencies are highly leveraged but are still able to borrow at thin spreads over Treasuries because their implied government guarantee. This precludes traditional market based solutions, such as rising borrowing costs, from limiting their growth, Greenspan said.

Short of privatisation – which Greenspan favours while acknowledging he is part of a minority – he said regulators should rein in the GSEs to prevent future "systemic difficulties, which we access as likely if GSE expansion continues unabated." (IFR, 2009)

During the last years before the credit crunch, securitization volumes have increased significantly, both in the US and in Europe. The activity is essential for economic development. A recognition of the benefits of the securitization activity can be seen in the policy adopted by the European Central Bank in 2008. During that year the ECB has bought a significant amount of all securitization issuances in Europe, making 2008 one of the best years for the activity in Europe. This book presents solutions using technology and innovation to foster the securitization business model to support the economic activity.

Appendix A
Economic Capital Allocation Approaches

Assume a loss distribution defined by L and a certain quantile α. The *credit value at risk* (CVaR) associated with the quantile is defined respectively as:

$$\text{CVaR}_\alpha(L) = \inf\{x > 0 \,|\, P(L \leq x) \geq \alpha\}. \tag{A.1}$$

Below we will define approaches using standard risk measures that are largely used in practice for allocating economic capital. Assume the conglomerate is comprised of n subportfolios whose allocations we want to determine. Below we show some of the different approaches used for ECAP allocation with some comments on the differences:

1. **VaR / Covar.** Although largely used by practitioners, this approach is typical for Gaussian loss distribution. The allocated capital of a certain subportfolio is given by:

$$\text{ECAP}_i(\alpha) = \frac{Cov[L, L_i]}{\sigma_T^2} \text{ECAP}_T(\alpha) \tag{A.2}$$

   where L_i and L are the losses of the subportfolio i and the total portfolio respectively. $\text{ECAP}_T(\alpha)$ and σ_T^2 are the total ECAP of the portfolio at the quantile α, and the total portfolio loss variance respectively.

2. **Pro-rata CVaR.** In this approach one uses the stand-alone CVaR_α of each sub-portfolio as a weight in the allocation of the total risk:[1]

$$\text{ECAP}_i(\alpha) = \frac{\text{CVar}_\alpha(L_i)}{\sum_{i=1}^{N} \text{CVaR}_\alpha(L_i)} \text{CVaR}_\alpha(L) \tag{A.3}$$

3. **Basel II.** In this approach we use the relative proportions resulting from the Basel II formulas to allocate CVaR. Assume, for example, that RCAP_i is the regulatory capital of subportfolio i then its allocated capital would be given by:

$$\text{ECAP}_i(\alpha) = \frac{\text{RCAP}_i}{\sum_{i=1}^{N} \text{RCAP}_i} \text{CVaR}_\alpha(L). \tag{A.4}$$

   The principle behind this approach is to keep Basel II proportions for ECAP allocation.

4. **Marginal optimization of total CVaR.** The idea is to search in the stand-alone loss distribution of each subportfolio the quantile for which the summation of the CVaR of the subportfolios would equal the CVaR of the whole portfolio, see Govaerts et al. (2005). One then searches the quantile β on the stand-alone loss distribution of the subportfolios such that:

$$\beta = \inf\left\{\beta\prime \in [0, 1] : \sum_{i=1}^{N} \text{CVaR}_{\beta\prime}(L_i) \geq \text{CVaR}_\alpha(L)\right\} \tag{A.5}$$

---

[1] As measured by the total cVaR that takes into account the whole correlation structure of the portfolio.

then $ECAP_i(\alpha)$ is defined as:

$$ECAP_i(\alpha) = CVaR_\beta(L_i) \qquad (A.6)$$

5. **CVaR contribution via expected shortfall.** In this approach, cVaR is allocated using the concept of Expected Shortfall (or conditional tail expectation CTE) contribution which is defined by:

$$ES_\beta(L_i) = E_P\left[L_i | L_i > CVaR_\beta(L_i)\right] \qquad (A.7)$$

and the allocation is given by:

$$ECAP_i(\alpha) = \frac{ES_\beta(L_i)}{ES_\beta(L)}CVaR(L). \qquad (A.8)$$

Observe that the quantiles for the $CVaR(\alpha)$ and for the ES_β do not need to be the same. For example, a bank might have its $cVaR_\alpha$ depending on a quantile of (say) 99.97% while allocating it following a quantile of 99%. This would mean riskier portfolios would demand more capital. Such decisions are strategic and depend on the policy of the bank.

6. **Expected shortfall equal to $CVaR_\alpha$.** In this approach we look for the ES quantile that is equal to the $CVaR_\alpha$. The allocation is done using the ES. Assume for example that:

$$\beta = \inf\left\{\beta\prime \in [0, 1] : ES_{\beta\prime}(L) \geq CVaR_\alpha(L)\right\} \qquad (A.9)$$

In this way $EC_i(\alpha) = EC_\beta(L_i)$. The main objective of this approach is to eliminate the problem of subadditivity of the CVaR measure.

Appendix B
Generalized Gauss Laguerre Quadrature

We outline two algorithms for the computation of abscissas and weights for generalized Gauss Laguerre quadrature.

B.1   EIGENVALUE PROBLEM

The first algorithm is based on an eigenvalue problem. We refer to Golub and Welsch (1969) and Wilf (1962) for a detailed discussion. The abscissas of the quadrature formula can be found as the eigenvalues of the symmetric tridiagonal matrix T, given by

$$T = \begin{pmatrix} \alpha_0 & \sqrt{\beta_1} & & & \\ \sqrt{\beta_1} & \alpha_1 & \sqrt{\beta_2} & & \\ & \ddots & \ddots & \ddots & \\ & & \sqrt{\beta_{n-2}} & \alpha_{n-2} & \sqrt{\beta_{n-1}} \\ & & & \sqrt{\beta_{n-1}} & \alpha_{n-1} \end{pmatrix} \tag{B.1}$$

where $\alpha_i = 2i + 1 + s$ and $\beta_i = i(i + s)$. The corresponding weights can be computed from the normalized eigenvectors. With

$$T v_j = x_j v_j \tag{B.2}$$

where $v_j^T v_j = 1$ we have that

$$w_j = \mu_0 v_{j,1}^2, \tag{B.3}$$

where $\mu_0 = \int_0^{+\infty} w(x; s) = \Gamma(s + 1)$.

The symmetric tridiagonal eigenvalue problem as in (B.2) can be solved efficiently using the classical algorithms for eigenvalues; see Golub and Van Loan (1989), Parlett (1980) or Wilkinson (1988) for details. This and other numerical algorithms are addressed in Press et al. (1992). Note that only the first component of the normalized eigenvector is required, hence an optimized eigenvalue solver can be used.

B.2   NEWTON-RAPHSON ITERATION

The second algorithm is based on the fact that good initial approximations for the zeros of the orthogonal polynomials are available (see Stroud and Secrest, 1966). The initial guess $\tilde{x}_1$ for the first root x_1 is

$$\tilde{x}_1 = \frac{(1 + s)(3 + 0.92s)}{1 + 2.4n + 1.8s} \tag{B.4}$$

and for the second root x_2 it is

$$\tilde{x}_2 = x_1 + \frac{15 + 6.25s}{1 + 0.9s + 2.5n}. \tag{B.5}$$

For the other roots x_i, the initial guess $\tilde{x}_i$ is

$$\tilde{x}_i = x_{i-1} + \left(\frac{1 + 2.55(i-2)}{1.9(i-2)} + \frac{1.26(i-2)s}{1 + 3.5(i-2)} \right) \frac{x_{i-1} - x_{i-2}}{1 + 0.3s}. \tag{B.6}$$

With these initial guesses a Newton-Raphson iteration is started; that is, subsequent approximations to the root $f(x_i) = 0$ are constructed as follows

$$x_i^{(k+1)} = x_i^{(k)} - \frac{f(x_i^{(k)})}{f'(x_i^{(k)})} \tag{B.7}$$

where $f'(x)$ denotes the derivative of the function $f(x)$ with respect to x. Since Newton-Raphson iterations converge quadratically, provided a good starting value is given, we have very accurate approximations to the root after a few iterations.

The polynomials can be evaluated efficiently using the recurrence relation

$$(n+1)L_{n+1}^{(s)}(x) = (2n + 1 + s - x)L_n^{(s)}(x) - (n+s)L_{n-1}^{(s)}(x), \tag{B.8}$$

which can be started with $L_0^{(s)}(x) = 1$ and $L_{-1}^{(s)}(x) = 0$. The derivative is easily obtained from the following relation

$$x \frac{d}{dx} L_n^{(s)}(x) = n L_n^{(s)}(x) - (n+s)L_{n-1}^{(s)}(x). \tag{B.9}$$

For these and other formulas involving Laguerre polynomials, see Abramowitz and Stegun (1964). The weights are given by

$$w_i = \frac{-\Gamma(s+n)}{n\Gamma(n)L_{n-1}^{(s)}(x_i)\frac{dL_n^{(s)}}{dx}(x_i)}. \tag{B.10}$$

Note that we only have to evaluate the gamma function once. Given $\Gamma(s + 1)$, we can make use of the recurrence relation $\Gamma(x) = (x - 1)\Gamma(x - 1)$ for other values of n.

References

Abramowitz, M. and Stegun, I. (1964) *Handbook of Mathematical Functions*. National Bureau of Standards.

AIG, Form 8-K Sec Filing, 11 February 2008.

AIG, Form 10-Q, Sec Filing, 30 September 2007.

Altman, E., Brady, B., Resti, A. and Sironi, A. (2006) The Link Between Default and Recovery Rates: Theory, Empirical Evidence, and Implications. *Financial Analysts Journal*, 78(6):2203–2227.

Altman, E. and Kishore, V. (1996) Almost Everything You Wanted to Know about Recoveries on Defaulted Bonds. *Financial Analysts Journal* 52(6):57–64.

Altman, E., Resti, A. and Sironi, A. (2001) Analyzing and Explaining Default Recovery Rates. Technical Report International Swap and Derivatives Association.

Andersen, L., Sidenius, J. and Basu, S. (2003) All your Hedges in One Basket. *RISK*.

Artzner, P., Delbaen, F., Eber, J.-M. and Heath, D. (1999) Coherent Measures of Risk. *Mathematical Finance*, 9(3).

Arvanitis, A. and Gregory, J. (2001) *Credit: The Complete Guide to Pricing, Hedging and Risk Management*, Risk Books.

Bahar, R. and Nagpal, K. (2001) Measuring Default Correlation. *Risk*, 129–132.

Baheti, P. and Morgan, S. (2007) Base Correlation Mapping. Technical Reports. Lehman Brothers.

Bak, P. (1996) *How Nature Works: The Science of Self-Organized Criticality*. Copernicus, New York.

Bak, P., Tang, C. and Wiesenfeld, K. (1987) Self-organized Criticality: An Explanation of 1/f Noise. *Physical Review Letters*, 59:381–384.

Bangia, A., Diebold, F. and Schuermann, T. (2000) Ratings Migration and the Business Cycle, with Applications to Credit Portfolio Stress Testing. Technical Report, The Wharton School, Univeristy of Pennsylvania.

Batchvarov, A., Collins, J. and Davies, W. (2003) ABS/MBS/CMBS/CDO 101: A Compendium of Pieces for New and Not So New Investors. Technical Report, Merril Lynch.

Baxter, M. (2006) Lévy Simple Structural Models Technical Report. Nomura.

Bertoin, J. (1996) *Lévy Processes*. Cambridge University Press.

Bingham, N. and Kiesel, R. (2004) *Risk-Neutral Valuation Pricing and Hedging of Financial Derivatives*. Springer.

BIS. (2005) An Explanatory Note on the Basel II IRB Risk Weight Functions. Technical Report, Bank for International Settlements.

BIS. (2006) Studies on Credit Risk Concentration. Technical Report, Bank for International Settlements.

BIS. (2008) Cross-sectorial Review of Group-wide Identification and Management of Risk Concentrations. Technical Report ISBN 92-9131-762-4, Bank for International Settlements.

Black, F. and Cox, J. (1976) Valuing Corporate Securities: Some Effects of Bond Indenture Provisions. *Journal of Finance*, 31:351–367.

Black, F. and Jones, R. (1987) Simplifying Portfolio Insurance. *Journal of Portfolio Management*, 31.

Black, F. and Karasinsky, P. (1991) Bond and Option Pricing when Short Rates are Lognormal. *Financial Analysts Journal*, 47(4):52–59.

Black, F. and Scholes, M. (1973) The Pricing of Options and Corporate Liabilities. *Journal of Political Economy*, 81:634–654.

Bluhm, C., Overbeck, L. and Wagner, C. (2003) *An introduction to Credit Risk Modeling*. Chapman & Hall/CRC.

Borland, L., Bouchaud, J., Muzy, J. and Zumbach, G. (2005) The Dynamics of Financial Markets – Mandelbrot's Multifractal Cascades, and Beyond. Technical Report.

Bremaud, P. (1981) *Point Processes and Queues: Martingale Dynamics*. Springer.

Brigo, D. and Chourdakis, K. (2008) Counterparty Risk for Credit Default Swaps. Technical report. Fitch Solutions.

Bruche, M. and Gonzalez-Aguado, C. (2008) Recovery Rates, Default Probabilities and the Credit Cycle. Technical Report, Center for Monetary and Financial Studies, Spain.

Calvet, L. and Fischer, A. (2001) Forecasting Multifractal Volatility. *Journal of Econometrics*, 25: 105.

Calvet, L. and Fischer, A. (2004) How to Forecast Long-run Volatility: Regime Switching and the Estimation of Multifractal Processes. *Journal of Financial Econometrics*, (2):49.

Carr, P. and Madan, D. (1998) Option Valuation using the Fast Fourier Transform. *Journal of Computational Finance*, 2:61–73.

Chava, S., Stefanescu, C. and Turnbull, S. (2006) Modelling Expected Loss. Technical Report, Texas AM Business School.

Chernih, A., Vanduffel, S. and Henrard, L. (2006) Asset Correlations: A Literature Review and Analysis of the Impact of Dependent Loss Given Defaults. Available on defaultrisk.com.

Cherubini, U., Luciano, E. and Vecchiato, W. (2004) *Copula Methods in Finance*. John Wiley & Sons Ltd.

Cifuentes, A., Efrat, I., Gluck, J. and Murphy, E. (1998) Buying and Selling Credit Risk: A Perspective on Credit-linked Obligations. In: *Credit Derivatives: Applications for Risk Management, Investment and Portfolio Optimisation*, Risk Books.

Cifuentes, A. and O'Connor, G. (1996) The Binomial Expansion Method Applied to CBO/CLO Analysis. Moody's Special Report.

Cont, R. and Tankov, P. (2004) *Financial Modelling with Jump Processes*. Chapman & Hall/CRC.

Cover, T. and Joy, A. (2006) *Elements of Information Theory*. John Wiley & Sons Inc.

Debuysscher, A., Szegö, M., Freydefront, M. and Tabe, H. (2003) The Fourier Transform Method. Technical Report. International Structured Finance, Moody's.

de Servigny, A. and Renault, O. (2002) Default Correlation: Empirical Evidence. Technical Report, Standard & Poor's.

de Servigny, A. and Renault, O. (2003) Correlation Evidence. *Risk Magazine*.

de Servigny, A. and Renault, O. (2004) *Measuring and Managing Credit Risk*. McGraw-Hill.

Dougherty, R., Edelman, A. and Hyman, J. (1989) Nonnegativity-, Monotonicity- or Convexity-Preserving Cubic and Quintic Hermite Interpolation. *Mathematics of Computation*, 52(186): 471–494.

Duffie, D. and Singleton, K. (1999) Modelling Term Structure of Defaultable Bonds. *Review of Financial Studies*, 12:687–720.

Eavis, P. (2009) U.S. Government Needs Map for Lost Citi. *Wall Street Journal*.

Embrechts, P., McNeil, A. and Straumann, D. (1999) Correlation and Dependence in Risk Management: Properties and Pitfalls. Technical Report.

Embrechts, P., McNeil, A. and Straumann, D. (2002) Correlation and Dependence in Risk Management: Properties and Pitfalls. In M. Dempster (ed.), *Risk Management: Value at Risk and Beyond*, Cambridge University Press: pp. 176–223.

Fabozzi, F. (2004) *Bond Markets, Analysis, and Strategies*. Pearson Prentice-Hall.

Fabozzi, F., Bhattacharya, A. and Berliner, W. (2007) *Mortgage Backed Securities: Products, Structuring, and Analytical Techniques*, John Wiley & Sons Inc.

Fischer, A., Calvet, L. and Mandelbrot, B. (1997) Multifractality of DEM/USD Rates. Technical Report 1165, Cowles Foundation Discussion Paper.

Frees, E. and Valdez, E. (1998) Understanding Relationships Using Copulas. *North American Actuarial Journal*, 2(1):1–25.

Frisch, U. (1997) *Turbulence: The Legacy of A. Kolmogorov*. Cambridge University Press.

Fritsch, F. and Carlson, R. (1980) Monotone Piecewise Cubic Interpolation. *SIAM J. Numerical Analysis*, 17:238–246.

Fu, Y., Gluck, J., Mazataud, P., Rosa, D., Schoder, R. and Toutain O. (2004) Moody's Revisits its Assumptions Regarding Corporate Default (and Asset) Correlations for CDOs. *Moody's Structured Finance*.

Garcia, J. (2006) Integrating Stress Tests and Scenario Analysis for Strategic Management of a Financial Institution. Risk Training, London.

Garcia, J., Gomes, M., Jyh, T., Ren, T. and Sales, T. (1993) Nonlinear Dynamics of the Cellular-automaton Game of Life. *Physical Review E*, (48):3345–3351.

Garcia, J. and Goossens, S. (2007) Lévy Base Correlation Explained. Technical Report.

Garcia, J. and Goossens, S. (2008) Explaining the Lévy Base Correlation Smile. *Risk Magazine*, pp. 84–88.

Garcia, J., Goossens, S. and Lamoot, J. (2007) Credit ALM: The Link Among Correlation, Credit Risk Systems and Standardised Indexes of Credit Derivatives. Technical Report.

Garcia, J., Goossens, S. and Lamoot, J. (2008) Credit Valuation Adjustment on Credit Default Swaps, In F. Cole, F. Mallor, E. Omey and S. Van Gulck (eds), *Proceedings of the Sixth International Conference on Simulation in Industry and Services*, pp. 109–119.

Garcia, J., Goossens, S., Masol, V. and Schoutens, W. (2009) Lévy Base Correlation. *Wilmott Journal*, 1(2):95–100.

Garcia, J., Goossens, S. and Schoutens, W. (2008) Let's Jump Together: Pricing Credit Derivatives. *Risk Magazine*, pp. 130–133.

Garcia, J., van Ginderen, H. and Garcia, R. (2003) On the Pricing of Credit Spread Options: A Two Factor HW-BK Algorithm. *Int. Journal of Theoretical and Applied Finance*, 6(5):491–505.

Gilkes, K. and Drexler, M. (2003) Drill-Down Approach for Synthetic CDO Squared Transactions. *Standard and Poors, Structured Finance*.

Glasserman, P. (2004) *Monte Carlo Methods in Financial Engineering*. Springer.

Glasserman, P. and Li, J. (2003) Importance Sampling for Portfolio Credit Risk. *Management Science*, 51:1643–1656.

Golub, G. and Van Loan, C (1989) *Matrix Computations*. The Johns Hopkins University Press.

Golub, G. and Welsch, J. (1969) Calculation of Gauss Quadrature Rules. *Mathematics of Computation*, 23:221–230.

Goodman, L. (2002) Synthetic CDOs: An Introduction. *Journal of Derivatives*, Spring, pp. 60–72.

Goodman, L., Li, S., Lucas, D., Zimmerman, T. and Fabozzi, F. (2008) *Subprime Mortgage Credit Derivatives*, John Wiley & Sons Inc.

Goodman, L. S. and Fabozzi, F. J. (2002) *Collateralized Debt Obligations: Structures and Analysis*. John Wiley & Sons Inc.

Gopikrishnan, P., Plerou, V., Amaral, L., Meyer, M. and Stanley, H. (1999) Scaling of the Distribution of Fluctuations of Financial Market Indices. *Physical Review E*, 60:5305.

Gordy, M. (2003) A Risk-factor Model Foundation for Ratings-based Bank Capital Rules. *J. Financial Intermediation*, 12(3):199–232.

Gordy, M. (2009) First, Do No Harm. A Hippocratic Approach to Procyclicality in Basel II. GARP Annual Convention.

Gordy, M. and Lütkebohmert, E. (2007) Granularity Adjustment for Basel II. Technical Report, Deutsche Bundesbank.

Govaerts, M., Van den Borre, E. and Laeven, R. (2005) Managing Economic and Virtual Economic Capital within Financial Conglomerates. *North American Actuarial Journal*, 9(3):77–89.

Grant, J. (2009) France Calls for Eurozone CDS Clearing House. *Financial Times*.

Gregory, J. (2009) Being Two-faced Over Counterparty Credit Risk. *Risk*, pp. 86–90.

Gupton, G., Finger, C. and Bhatia, M. (1997) Credit Metrics – Technical Documentation. *JP Morgan*.

Hamilton, J. (1989) A New Approach to the Economic Analysis of Nonstationary Time Series and the Business Cycle. *Econometrica*, 57:357–384.

Hayre, L., Saraf, M., Young, R. and Chen, J. (2008) Modelling of Mortgage Defaults. *Fixed Income Strategy and Analysis*, Citigroup.

Heitfield, E., Burton, S. and Chomsissengphet, S. (2005) The Effects of Name and Sector Concentrations on the Distribution of Losses for Portfolios of Large Wholesale Credit Exposures.

Hill, M. and Vacca, L. (1999) Collateralized Debt Obligations: An Introduction to Arbitrage CBOs and CLOs. Bank of America.

Hooda, S. (2006) Explaining Base Correlation Skew Using Normal-Gamma Process. Techinical Report. Nomura.

Hull, J. (2003) *Options, Futures and Other Derivatives*. Pearson Prentice-Hall.

Hull, J. and White, A. (1994a) Numerical Procedures for Implementing Term Structure Models I: Single Factor Models. *Journal of Derivatives*, 2(1):7–16.

Hull, J. and White, A. (1994b) Numerical Procedures for Implementing Term Structure Models II: Two-factor Models. *Journal of Derivatives*, 2(2):37–48.

Hurst, H. (1956) Methods of Using Long-term Storage Reservoirs. *Proceedings of the Institution of Civil Engineers*, (5):519–590.

IFR (2008a) Moody's CPDO Team Faces Disciplinary Action. *International Financing Review*, 1741:10.

IFR (2008b) Moody's Fights growing CPDO Storm. *International Financing Review*, 1735:45.

IFR (2009) Greenspan Fires on the GSEs. *International Financing Review*, 1772:18.

Jarrow, R., Lando, D. and Turnbull, S. (1997) A Markov Model for the Term Structure of Credit Spreads. *The Review of Financial Studies*, 10(2):481–526.

Jones, D. (1998) Emerging Problems with Basel Capital Accord: Regulatory Capital Arbitrage and Related Issues. *Journal of Banking and Finance*, 24:35–58.

JP Morgan (2006) *Credit Derivatives Handbook*.

Kalemanova, A., Schmid, B. and Werner, R. (2007) The Normal Inverse Gaussian Distribution for Synthetic CDO Pricing. *Journal of Derivatives*, 14(3):80–93.

Kalra, R., Yim, G., Hrvatin, R., Segger, H., Gill, K., Hardee, R. and Bund, S. (2006) *ABS Leveraged Super Seniors: Structuring and Modelling*. Technical Report. Structured Credit Criteria Report, Derivative Fitch.

Karatzas, I. and Shreve, S. (1991) *Brownian Motion and Stochastic Calculus*. Springer.

Kothari, V. (2006) *Securitization: The Financial Instrument of the Future*. John Wiley & Sons Inc.

Krugman, P. (2008) Paul Krugman says: I'd blame Alan Greenspan and Phil Gramm. http://www.youtube.com/watch?v=YwqcLbZJ4HA.

Kyprianou, A. (2006) *Introductory Lectures on Fluctuations of Lévy Processes with Applications*, Springer.

Laing, J. (2005) The Bubble's New Home, *Barron's*, **20**, June.

Lando, D. (1998) On Cox Processes and Credit Risky Securities, *Review of Derivatives Research*, 2(2/3):99–120.

Li, D. (1999) The Valuation of the nth-to-default Basket of Credit Derivatives, Technical Reports. Risk Metrics Group.

Livesey, M. and Schloegl, L. (2006) Recovery Rate Assumptions and No-Arbitrage in the Tranche Market, Technical Reports. Lehman Brothers.

Lo, A. (1991) Long Term Memory in Stock Market Prices, *Econometrica*, 59, 1279.

Lucas, D. (1995) Default Correlation and Credit Analysis, *Journal of Fixed Income*, 4(4):76–87.

Lucas, D. (2001) *CDO Handbook, Global Structured Finance Research*, JPMorgan.

Mandelbrot, B. (1963) The Variation of Certain Speculative Prices, *Journal of Business*, 36:394–419.

Mandelbrot, B. (1982) *The Fractal Geometry of Nature*, W.H. Freeman & Co., NY.

Mandelbrot, B. (1997) *Fractals and Scaling in Finance*, Springer, New York.

Mandelbrot, B. (1999) A Multifractal Walk Down Wall Street, *Scientific American*, February.

Mandelbrot, B. (2002) *Gaussian Self-Affinity and Fractals: Globality, the Earth, 1/f Noise, and R/S*, Springer Verlag, New York.

Mandelbrot, B. and Hudson, R. (2004) *The (Mis)Behavior of Markets: A Fractal View of Financial Turbulence*, Basic Books.

Markowitz, H. (1952) Portfolio Selection, *Journal of Finance*, 1(7):77–91.

Martin, R. and Tasche, D. (2007) , Shortfall: A Tail in Two Parts, *Risk*, 20(2):84–89.

Martin, R., Thompson, K. and Browne, C. (2001) Price and Probability, *Risk*, pp. 115–117.

McGinty, L., Beinstein, E., Ahluwalia, R. and Watts, M. (2004) Introducing Base Correlations. Technical Report. JPMorgan.

Merton, R. (1974) On the Pricing of Corporate Debt: The Risk Structure of Interest Rates, *Journal of Finance*, 29:449–470.

Moody's (2002) *Modeling Default Risk*, KMV Publishing.

Moosbrucker, T. (2006) Pricing CDOs with Correlated Variance Gamma Distributions, *Journal of Fixed Income*, 16(2):62–75.

Morgan Stanley (2007a) *Structured Credit Insights – Instruments, Valuation and Strategies*. Morgan Stanley.

Morgan Stanley (2007b) *Structured Credit Insights – Single Name Instruments & Strategies*. Morgan Stanley.

Morokoff, W. (2004) An Importance Sampling Method for Portfolios of Credit Risky Assets. In R. Ingalls, M. Rossetti, J. Smith, and B. Peters (eds). *Proceedings of the 2004 Winter Simulation Conference*, pp. 1668–1676.

Nelsen, R. (1999) *An Introduction to Copulas*, Lecture Notes in Statistics, Springer.

Neugebauer, M. (2004) Analysis of Synthetic CDOs of CDOs, Technical Reports, Fitch, September.

Nickell, P., Perraudin, W. and Varotto, S. (2000) Stability of Rating Transitions, *Journal of Banking and Finance*, 24:203–227.

O'Kane, D. (2008) *Modelling Single-name and Multi-name Credit Derivatives*, John Wiley & Sons Ltd.

O'Kane, D. and Livasey, M. (2004) *Base Correlation Explained*. Technical Reports 2004-Q3/4. Lehman Brothers.

Øksendal, B. (1998) *Stochastic Differential Equations*. Springer.

Parcell, E. and Wood, J. (2007) Wiping the Smile of your Base (Correlation Curve), Technical Reports. Derivative Fitch.

Parlett, B. (1980) *The Symmetric Eigenvalue Problem*. Prentice-Hall.

Plerou, V., Gopikrishnan, P., Amaral, L., Meyer, M. and Stanley, H. (1999) Scaling of the Distribution of Price Fluctuations of Individual Companies, *Physical Review E*, 60:6519.

Press, W., Flannery, B., Teukolsky, S. and Vetterling, W. (1992) *Numerical Recipes in C: The Art of Scientific Computing*. Cambridge University Press.

Pykhtin, M. (2005) *Counterparty Credit Risk Modelling: Risk Management Pricing and Regulation*. Risk Books.

Ross, S. (1996) *Stochastic Processes* 2nd edition, John Wiley & Sons Inc.

Sato, K. (2000) *Lévy Processes and Infinitely Divisible Distributions*, Cambridge University Press.

Schönbucher, P. (1999a) A Tree Implementation of a Credit Spread Model for Credit Derivatives, Technical Reports. University of Bonn.

Schönbucher, P. (1999b) Credit Risk Modelling and Credit Derivatives. PhD Thesis, University of Bonn.

Schönbucher, P. (2003) *Credit Derivative Pricing Models*, John Wiley & Sons Ltd.

Schoutens, W. (2003) *Lévy Processes in Finance: Pricing Financial Derivatives*. John Wiley & Sons Ltd.

Schwed, F. (1940) *Where Are the Customers' Yachts? or A Good Hard Look at Wall Street*, Simon & Schuster.

Shreve, S. (2004a) *Stochastic Calculus for Finance 1: The Binomial Asset Pricing Model*, Springer.

Shreve, S. (2004b) *Stochastic Calculus for Finance 2: Continuous Time Models*. Springer.

Sklar, A. (1973) Random Variables, Distribution Functions and Copulas, *Kybernetika*, 9:449–460.

Steffen, M. (1990) A Simple Method for Monotonic Interpolation in one Dimension. *Astronomy and Astrophysics*, 239:443–450.

Stroud, A. and Secrest, D. (1966) *Gaussian Quadrature Formulas*. Prentice-Hall.

Taleb, N. (2007) *The Black Swan: The Impact of the Highly Improbable*. Random House.

Tasche, D. (2004) Allocating Portfolio Economic Capital to Sub-Portfolios. In A. Dev (ed.) *Economic Capital: A Practicioner Guide*. Risk Books. pp. 275–302.

Tett, G. and Larsen, P. (2008) Finger Pointed at CDO Index. *Financial Times*, April.

Torresetti, R., Brigo, D. and Pallavicini, A. (2007) Implied Expected Tranched Loss Surface from CDO Data. Technical Report. Banca IMI.

Toutain, O., Rosa, D., Fu, Y., Mazataud, P., Jolivet, G., Lassalvy, L., Sieler, J., Levington, G., Witt, G. and Yoshizawa, Y. (2005) Moody's Revisits Its Assumptions Regarding Structured Finance Default (and Asset) Correlations for CDOs. *Moody's Structured Finance*, June.

Vasicek, O. (2002) Loan Portfolio Value. *Risk*, pp. 160–162.

Walker, M. (2006) CDO Models – Towards the Next Generation: Incomplete Markets and Term Structure. Technical Report.

Wilf, H. (1962) *Mathematics for the Physical Sciences*. John Wiley & Sons Inc.

Wilkinson, J. (1988) *The Algebraic Eigenvalue Problem*. Oxford University Press.

Witt, G. (2004) Moody's Investor Service, Moody's Correlated Binomial Default Distribution. August.

Wolff, R. (1989) *Stochastic Modelling and the Theory of Queues*. Prentice-Hall.

Yang, Y., Hurd, T. and Zhang, X. (2006) Saddlepoint Approximation Method for Pricing CDOs. Technical Report. McMaster University.

Zelter, F., Kendra, K., Gill, K., Bund, S., Cromartie, J. and Hardee, R. (2007) Global Criteria for the Review of Structured Finance CDOs with Exposure to US Subprime RMBS. Technical Report, Fitch, November

Zhou, R. (2008) Bond Implied CDS Spread and CDS-Bond Basis. Technical Report.

Index

*Index compiled by Terry Halliday
(HallidayTerence@aol.com)*